"When the theologians of the sacerdotal school elaborated the doctrine of man that is summarized in the startling expression of the first chapter of Genesis—'Let us make man in our image and likeness'—they certainly did not master at once all its implicit wealth of meaning. Each century has the task of elaborating its thought ever anew on the basis of that indestructible symbol which henceforth belongs to the unchanging treasury of the Biblical canon."

—Paul Ricoeur

LIBRARY OF CHRISTIAN STEWARDSHIP
(Published by Friendship Press)

IMAGING GOD

DOMINION AS STEWARDSHIP

Douglas John Hall

WM. B. EERDMANS PUBLISHING CO. • GRAND RAPIDS
FRIENDSHIP PRESS • NEW YORK
FOR
COMMISSION ON STEWARDSHIP
NATIONAL COUNCIL OF THE CHURCHES OF CHRIST
IN THE U.S.A.

For Nordan Murphy, whose encouragement and
dedication to the deeper understanding of stewardship in
the churches is the major raison d'être *of this study.*

Copyright © 1986 Commission on Stewardship, National Council of Churches

Published by Wm. B. Eerdmans Publishing Co.
255 Jefferson Ave. SE, Grand Rapids, MI 49503
and
Friendship Press
475 Riverside Dr., New York, NY 10115

Printed in the United States of America

Eerdmans ISBN 0-8028-0244-3
Friendship ISBN 0-377-00166-X

Contents

PREFACE

The rapid deterioration of our natural environment under the impact of a rampant technological society has prompted two conspicuous responses from the Christian theological community. One is, of course, the attempt to articulate a theology of nature. The other, with which the first is frequently combined, is the endeavor to reinstate the primacy of God in order to offset what to our newly acquired Christian guilt concerning nature appears an unwanted and unwarranted anthropocentricity within the Judaeo-Christian tradition.

While the present study has benefited from both of these emphases in recent Christian theology and ethics, it duplicates neither of them; and in some ways it may be considered critical of both. For I do not think that the best way — within the parameters of this belief system — to redress the neglect and denigration of nature to which our cult has contributed is by displacing the human creature in favor of either God or nature. We cannot avoid the fact that the tradition of Jerusalem gives a place of centrality to this speaking animal:

> What is man . . . ?
> Yet thou has made him little less than God
>   and dost crown him with glory and honor.
> Thou hast given him dominion. . . .

To try to negate or reduce that prominence may be a betrayal, not only of our tradition but also of our civilization. There is already enough in the world by way of human self-loathing and other forms of the sin of sloth!

The predisposition of this book, therefore, is not toward the diminishment of the human; rather, it seeks to reimagine our species in such a way that something approximating its grateful responsibility in and for the world — its stewardship! — can be understood as the aim of the Christian message.

To this end I have dared to take up the little term that many of our contemporaries feel is the nub of the problem: *imago Dei*. Adding what may seem foolhardiness to daring, I have then combined it with that even more "dangerous" word of the P-writer of Genesis, *dominion.* I hope, however, that what has come out of this unlikely mix is an interpretation of human being, and of all being, that retains in a provocative way the biblical centrality of *Homo sapiens* while at the same time raising both nature and God to a new kind of prominence in the dialogue that is life.

This book is the third in a series that the National Council of Churches' Commission on Stewardship has invited me to write, and I should like to express my sincere gratitude to all concerned with the publication of these works. I have addressed this one, unlike the two previous books, more explicitly to those who have some formal theological education, though I believe that it is easily accessible to any Christians who are serious about their faith.

My university, McGill, provided me with a research grant to assist in the preparation of this study, which is based on lectures originally given at Garrett-Evangelical Seminary in Evanston, but greatly expanded and altered. To the two research assistants whose background study has immeasurably enriched my work — Christopher Levan and Rhoda Palfrey Hall — I acknowledge my sincere appreciation.

Notre-Dame-de-Grâce, Montréal   D. J. H.
Advent, 1985

INTRODUCTION

Reimagining Ourselves

We become what we think of ourselves. . . .
What determines one's being is the image one adopts.[1]

Abraham Heschel

I. SOMETHING IS WRONG

Every twenty-four-hour day, citizens of the United
States of America consume 2,250 head of cattle in the form of
McDonald's hamburgers.[2]

I admit that this is not the kind of sentence normally found on
the first page of a book that intends to be regarded as an exercise in
serious theology. It may, however, be an appropriate beginning to
a study that takes as its first presupposition the belief that there is
something fundamentally wrong with our civilization. I hope that
it will also establish, in a symbolic way, the dimension of societal
"wrongness" this study will attempt to elucidate, namely, the distorted relationship between human and nonhuman nature.

Christian theology is, of course, accustomed to the notion that
something is wrong. There would be little reason for doing theology if everything were all right. Still, one hesitates on the brink of
such an analysis as this; for, oddly enough, many who are readers
or potential readers of Christian theology (since they are Christians)
seem not to want to hear that anything is seriously wrong. Large
numbers of people on this continent go to church for the precise reason of avoiding any such suggestion. They are quite literally seeking
"sanctuary," a little island of calm away from the news broadcasts
and urban squalor and graffiti where they can confirm their desperate determination to believe that "God's in his heaven, all's right with
the world."

Let me assure anyone belonging to that company that I have
profound sympathy for their quest. It is entirely understandable and

1

human—it is even "Christian" in a real sense—that we should want everything to be "right with the world" and that we should seek out places and persons and films and books and the like that help us believe it is so.

The trouble is, it isn't so! And when so many of us citizens of First World societies—where it is still possible, with a little luck, to sustain the illusion of well-being—make it our aim to assure ourselves regularly that nothing is seriously amiss, we simply compound the deepening crises of our planet. Not only do we deceive ourselves, but we perpetuate systems of injustice, oppression, and want by which other human beings are daily humiliated. Our illusion of calm is purchased at a very high price. The immediate cost of it is borne by the world's have-nots, like the Haitians and Guatemalans, whose grazing land and cheap labor sustain the cattle we transform into hamburgers. The longer-range cost will be carried by our children, and by all the children of the world. For we are accumulating a fantastic debt to truth; and societies, like individuals, must eventually pay that debt.

We are given notice of the debt even in a statistic as apparently innocuous as the one cited above (any number of other similar data would achieve the same end). For not only does it contain a hidden datum about our relationship to the Third World, it speaks volumes concerning our own lifestyle as a people, the image of ourselves as a species that is fostered by our social institutions, our moral and aesthetic sensibility, our conception of nature, and so forth. In order to appreciate something of what is concealed in such a statistic, one has merely to ask whether our high consumption of meat is necessary. Quite apart from the relative merits of an herbivorous as opposed to a carnivorous diet, what are the consequences of our actual diet as a people? The answer—or at least an important part of it—is: (a) "Americans eat so much unnecessary protein that we could reduce our livestock population by one-quarter and still feed every one of us half a pound of meat or poultry a day—enough to meet our entire protein allowance from meat alone"; and (b) because of our preference for meat, especially beef, we waste by far the greater share of the energy that is needed to produce what we have learned to demand.

> If we exclude dairy cows, the average conversion ratio for U.S. livestock is 7 pounds of grain and soy fed to produce one pound of edible meat. According to this estimate, of the 140 million tons of grain and soy we fed our beef cattle, poultry, and hogs in 1971,

one-seventh, or only 20 million tons, was returned to us in meat. *The rest, almost 118 million tons of grain and soy, became inaccessible for human consumption.* Although we lead the world in exports of grain and soy, this incredible volume "lost" through livestock was twice the level of our current exports. It is enough to provide every single human being on earth with more than a cup of cooked grain each day of the year![3]

The great issues of justice, as well as those of ecology, stare at us from our plates every time we sit at table.

While I sympathize, then, with the human need to be optimistic about the world, I am trying very hard to prevent that desire for personal reassurance from getting in the way of honesty about our actual condition. Is it in any case necessary for Christians to close their eyes to what is wrong with our world? Must the people of the Cross keep their gaze fixed only upon what is "bright and beautiful" in order not to fall into despair?

It is time for serious persons of faith to give a resounding no to such questions. The alternatives with which we as the body of Christ work are not optimism and pessimism; they are truth and hope. Optimism is the product of a frantic need to think exclusively "positive," that is, untroubling, thoughts about reality. It must therefore shut out all the "negative" data that threaten to overwhelm it. Christian hope, which is first of all hope in God and not in human institutions, systems, ideologies, and "dreams," does not have to lie to itself about what is really there in the world. Being shaped by the story of one who was "crucified, dead and buried," and by his living presence, faith dares to hope that God is working out his purposes in the midst of the whole bizarre admixture of positive and negative data, joy and pain, anticipation and anxiety that constitutes our life in this world. Such faith is not smug, nor is it presumptuous: to live with it is to be carried willy-nilly into God's redemptive work in the world. That work, to use the Gospel of John's metaphor, is the work of a light that is operating in darkness. Faith then, if it is genuine and not mere sentimentalism, transports one into the heart of the world's darkness. It does not function to insulate one from what is wrong; rather, it brings with it a greater courage to confront the world's wrongness, to accept what must be accepted, and to change what can be changed.[4]

In 1957 one of the neglected prophets of our era, Suzanne de Dietrich, wrote:

The chaos of our existence, the chaos of the historical period in which we are living, simply emphasizes the disorder of a creation that has gotten separated from its Creator, of a humanity that has revolted against its Lord, and that, confronted with the options of life and death, has chosen death. Our earth appears to have been handed over to some demonic power, and, humanly speaking, we are tempted to say that the battle is a hopeless one. . . . [5]

Humanly speaking! Madame de Dietrich did not mean that as a denigration of humanity. The human soul of every one of us cringes before the seemingly irresolvable problems of earth, problems that appear still more complex and hopeless than they did in the midst of the postwar recovery of the 1950s, when de Dietrich wrote this. But her book, *God's Unfolding Purpose*, is not based on the assumption that the world must *look* hopeful in order for Christians to look upon it with hope. The all-too-human sense of hopelessness that steals over us whenever we allow ourselves to take in, for a moment, the "chaos" of our epoch—this twentieth-century angst that, in order to avoid, we cover with false cheerfulness or world-weary indifference—is met by another impulse and influence. As Christians we attribute that combative influence, not to our own survival instincts but to grace—sheer grace! God is at work in the world, appearances notwithstanding. God's "unfolding purpose" incorporates into itself the very "clouds ye so much dread"—without thereby sanctioning either the "clouds" or the dread.

> *God's* purposes will ripen fast,
>   Unfolding every hour;
> The bud may have a bitter taste,
>   But sweet will be the flower.

Not, however, saccharin sweet. The hope that is born of grace is revolutionary hope because it is at the same time uncompromisingly realistic about what is wrong. Hope does not begin, for the Christian, at the point where faith turns to the proclamation of the light. It is already fully operative in its attempt to comprehend the darkness. For "darkness realized is creative of a receptive theatre for the drama of God's salvatory action in Christ."[6] Courage to name the powers of darkness is of the essence of the prophetic and apostolic faith of our tradition. And in times of crisis, not to name those powers—to speak instead of "peace, peace, where there is no peace"(Jer. 6:14; 8:11)—is the surest sign of apostasy. "The job of thought at our time is to bring into the light [the] darkness as dark-ness."[7] The only kind of darkness that faith needs to fear and avoid is unacknowledged darkness, the unnerving and shadowy blur on the edges of our consciousness that we expend so much of our psychic energy ignoring. Darkness entered into, darkness realized, is the point of departure for all profound expressions of Christian hope. "Meaningless darkness" becomes "revelatory darkness" when it is confronted by the courage of a thoughtfulness and hope that is born of faith's quest for truth.[8]

To illustrate: When Robert McAfee Brown writes about the possibility of *Making Peace in the Global Village*, he has to devote a good deal of space to the analysis of the unpeace that grips our globe. And to those who do not like to be reminded of global violence (especially in a book of theology) he cautions: "There emerges a very simple starting point about which Christians and non-Christians can agree. Juan Luis Segundo, a Jesuit from Uruguay, has captured it: 'The world *should not be* the way it is.' " "Anybody," Brown concludes, "who disagrees can stop reading immediately. Nothing that follows will make any sense."[9]

That "something is wrong" is not the last word of this present study, any more than it is of Professor Brown's. But it has to be the first word. And if this first word cannot be borne, then probably the last word will not make any sense.

II. WE OURSELVES MUST BE CHANGED

Something is wrong. The world should not be the way it is. But *what* is wrong?

In answer, we could indulge in an interminable list of worldly woes, and there would be no end to the witnesses and victims of these sorrows on whose testimony we could draw. From every known science of humanity — from psychology and sociology, from political science and economics, from ecology and the life sciences, from physics and chemistry, from history, from the arts — we could summon devastating evidence of the wrongness of things. If anything distinguishes our century from the previous one, it is the entire willingness of intellectuals and experts in every field of human endeavor to testify to the wretchedness of the human condition. Theology is no longer alone in pursuit of the ancient science of hamartiology.

But theology is bound by its subject matter always to attempt to get to the bottom of things. Of course, it is not at liberty chauvinistically to ignore or despise the data of those who investigate concrete issues and aspects of the totality. But theology is by definition a holistic mode of reflection, an interdisciplinary discipline. Therefore, it must play the fool (it is patently foolhardy to risk such generalizations in a specialist culture!) and move from secondary to primary causation.

This is what I mean: If, as one who attempts to reflect on the human situation through the medium of the Christian story, I ask myself "What is wrong?" I invariably find myself answering, "We ourselves are wrong." Now it is undoubtedly an awkward turn of phrase for me to say, "I find myself answering . . ."; nonetheless, it describes rather precisely the process that takes place in my mind. For it is as if the conclusion formed itself. I do not mean that it comes to me without any forethought, experience, observation, hypothesizing, or testing on my part—as sheer revelation, so to speak, or simply because the "doctrine of sin" is a prominent feature of the dogmatic tradition in which I stand.

There is, as I have already noted, plenty of evidence in our context to substantiate the conclusion that we ourselves are wrong. But I know that I did not and do not reach this conclusion by an ordinary process of unbroken reasoning from one thing to another; sheer empirical observation could not of itself generate this conclusion. For one thing, I could point out that there is much that is "right" about us—that our society, by comparison with many others past and present, is at least in many respects more desirable. I recognize, therefore, that in being led to the conclusion that we ourselves are wrong I have made a judgment. A kind of leap is involved in this, something perhaps on the order of Kierkegaard's "leap of faith." Gradually, or perhaps suddenly, one finds oneself the perpetrator of a judgment, a decision. How did it happen? Probably one can say something about the atmosphere in which the judgment came to be; but it remains, like all real decisions, a mystery of will. Faith also has to learn to live with this mystery, and the criticism that it inevitably begets.

Yet today the judgment that "we ourselves are wrong" does not seem so absurd as it has seemed during other periods in history, such as the nineteenth century. Given the generally promethean expectations of the Victorian era, Christians like P. T. Forsyth and Dean Inge, who felt impelled to point up the wrongness of the age, were regarded by many as mere malcontents. Today the judgment seems less arbitrary. Living in the midst of a consumer society that is more and more acquisitive yet increasingly insecure despite its possessions, its caloric intake, its armaments, and its bravado; living with statistics far more unsettling than the datum concerning beef cattle with which I introduced this statement—data about teenage suicide and environmentally caused disease and spouse abuse and joblessness; living with television pictures of emaciated Ethiopians on the one hand and the "beautiful," superficial characters of "Dallas" and "Dynasty" on the other, many ordinary people find themselves thinking: "There is something wrong, and it is us." Just as traditional Christian hamartiology always claimed! The idea of Sin—not just sins, but Sin—that was so embarrassing to our liberal forebears takes on new and profound significance for many today, by no means all of whom are Christians. In fact, it is hard to know what to make of our global situation without recourse to something like this ancient Hebrew concept.

Having said that, however, I must immediately note that such a judgment is by no means universally felt. Even among Christians on this most Christian of continents (perhaps especially among Christians) there is still a marked resistance to a radical doctrine of sin. In that respect there often seems to have been little change since Reinhold Niebuhr first began to write about the human condition in terms of sin. Numerous people around us appear able to observe the same phenomena I have briefly cited above and yet avoid the conclusion that there is something fundamentally wrong with us. The more aggressive and articulate among them will not hesitate, in the face of any such conclusion, to point out that it involves a highly subjective component: that in making it, one has gone from observation of data to a stance of personal opinion, a value judgment.

They are absolutely right. The whole notion that there is something wrong with us *is* a value judgment. That is to say, it presupposes certain positive "values," some understanding, however dim, of what "right" would mean, of what "should be." Even to employ the language of "wrongness," quite apart from compounding valuation with offense in the use of the term "sin," is to invite reaction. One can at least expect to hear that such an opinion is strictly subjective and incapable of verification. In all probability, one's critics will be less polite and simply quip that one is jaundiced, jaded, embittered, moralistic, old-fashioned, idealistic, intolerant, pessimistic, and so forth. The more astute among one's detractors may add that it is hardly surprising that as Christians, who have some vested interests in discovering the world to be sinful, we have actually found it so.

At this point, however, it may be pertinent to usher in the experts whose evidence we earlier declined. If the conclusion that we ourselves are "wrong" is such an egregious value judgment, how does it happen that many of the people in our society who "find themselves thinking" just this kind of thought are natural scientists—the very people who taught us about the importance of "hard data" and "scientific method" and keeping human emotions out of the process of rational and empirical investigation? More than any other single segment of the general public today—certainly more than government leaders, lawyers, philosophers, and educators—more, even, than most mainline preachers, it is the scientists who are telling us that our world is in critical shape and that the human element is chiefly to blame for it. In fact, there has been a conspicuous about-face in the scientific community within the past two or three decades. Of course, there are still scientists who beat the drum for Progress, or simply serve the status quo ("ours not to reason why"), or maintain a hands-off posture where all social and moral issues are concerned. But a vociferous segment within all the physical sciences, backed up by many social scientists, has been imbued with a spirit of alarm in our time, and with a new sense of public responsibility.

A later age may judge that the great moralists of the latter half of the twentieth century were scientists rather than either humanists or the representatives of religious traditions. Like all genuine moralists, they are made fearless because they sense that their cause is more important than their own reputations or the feelings of those to whom they must make their testimony. David Suzuki is typical of the scientist as moralist. Before the introduction of his television series *A Planet For The Taking*, he told a reporter: "This series is going to hammer the shit out of people. It's going to make them very unhappy, very uncomfortable. It's going to make some people mad as hell. But that's the beginning it seems to me of the change."[10] Demographers, botanists, zoologists, ecologists, medical scientists, and many others are conspicuous today among those who are seized by prophetic indignation and the impulse to transform the world. They are supported, moreover, by another important segment of our society, representing a quite new social phenomenon: the "citizen scientists,"[11] that is, those who, though they have not been equipped for it by education or profession, become lay scientists because they are driven to find out what is wrong with their world, what is poisoning their water and contaminating their food and killing their trees and ruining the future of their children and grandchildren.

An obvious reason why the scientific community has been alerted to the need for truth and transformation in the public domain is that scientists are students of nature. In the natural world they examine in detail they have discovered conspicuous and often desperate problems: the depletion of vital resources, the extinction of whole species, manifold pollution of ecosystems, and so forth. Now, to designate scientific "facts" as "problems" is already an unscientific thing to do. But there is still in the scientific community a sufficient residue of love for what is examined—perhaps remarkably—that such facts are regularly designated problems, and by the scientists themselves.

Another reason for the growth of concern among scientists is one that was pointed out by C. P. Snow over two decades ago: unlike the literary people who are mostly oriented toward the past, the natural scientists are oriented toward the future.[12] This futuristic bent may have fostered a kind of "social optimism," as Snow believed, in scientists of an earlier period; for their general lack of awareness of the past, combined with the modern outlook of which they were the vanguard, conditioned them to place a good deal of faith in human rationality and technical ability. But the future that scientists now contemplate is far removed from the brave new world entertained by their nineteenth-century precursors. The future they envision, many of them, is more shocking than the future that appears to nonscientists, because its details are more explicit. Extrapolating from their known data, the scientists of our time have rendered obsolete the language of myth and poetry for describing the earth's end. We now possess an apocalypse based on data that can be fed to computers; and it is every bit as awesome as the ancient visions of Last Things—and for the contemporary mind a great deal more convincing.

There is, however, an entirely new factor in the modern apocalypse: the end of the world is ushered in, not by divine intervention or the long-range planning of an ultimately benevolent providence, but by human error, stupidity, malevolence, or the lure of oblivion. When the scientists look for the causes of the bleak prospects they spy through their sophisticated instruments, they do not see an angry or omnipotent Deity but a selfish and myopic little biped who has more knowledge than wisdom, and who is almost wholly devoid of mercy. Loren Eiseley speaks for many other scientists today when he writes: "Man is not as other creatures and . . . without the sense of the holy, without compassion, his brain can become a gray stalking horror—the deviser of Belsen."[13] How often it happens today that ordinary scientific researchers are transformed from the rather bland personalities preferred by their disciplines into passionate preachers of higher morality or frustrated prophets of doom![14]

That something is wrong, then—and with us—is not the conclusion of only the inheritors of the dogma of original sin these days. What few scientists grasp, however, is that the problem with "us" is not just the way we behave but the way we are. This is where theology, whether trained or intuitive, has to go beyond the empirical sciences in its attempt to get to the bottom of things.

The Christian tradition holds that it is our being itself, not only our activities, that constitutes the problem. The biblical concept of sin is gravely trivialized if we reduce it to the "thoughts, words, and deeds" that liturgical prayers of confession habitually conjure up: that is, to namable, isolable incidents or traits, things that we have "done" or "left undone," which can be confessed according to various categories and hence ritually pardoned. Such "sins" may be external symptoms of sin (though in practice they are frequently foils by which we camouflage our more serious malaise); sin as such is something at the heart of us, so deeply ingrained in our persons that it is impossible to isolate, or even to describe, very satisfactorily. It belongs to the mystery of the self and refers in a particular sense to the distortion of the self's relationships.

> Sin is occasioned precisely by the fact that man refuses to admit his "creatureliness" and to acknowledge himself as merely a member of a total unity of life. . . .
>
> Man is an individual but he is not self-sufficing. The law of his nature is love, a harmonious relation of life to life in obedience to the divine center and source of his life. This law is violated when man seeks to make himself the center and source of his own life. His sin is therefore spiritual and not carnal, though the infection of rebellion spreads from the spirit to the body and disturbs its harmonies also.[15]

Contemporary theology has attempted to offset the moralistic connotations of the term "sin" by employing such concepts as alienation, estrangement, indifference, and so forth. Sin certainly has to do with what happens between persons—between the "I" and all "the others," human and extrahuman, vis-à-vis the ones with whom we live, move, and have our being. It refers to a deep-seated flaw in the manner in which we express our being over against these others. It concerns the preconception of self that we bring to every meeting with what is not the self. Sin means that what is wrong with us is wrong at the level of our self-image. It is there in our imagination before it ever forms itself into "thoughts, words, and deeds." It is a warped imagining of the self.

But let us become concrete. Otherwise, we create the impression that by "sin" Christians mean something so general and so immutable that it defies historical distinctions and is simply part of that "eternal theology" that Christian orthodoxy forces upon every discussion of the human condition. Of such an understanding of sin Dorothee Sölle has correctly said that it is "innocuous and distresses no one in its indiscriminate universality, for it identifies sin, not theoretically but *de facto*, with a universal human fate comparable perhaps to smallpox, against which we are protected by vaccination."[16]

Sin, we have said, has to do with human self-imagining. But images of the self are not, in any simple way, mere products of individual or personal imagination. To be sure, each of us is molded by quite specific and unique circumstances, experience, desires, phobias, and so forth. But at the same time we are all profoundly conditioned by the social context to which we belong, and so by the kinds of public expectations and patterns of conduct and goals and taboos that are woven into the general cultural fabric. This is why Christian theology, when it endeavors (as it always must) to rethink the meaning of sin, is obliged to move out beyond the personal into the societal sphere. It is not only a matter of what is wrong with me but what is wrong with us (as I have purposely phrased it all along). In the words of the prophet Isaiah, "I am a man of unclean lips, and I dwell in the midst of a people of unclean lips" (6:5).

Together with modern Western humanity generally, but more consistently than most other Western societies, North Americans have been conditioned by the circumstances of history and geography to develop and nurture a very expectant, or "high," self-image. As a people, we entertain great expectations. For example, we think ourselves the possessors by nature of certain "inalienable rights." These include not only the minimal human rights being championed today by all enlightened peoples of earth;[17] they also extend into areas of privilege undreamt of not only by the past ages of our race but by the vast majority of living human beings. Not only do we assume the right to private property of every description, we reward those who through cunning, industry, or stealth accumulate more of it than do their fellows. Not only do we assume the right to use all of nature for personal and national aggrandizement, we assume the right to "develop" (plunder?) the planet's limited resources so unstintingly that we are depriving future generations of their "rights." Not only do we assume the right to defend ourselves and what is "ours" through violent means if necessary, we do so with the knowledge that such a defense of "our own" would probably cripple the entire globe and perhaps leave the biosphere uninhabitable.

While a significant minority among us have begun — on account of various obvious crises brought on by the rampant extension of such "rights" through the deployment of high technology — to raise serious questions about the principles involved, the vast majority of our citizens continue to take such rights for granted. The "American" belief system is so axiomatic with them that it does not function at the level of conscious reflection at all. Without asking themselves any questions whatsoever, multitudes on this continent munch their hamburgers, drive their acid-rain-producing vehicles five blocks to the local church or supermarket,[18] pay their taxes to governments that use well over 50 percent of tax moneys for "national defense," and all the while imbibe from the "hidden persuaders" yet more exaggerated images of what they and their progeny have a "right" to.

Perhaps in a world where every man, woman, and child had the opportunity of entertaining these same assumptions it would be permissible for thinking persons to consider such an *imago hominis* (image of the human) an innocent delusion. But despite the fact that some of our political and economic leaders seem to have persuaded themselves that the American pattern will work for any people with a little "gumption," the truth is that the overwhelming majority of the earth's present human population (I do not even speak about the past) has never experienced the smallest reason why they should imagine themselves along these grandiose lines. A large percentage of them can only cling with the greatest determination and courage to the belief that they have a right to life as such. For the most part, however, they do not think in these terms at all. Their language is not that of rights but of possibilities; and, by comparison with what we deem possible, their aspirations are meager indeed.

There is a disturbing connection between those aspirations of the two-thirds poor and our First World *imago hominis*. The connection is implied, for example, in the oft-cited statistic that 6 percent of the world's population consumes 40 percent of its raw materials.[19] But such statistics hide something in spite of their potential for revelation. They hide the fact that what we are dealing with here is a matter of being and not only of having or doing. They hide the reality that the group designated as the "six percent" (i.e., North Americans) are human beings who not only have certain things, and do certain things with what they have, but *are* certain kinds of human beings. Such statistics are often misleading because they contribute to the deceptive impression, widely held, that the imbalance they designate could be rectified by a different way of dividing up the planet's resources (having) or a different way of conducting our lives individually and socially (doing).

Now when such implications are drawn up imaginatively (as by those who call for a "new economic order," for instance), they are perfectly right as far as they go. But they do not go far enough. For in casting the remedy in terms of a rearrangement of materials and certain adjustments in social behavior, they overlook the foundational fact that our First World patterns of lifestyle and possession emerge out of a profoundly entrenched image of who we are. It is our being-who-we-are that constitutes the problem. We resent this message deeply when it is proclaimed to us by the victims of our high self-image. But no significant changes in the arrangement of the world will occur until we ourselves have felt the truth of this judgment. As we are, we are a highly problematical people. And the problem is there inside us before it is incarnated in defense programs, international economic manipulations, domestic consumer patterns, and so forth. What is wrong with us is wrong at the level of our *being* as such—not, of course, the fact that we exist but the manner in which we body forth our existence. There can be no serious or permanent alteration of the catastrophic course upon which twentieth-century civilization is set without a *metanoia* in the soul of First World peoples in general, and North Americans in particular. For the changes that are requisite for planetary survival and shalom are not surface rearrangements like the redistribution of material goods and services, but a transformation at the level of personal and social being. In short, we must get a new image of ourselves: we ourselves must be changed!

III. RELIGION AND IMAGE-MAKING

Since I began with a symbolic statistic about American eating habits, let me introduce at this point another symbolic statistic: a recent Princeton University survey indicates that 41 percent of Americans go to church regularly, and that 81 percent of them say they would like to see a revival of religion in their nation.[20] Another survey declares that, as of 1985, 44 percent of adult Americans regard themselves as "born-again Christians."[21]

There are two implications in these data that are significant for our present inquiry. One of them is a necessary aspect of the *critical* thinking in which responsible Christians must engage if they are to make good their membership in the prophetic faith of the Judaeo-Christian tradition; the other is essential to the *constructive* task of theology and faith. We shall consider them in that order.

The Role of Religion in the Formation of Images. Many and diverse influences are, of course, brought to bear on the way a people imagines itself: its natural environment, its weather patterns, the size of its population in relation to the land space it occupies, its resources, its relative strength and prosperity in relation to its neighbors, its admixture of races and age groupings, its economic stability, its age, its success in achieving its stated goals, and more. But nothing has been as influential in the creation of images of the human, historically speaking, as religion. The reason is obvious: religion is a people's expression of its own "ultimate concern" (Tillich). The deity or deities of a religion embody the highest values, virtues, and goals of its adherents. From Feuerbach onward, secular explanations of "the religious phenomenon" have insisted that the gods are in fact nothing but "projections" of human desires. The defenders of religion maintain that, on the contrary, human ideals are reflections of the transcendent. But in either case it is acknowledged, implicitly, that the connection between our most commanding conceptualizations of ourselves and our understanding of the divine is a very close one. Whether we create God in our own image, or God creates us in his image, is certainly an important question. But in terms of the link between divinity and human self-understanding, the connection must be seen as a strong one in either case. We emulate—or strive to—what we worship. "Be perfect, as your father in heaven is perfect" (Mt. 5:48).[22]

An uncomfortable prospect thus presents itself to Christian reflection in North America today: that our problematic manner of imagining ourselves as a people is somehow linked with our religious belief, our Christianity. Unless we are willing to believe that the problem side of our being emanates from the non-Christian elements in our midst — that the 41 percent who go to church regularly are strictly distinguishable from those who consume all those hamburgers — we must be ready to explain how the worship of the Christian God is related to our being this kind of society. Clearly, by contemporary standards at least, we are an exceptionally religious people. In other parts of the industrialized, urbanized West, the movement away from the land and into increasingly technicized cities has been accompanied by a conspicuous decline in religion. While by comparison with our own past, we too are a secular society, in relation to other cultures of the affluent North we are still a believing people. There are bibles in 98 percent of American homes. Though our society is pluralistic, the dominant religious influence is still Christianity — to the extent that those who seek election to high public office, regardless of their personal preferences, are obliged to seem to be committed (or even "born again") Christians. If cultures are products of their cults, if images of the human are reflections of a people's imaging of the divine, then North American life must be said to reflect the Christian religion. Are we thus to conclude that Christianity itself has given birth to a society whose citizenry can be nonchalant about the fact that it, a small fraction of the planet's human occupancy, can lay claim to almost half of the earth's natural resources?

The characteristic Christian reaction to this sort of innuendo is understandably defensive. One wants to rush immediately to the defense of a faith tradition that, far from upholding selfishness and aggressiveness, has clearly identified such behavior as sinful, extolling instead the virtues of love and sensitivity and self-sacrifice. One wants to remind the modern critics of Christendom that at the center of this faith stands one who "did not count equality with God a thing to be grasped, but emptied himself, taking the form of a servant . . ." (Phil. 2:6–7). One wants to point out that stewardship is, after all, one of the fundamental ethical teachings of this tradition.

Unfortunately, the historical-sociological data that are being rather unceremoniously flung in the face of First World indifference today by the victims of that indifference cannot be offset by such theological-biblical argumentation. It remains indelibly fixed in the minds of our critics that the world of the people who "have" on this planet is historically and avowedly a Christian world. It remains that this "Christian" First World has forged an *imago hominis* depicting the human in a posture of mastery vis-à-vis the nonhuman; that it has spawned successive empires that conceive it to be their "manifest destiny" to subdue not only nature but other peoples; and that the epicenter of this First World, the United States, is at the same time the most devotedly "Christian" nation and the most technicized, well-fed, and fully armed people on the planet. Our more charitable detractors are willing to admit that it is necessary to account for some of these factors by pointing up the discrepancy between religious ideals and their actual observance — a discrepancy by no means unique to Christians. Still, I should like to suggest that we Christians should resist the temptation to excuse ourselves on these grounds. It is not always helpful to exonerate our doctrine by blaming ourselves. Might it not be that what is wrong with us as a people is not just that we have fallen short of our Christian code but that our Christian code is itself in need of critical rethinking? Perhaps the fault lies deeper than the sins of omission and commission that we measure against the standard of becoming "imitators of God." Perhaps our conception of God is itself a significant aspect of the problem. Perhaps we are imaging an unworthy god.

The Role of Religion in the Re-formation of Images. The second implication of the data encoded in the religious statistic quoted above is that in a culture that is still as open to explicit religious influence as ours appears to be, those who bear responsibility for the interpretation of the faith can have a significant impact on the re-formation of existing images of the human. If there really is at the heart of the Christian faith a conception of the identity and destiny of the human creature different from the *imago hominis* that our culture has apprehended as Christian, then it is incumbent upon those who perceive this difference to communicate it as clearly and forcefully as possible. There could be no more responsible *political* act in North America today than to recall an avowedly Christian people to the authentic rudiments of its own belief tradition.[23] Insofar as religion in general, and the Christian religion in particular, is still respected in our context, even interpretations of this tradition that are openly critical of existing social, political, and moral practices can have an impact. The recent pronouncements of the Roman Catholic bishops in Canada and the United States on war and unemployment demonstrate the truth of this claim.

There is, however, a precondition that must be met by any who want to take up the task of re-forming our society's image of the human, and that is the twofold recognition that a) the present form of our self-understanding is both wrong and dangerous, and b) there are resources within the tradition and spirit of biblical faith that provide the basis to challenge the existing *imago hominis*.

It is unfortunate that to date these two conditions have been met only by minorities within the churches. Dominant forms of the church still function in our midst to confirm, or at least to leave untouched, the basic values and pursuits of the majority culture. In the case of much of the so-called conservative or evangelical Christianity that has gained control of the media, religion not only underwrites the assumptions and policies of those in power but, in significant instances, has become the most vociferous and effective promoter of the imperial aspirations of the ruling parties. What religious conservatism on this continent wills most consistently to conserve is not really "Bible Christianity" but the economic and ideological status quo of an imperium that thinks itself destined for world rule. The "Jesus Christ" of evangelicalism is a cultic symbol enshrining and legitimating the political hubris of Superpower.

Where the older forms of classical Protestantism and Catholicism are concerned, there are, to be sure, signs of a provocative divergence from the "culture religion" (Berger) they have been content to be in the immediate past. Nonetheless, they are hesitant to take upon themselves the role of critic. For one thing, that role is largely foreign to their Constantinian past. For another, the membership of these established denominations is still largely identified with those economic classes that benefit most from the status quo. To take up the posture of prophet and reformer; to begin from the vantage point of a belief that "the world is not the way it should be"; to identify what is wrong with something at the very core of "our way of life"; to set out to rethink and reshape the social order around a very different image of the human — all of this calls for not only unusual insight and conviction but the courage to step outside of one's own comfortable religious conventions and class associations and to accept the subtle but real suffering that must be the inevitable consequence of such a "betrayal" of one's own.

Perhaps this prophetic vocation is too demanding altogether for most Christians; but it is the second basic presupposition of this book (i.e., it will simply be assumed). If the first presupposition is that there is something wrong with our civilization, the second is that there is sufficient wisdom, energy, and courage in the churches both to identify what is wrong and to begin to change it. Enough signs have been given us to warrant risking such an assumption. Clusters of Christians everywhere have already done courageous and unprecedented things in the area of social ethics. Individual Christians such as the Berrigans, Jim Wallis and the Sojourners, Jean Vanier, and many others have provided us with models of responsible behavior in a perilous world. Ordinary congregations across the continent have asked for serious theological, biblical, and social study. Even our various church hierarchies (in some cases one may say especially the hierarchies) have given both symbolic and concrete notice to the entrenched powers of economic oppression, war, sexual stereotyping, racism, and so forth, that they no longer intend to serve as their cultic functionaries. In short, it is possible to believe that a significant minority of committed Christians on this continent can and will, from now on, be able to give much-needed leadership in the critical and constructive vocation of altering this problematical First World society from within.

I do not use the term "leadership" lightly in that statement. If it is true that religion is the most potent ingredient in the formation of images of the human, it is precisely to responsible leadership that Christians are called in a society whose *imago hominis* requires re-forming. I do not mean to invoke the hoary concepts of Christian leadership that were products of religious triumphalism. The new leadership that is required of reflective disciples of Christ is a form of servanthood, and it does not hold much promise of fame and fortune. It is a matter of stewardship. As "stewards of the mysteries of God" (I Cor. 4:1) — not simply of material resources but of truth — we can, if we will, draw upon sources of criticism and construction to which very few in our technological society have spiritual or intellectual access. While we dare not suppose that all 81 percent of the Americans who say that they would like to see a return to religion are looking for the kind of religious leadership to which I am referring here, we can surely assume that some of them are. The onus is on us to drop our masquerade of bland and unthreatening servitude, of supplying without question what we think people want, and become really faithful servants of a gospel that may indeed refuse to cater to people's wants but nevertheless addresses their real needs.

IV. THE INTENTION OF THIS STUDY

I intend this book to be a kind of reflective background for one aspect of this total Christian vocation of reformative leadership: the need to identify what is wrong with our understanding of the relationship between humanity and extrahuman nature, to assess the character and extent of empirical Christianity's culpability in this wrong relationship, and to point to an alternative Christian conceptualization of this relationship. I shall attempt to accomplish this in the following way: In the first chapter I shall indicate broadly what I conceive to be the culpability of Christianity as we have understood and practiced it with respect to the crisis of nature. In the four subsequent chapters I shall concentrate on a particular theme within the greater discussion of the relationship between human and nonhuman dimensions of the natural order. This theme is bound up with the biblical symbol—woven into dogma by evolving Christian doctrine—of the *imago Dei*, that is, the belief that the human creature was made "in the image of God."

In this introductory statement we have been considering the importance of human self-imaging and the role of religion in the forming and re-forming of images of the human. Whatever else religion may be, it is also anthropology—in the sense that it fosters conceptions of human authenticity on whose basis moral codes can be drawn up and the actual behavior of individuals and societies assessed, challenged, and altered. Religion speaks not only of the divine but of the divine intention for the human. In fact, already when it speaks of the divine it is speaking indirectly of the human.

Within the Christian religion there is no more important expression of this latter function of religion than the doctrinal symbol *imago Dei*. Though the term was borrowed from Hebraic literature (Genesis), it has played a more explicit and official role in Christian doctrine than in Hebraic faith. Through this dogmatic device historic Christianity attempted to explain what it believes to be the essence of human being and human vocation.

Imago Dei is not the only historical doctrinal expression, of course, that needs to be explored in connection with the theology of humanity's relationship to the natural order; but it is perhaps the central one. This is partly because of the sheer weight of dogmatic emphasis associated with this symbol. It became virtually a technical theme of Christian dogmatics very early in the development of church doctrine, whereas other biblical concepts having to do with the same attempt to express the "true nature" of the human creature remained at the metaphoric or symbolic level. A term like "steward," as I have argued elsewhere,[24] is a fascinating biblical symbol with excellent apologetic prospects in our time. Yet "steward" did not achieve anything like the official doctrinal status that the Jahwist's term "image of God" occupied from an early stage.

Another reason *imago Dei* is so significant for our purposes (and this is no doubt also the reason it achieved such a sublime status historically) is that it is intrinsically evocative. Since "imaging" plays a very vital role in human life (one could even define the human being as an image-making creature), a symbol like *imago Dei* holds immediate, existential interest.

But a third reason for the significance of this doctrinal device is more closely linked to the present project. The truth is that if the original Hebraic metaphor achieved a prominence within Christianity that it did not have in Judaism, it is because it became one of those biblical expressions that had to bear the enormous weight of meanings derived from nonbiblical sources—initially from the world of Greek and Roman civilization, and subsequently from various philosophical and moral developments in European history. Part of my argument in the ensuing pages will be that it was precisely in connection with the imputation to this biblical concept of Hellenistic and other connotations that an understanding of the human was introduced into our civilization that led, over the centuries, to the present crisis of nature. Since, under non-Hebraic influences, the *imago Dei* became the principal doctrinal device for distinguishing "man" from the other creatures, any attempt to unearth the ideational sources of the crisis of the biosphere must undertake a critical analysis of this symbol's history.

It is also my contention, however, that the *imago Dei* concept can be redeemed. Not everything that could be said about this symbol has been said, and however entrenched certain interpretations of it may be, this "startling expression of the first chapter of Genesis" defies and transcends all of its historic explanations. It points toward a mystery of human identity that must be rediscovered by each generation of the believing community and worked out with regard to the specific problems and possibilities confronting that generation. As Paul Ricoeur has said, "Each century has the task of elaborating its thought ever anew. . . . "[25] In our search for an image of the human that can challenge what is "wrong" with us, we may yet, I believe, gain insight from this ancient biblical expression. Placed within the context of a Hebraic-Christian ontology of being-in-relationship—and liberated from its own dogmatic past—the *imago Dei* can help to fashion an alternative way of imagining ourselves as human beings within the larger order of nature to which we belong.

CHAPTER ONE

Christian Culpability in a Groaning Creation

The earth mourns and withers,
  the world languishes and withers;
  the heavens languish together
    with the earth.

The earth lies polluted
  under its inhabitants;
for they have transgressed the laws,
  violated the statutes,
  broken the everlasting covenant.

Therefore a curse devours the earth,
  and its inhabitants suffer
  for their guilt;
therefore the inhabitants of the earth
  are scorched,
  and few men are left.

Isaiah 24:4–6

I. ON TELLING THE TRUTH

The outspokenness of the prophets of Israel concerning what is wrong with their world reminds us of our vocation as Christians to bear witness to the truth as we are able to perceive it. Not to give voice to what we see happening in our midst is to serve the one whom Jesus called "the father of lies" (Jn. 8:44); and, as Dietrich Bonhoeffer said in his memorable essay on this subject, "Even a deliberate silence may constitute a lie. . . ."[1]

Truth is not always comforting. Indeed, if our paradigm for truth is the One who made the apparently audacious but ultimately

21

humble claim that truth had been incarnated in his life (Jn. 14:6), then we must suppose that the abode of truth is never far away from Golgotha and that those who point to it will not likely flourish. Not only governments, ancient and modern, but average citizens as well seem to have preferred comfort to truth from time immemorial. But what kind of comfort is it that is purchased at the expense of truth, functioning as an oily surface of civility over a sea of falsehood? "We go astray," writes Dorothee Sölle, "if we separate consolation and truth and allow religion to console but forbid it to partake in truth. If the Church confines herself to consoling . . . and no longer regards herself as capable of truth, then she will be offering but shallow comfort, limited to the individual person and deferred to the beyond. . . . The Spirit of God will console only by illuminating truth, not by abandoning it."[2]

The truth that evokes this attempt to reformulate the relationship between human and extrahuman nature is a planet that suffers visibly from the pursuits and distorted values of its most "successful" inhabitants. Living in the midst of these technologically aggressive human societies, we cannot expect to draw attention to this truth without incurring some of the rejection, perhaps even the wrath, that has always been the lot of the prophetic community. If we are in earnest about our inquiry into an appropriate theology of humanity and nature, we shall not, as participants in such a social context, be engaging in a polite academic exercise. We shall be reminded at every turn of the fact that the crisis of nature, which is the point of departure for our inquiry, is a crisis brought on the world by the very goals and beliefs of the society to which we ourselves belong and which we no doubt represent in many ways.

There can thus be no calm, neutral, or detached discussion of the theology of nature in First World Christianity today. To engage knowingly and intentionally in the search for a responsible understanding of the relationship between the human species and the rest of creation, and to do so within the dominant cultures of the Northern Hemisphere, is to engage in an exercise in critical theology. To critical theology belongs the prospect that one shall have to accuse one's own, extending the finger of guilt at the very processes, institutions, and structures that sustain one—or seem to.[3] To tell the truth in the rich societies of planet earth today is to invite the sort of angry response that few of us who have been reared in middle-class Christianity can regard as though it were a natural consequence of obedience to Christ. But a renewed interest in Scripture (a consequence that sometimes follows from exposure to angry responses to the Christian witness) will remind us that truth-telling on the part of the people of God almost inevitably incurs worldly indignation. Given the indelible connection between truth and suffering in both biblical testaments, one may indeed wonder how so much empirical Christianity could have avoided the world's wrath.

Of course, we are all personally implicated in the guilt to which we must bear witness. And therefore we shall know the secret causes of the world's rejection of truth within our own hearts before we meet it outside ourselves in our society. But despite our own obvious or subtle involvement in the lie, we must tell the truth. Not only are millions outside these rich nations of ours depending on the confessional forthrightness of a few within them;[4] we ourselves require truth "in our inward parts" (Ps. 51:6). We require it for our own integrity, for the purgation of our spirits, and for sheer survival—our own and our progeny's.

II. THE JUDGMENT BEGINS AT THE HOUSEHOLD OF GOD

Just here, however, we encounter a certain nuance—in fact a disconcerting twist—in the whole business of Christian truth-telling; and it is just this nuance that provides the clue to the kind of theological reflection we must engage in as we consider how best to build a theological foundation for the stewardship of nature.

It is always tempting for those who—probably against their wills—are caught up in the prophetic tradition of truth-telling to begin straightaway to locate the causes of what is wrong outside the sphere of faith and church. But the uncanny thing about biblical religion is that it refuses to permit easy divisions of the world into guilty and innocent; and even more unsettling is that it seldom identifies the innocent ones it occasionally speaks of with the community of belief as such. More often, the innocent are those being neglected or hurt by "the elect"! Therefore, those who want to get to the bottom of things in biblical terms must reckon with the prospect that they will themselves have to feel the sting of the divine *krisis* (judgment) in the process; that they will have to discover anew how "we ourselves are wrong," our Christianity notwithstanding. For "the time has come for the judgment to begin with the household of God" (I Pet. 4:17).

Have Christians themselves been faithful stewards of God's

earth? Given our past, it does not become Christians to rush in with righteous indignation, accusing the technologists and entrepreneurs and industrialists of careless and rapacious ways. It would be better for us to begin in the spirit of self-examination and *metanoia*. As a beautiful Philippine proverb has it, "Whoever would shed light must endure the burning."

There are many ways in which Christians have contributed to the manifold crises of our planetary environment. In keeping with my warning in the Introduction, I am not referring here only to Christian behavior with respect to the natural order, which seems barely distinguishable from any other sort of human behavior in the Western world. I am suggesting that we have contributed to the crisis of the biosphere through what we believe, not only what we have done. It is with belief itself that critical theology must begin. The problems of the biosphere are effects; we are looking for causes. Theology has always known that the search for causes, if it is earnest, regularly conducts one into the very heart of one's belief system.

The logic of our situation as Christians in the First World today is not difficult to understand, however difficult it may be to accept. We belong to a civilization whose dreams and deeds have produced widespread industrial pollution, rampant abuse of ecosystems, the depletion of vital resources, appalling waste, the demise of countless species of plants and animals, incipient destruction of the ozone layer, and much more. Civilizations are spun out of visions, world views, images of the human; and these are always, in some measure, the products of religion.[5] To state it differently: behind every culture there is some cult. Christianity is clearly the primary historical cult behind the culture we identify as "Western." The critical question inherent in this relationship is obvious: what is and has been present in the Christian cultus — or what is absent? — that might account for some of the problems that have surfaced in our time within this First World context?

It would be frivolous, of course, to posit that Christianity is as such directly responsible for the crisis of the environment. That is why the explanations of many who have followed the lead of Lynn White's provocative 1967 article "The Historical Roots of our Ecologic Crisis"[6] are finally not very convincing. Obviously, some of those who took up the thesis that White rather modestly introduced have been more strident in their accusations than Professor White himself was. One of them writes:

> Our Greek derivation in western civilization gave us the reason
> which has guided our science, but the Judaic-Christian back-
> ground gave us a man-centred world. Our technology is a monu-
> ment to the belief that Jehovah created us in his image, a belief
> which of course had to be put that way to express the truth that
> man created Jehovah in *his* own image. The resources of the planet
> were for man, without a doubt. They could have no higher end
> than to serve man at the behest of Jehovah.[7]

White himself, as Thomas Sieger Derr has pointed out, "carefully
avoids positing a direct causal connection between [Christianity and
the technological society]":

> It is only at the end of his paper that he drops his caution and
> somewhat inconsistently seems to equate "exploitation of nature"
> with Christianity, speaking of an "orthodox Christian arrogance
> toward nature." It is this plaint, and this phrase, which the unwary
> and the unthinking and the unknowing have picked up and
> repeated in the current debate.[8]

As I have tried to show elsewhere,[9] biblical religion cannot without
gross oversimplification be accused of being *the* cause of our current
environmental problematic. At the same time, Christians should not
too quickly and confidently rise to the defense of their belief system
in the face of the "sharp historical questions"[10] Professor White and
others have raised.[11] While it is perhaps too blatant to announce, as
White does, that "Christianity bears a huge burden of guilt," we cannot escape the charge of a certain culpability in relation to the use
and abuse of nature. Deliberate hostility toward the creation is not
the charge. But it is at least possible that the custodians of our religious tradition have used it, and permitted it to be used, to create a
spiritual-intellectual atmosphere in which certain attitudes and practices of a questionable and dangerous character could emerge. It
would not be the only instance of what José Miguez-Bonino calls
"the ideological misuse of Christianity."[12]

First World Christians today are particularly required to face
up honestly to some of our reputedly "Christian" precepts and practices that may have set the tone for the highly ambitious goals of our
civilization and the nightmares into which some of those dreams
have turned.

> "Western man," says Dr. Rene Dubos, "tends to consider himself
> apart from and above the rest of creation. He has accepted to the

letter the Biblical teaching that man was given by God 'dominion over the fish of the sea, and over the fowl of the air, and over the cattle, and over all the earth' (Genesis 1:26)."[13]

Only as we expose ourselves to the dangers inherent in some of our widely held beliefs — such as the popular belief concerning human "dominion" — can we entertain correctives that could help to provide a more faithful basis for prophetic and constructive ministry in our contemporary global context. The correctives, we may well discover, do not have to be imported from outside the tradition but may be found in forgotten or submerged dimensions of our faith itself.[14]

In what follows in this chapter, we shall consider three areas of Christian theology where, whether intentionally or by default, Christianity may have helped to lay a foundation for the crisis of the biosphere. It will become obvious in the development of these themes that they are subtly interwoven; they are, in fact, aspects of a rather consistent world view, in which we may detect a distinctive preconception of the nature of the relationship between the human species and the rest of creation.[15] As such, this discussion will provide a broad backdrop for our subsequent treatment of the *imago* motif.

III. THE FATE OF THE WORLD

Is the welfare and destiny of this world a matter of "ultimate concern" (Tillich) to Christian faith? This is the confronting question of our first doctrinal consideration, and as such it is the foundational question of the whole inquiry. For unless the fate of this world does matter to Christians, and in a fundamental way, it is futile to expect adherents of this particular belief system to occupy themselves overmuch with the understanding, nurture, and preservation of nonhuman species and of the earth itself. We shall proceed with the discussion of this question in four stages.

Christian Ambiguity about this World. The answer to the question of whether this world's welfare and destiny ultimately matter to Christian belief is — unfortunately, though perhaps necessarily — a highly complex one; and this complexity, while sheltering some very profound thoughts about the character of "this world," in practice leads more frequently to a debilitating ambiguity than to profundity. Christians throughout history have manifested an extreme uncertainty about the appropriate Christian attitude toward this world, to say the least. Rarely — very rarely — have they spoken, written, or behaved as if the world should simply be loved. On the whole, the impression lingers both inside and outside the churches that true Christian piety would be marked by a certain detachment from the world, perhaps even indifference toward it. The more zealous of ascetic Christians would want to say disdain!

This impression appears to be substantiated by some of the New Testament's own commentary on the question.[16] Even Paul, whose position (as both J. C. Beker and H. Paul Santmire contend) can be read in a manner favorable to an "ecological" interpretation of the gospel,[17] sometimes seems to provide scriptural warranty for an antiworld kind of spirituality. Thus he advises those "who deal with the world" to conduct themselves "as though they had no dealings with it." For, he warns, "the form of this world is passing away" (I Cor. 7:31). His well-known argument for celibacy, which follows immediately upon this statement, rests on the premise that "the married man is anxious about world affairs, how to please his wife, and his interests are divided," whereas the "unmarried man is anxious about the affairs of the Lord" — a statement that goes more than halfway toward implying that the Lord's affairs and the world's affairs are basically incompatible (vv. 32ff.)

The Johannine literature is, of course, much more consistent than is the Pauline in embracing a faith that distances itself from the world. "John," writes Santmire, "often seems to suggest that salvation means the removal of believers from this world to some higher heavenly sphere. . . . The Pauline vision of the Christian standing in solidarity with the whole creation at the very end is thereby eclipsed. . . . The spiritual motif has triumphed over the ecological motif."[18] "Do not love the world or the things in the world," this writer cautions. "If any one loves the world, love for the Father is not in him. For all that is in the world, the lust of the flesh and the lust of the eyes and the pride of life, is not of the Father but is of the world. And the world passes away, and the lust of it . . ." (I Jn. 2:15–17).

But authors of the New Testament can go even further in their injunctions against mixing faith in God with world-orientation. "Do you not know," asks James (4:4), "that friendship with the world is enmity with God? Therefore, whoever wishes to be a friend of the world makes himself an enemy of God." Peter (II Pet. 1:4) refers to the "divine power" that has enabled believers to "escape from the corruption that is in the world because of passion, and become partakers of the divine nature." Paul, again, reminds believers that they have not received *ta pneuma tou kosmou* ("the spirit of the world") but "the Spirit which is from God" (I Cor. 2:12) — the two being mutually antagonistic. Through Christ, he cries, "the world has been crucified to me, and I to the world" (Gal. 6:14).[19]

When such a sense of the "evil" (I Jn. 5:19), "darkness" (Eph. 6:12), "hate" (Jn. 15:18), and general undesirability of the world is combined with a highly spiritualistic conception of the character of redemption, it quite naturally engenders attitudes that shun proximity to this world and, especially under apocalyptic conditions, are likely to express themselves in aggressive forms of world-negation. The celebration of the world's destruction on the part of important and vociferous Christian groupings within our own society today stands, I fear, in inescapable continuity with a motif that is present throughout ecclesiastical history. To this age-old religious "sense of an ending" popular apocalypticism is now able to apply the dread mechanics of post-Hiroshima warfare. In this rendering of the Christian message — an interpretation that cannot be divorced from certain scriptural sentiments no matter how inimical it may be to the fundamental thrust of the biblical message — the fullness of salvation can be entertained only in company with the prospect of world demolition and damnation. "The Rapture" can occur only as the prelude to earth's obliteration.[20]

Unfortunately, the religious logic that manufactures such conclusions about the divine purposes has never been clearly distinguishable from what is perceived by many as the deepest kind of Christian spirituality. The fact that the term "spiritual" itself connotes, in the popular imagination, the direct antithesis of such categories as "material," "physical," "worldly," "earthy," "bodily," and even "human," betrays the extent to which Docetic and Manichaean forms[21] of belief have displaced the concrete mysticism inherent in the biblical concepts both of creation and redemption. When present-day neoapocalypticism connects salvation with world demolition, it is simply giving expression (one kind of expression) to a sentiment so profoundly embedded in the history of Christian spirituality that it requires a concerted effort of both mind and will even to detect it.

The basis of this sentiment is that it is the world that we must be saved from. Thus, while "mainline" Christianity abhors the thought that God would use a nuclear holocaust to effect the *escha-*

ton, this same Christianity perpetuates models of "true spirituality" that accentuate nonmaterial, supranatural, and—above all—transpolitical virtues, thus sustaining the impression that genuine faith transports the believer to realms of security inaccessible to mere creaturely existence. When Hal Lindsey and his followers celebrate the approach of "the Rapture," they are carrying this same supramundane interpretation of belief to lengths that are no doubt both drastic and dramatic; but they are nonetheless on a plane strictly continuous with the milder and more sentimental versions of the redeemed life preferred by the bourgeois remnants of classical Protestantism.

The truth is, the hagiography of Christendom abounds in demonstrations of the principle that spiritual salvation implies physical destruction. If this principle applies at the level of the microcosm (the individual "soul"), then why would it not apply to the macrocosm (the world as a whole)? While there have been countervailing tendencies (such as the warnings of the early church that its members should not actually seek martyrdom), the allure of martyrdom, that is, of the violent destruction of "the flesh," has been more than an occasional trend within Christian history. Thus, in a catalogue of tortures that may be rhetorically unique yet captures a long and honored tradition of high spirituality, Ste. Thérèse of Liesieux wrote:

> From my childhood I have dreamt of martyrdom. . . . But I don't want to suffer just one torment. . . . I want to be scourged and crucified. I want to be flayed like St. Bartholemew. Like St. John, I want to be flung into boiling oil. Like St. Ignatius of Antioch, I want to be ground by the teeth of wild beasts. . . . With St. Agnes and St. Cecilia, I want to offer my neck to the sword of the executioner and like St. Joan of Arc murmur the name of Jesus at the stake. My heart leaps when I think of the unheard tortures Christians will suffer in the reign of anti-Christ. I want to endure them all.[22]

Not many saints and martyrs could equal the enthusiasm of this heaven-bent soul (of whom it was said that she was filled with "secret joy" when, on her last Good Friday, she awoke to find "a haemorrhage of blood" issuing from her mouth over her bed clothes and pillow);[23] yet the eagerness to have done with the life of this world is by no means unique to Thérèse of Liesieux. Even the comparatively balanced spirituality of Thomas à Kempis constantly pits the love of God against orientation toward the world: "The soul that loves God despises all things that are less than God. . . . The love of things created is deceitful and inconstant; the love of Jesus is faithful and enduring. He that clings to the creature shall fall with its falling."[24] Generations of readers of this most popular of all devotional books have been counseled to "learn now to die to the world, that then you may begin to live with Christ. . . . For a perfect contempt of the world, a fervent desire to advance in virtue, the love of discipline, the labour of penance, readiness of obedience, self-denial, and the bearing of any kind of adversity for the love of Christ: these things will give us great confidence in dying happily."[25]

It is not necessary to paint a picture of unrelieved world-negation, for our intention here is only to demonstrate something of the nature of empirical Christianity's ambiguity concerning this world. Certainly there have been forces at work in our religious past that militated against a complete otherworldliness. A faith centered in the Incarnation, that is, in the movement of the divine toward the world, could hardly ignore the implications of such a paradigm for Christian behavior within history. At the same time, it was also quite possible to treat the journey of the divine *logos* earthward as a necessary prelude to our transportation heavenward. Athanasius' famous dictum, "God became human in order that we might become divine," however it was intended, readily translates precisely into the sort of spirituality that looks upon the quitting of earth as the *telos* of the salvational process.

An example of the two tendencies working within the same contextual framework is provided by nineteenth-century Protestant liberalism. On the one hand, liberalism could be heralded as the rediscovery of the world as the object of God's ultimate concern. This emphasis, which had been prepared for by the humanistic tradition whose genesis is inseparable from the Reformation itself, came to a flowering in the quest for the historical Jesus, the teaching of "the brotherhood of man" as corollary of "the fatherhood of God"—and (programmatically) the social gospel movement. Yet the world-orientation that expressed itself in "social service" was never able radically to qualify the incipient otherworldliness of the piety that informed both the internal spirituality of liberalism and its "evangelism." In denominations like my own, which were profoundly influenced by liberal interpretations of the faith, the attempt was frequently made—at the administrative as well as the theoretical level—to combine "evangelism and social service."

I believe that some creative and lasting influences have come to us from such attempts. But subsequent divisions of ecclesiastical bodies into mutually suspicious camps of those stressing social activism and, on the other hand, those concerned for the salvation of human souls indicate how difficult it is, within the Christian context, to affirm a faith in God that is at the same time and with equal intensity a commitment to God's world. Ambiguity about the latter commitment is indeed most in evidence, so far as nineteenth-century Protestantism is concerned, where commitment to God seems most sure of itself, for instance in the hymns of the epoch. Many of the most beloved sacred songs of the century that discovered the humanity and worldly compassion of Jesus present "the world" as an impediment to belief. A stanza of the well-known "O Jesus, I Have Promised" by John Ernest Bode (1816–1874) typifies this dichotomy:

> O let me feel Thee near me!
>   The world is ever near;
> I see the sights that dazzle,
>   The tempting sounds I hear;
> My foes are ever near me,
>   Around me and within;
> But, Jesus, draw Thou nearer
> And shield my soul from sin.

Another favorite draws once more upon the well-established contrast between "the Lord" and "the world"

> Who is on the Lord's side?
> Who will serve the King?
> Who will be His helpers
> Other lives to bring?
> Who will leave the world's side?
> Who will face the foe?
> Who is on the Lord's side?
> Who for Him will go?
>
> (Frances Ridley Havergal, 1836–1879)

Normative Protestant sentiments of the epoch could not condone withdrawal from the world, such as was practiced in some Roman Catholic orders; yet the individualism and privatism of the kind of piety that loved to "walk in the garden alone" constituted a type of withdrawal at least comparable in its effects, and perhaps in the long run more decisive. Advocates of the social gospel could press for earthly stewardship, but this did not prevent popular piety from embracing a spirituality ("service above") that left this present world—to say the least—on the periphery of Christian conscience:

> Take time to be holy,
>   The world rushes on,
> Spend much time in secret
>   With Jesus alone. . . .
>
> Thus led by His Spirit
>   To fountains of love,
> Thou soon shalt be fitted
>   For service above.

(W. D. Longstaff)

While the "worldliness" of the Hebrew scriptures, the centrality of Incarnation and Cross, and the love ethic prevented historic Christianity from adopting an unequivocally world-negating posture, Christian duplicity in relation to this world is certainly one of the most salient features of the history of Christian thought. Even where it is not articulated in word or deed, this ambiguity is present, as Hendrikus Berkhof has noted, in the church's "silence about this world," especially about the world's renewal:

> It could be defended that faith actually has nothing to do with the world. This view is so wide-spread that theology textbooks hardly ever devote special attention to this theme. . . . Particularly the doctrine of renewal has suffered from this neglect. On the one hand it reduces it to a study of man who is detached from his world and therefore is all too often unreal, not a real creature of real flesh and blood; on the other hand, by its silence about the world it suggests that this world is irrelevant for the faith, either because it is capable of saving itself or because it is unsaveably lost.[26]

Yet, as Berkhof goes on to note, this silence cannot be justified on biblical grounds; for despite world-negating references such as those to which I have drawn attention above, the overall thrust of both Testaments is toward a noteworthy zeal for the fate of the world. How, then, can this ambiguity of historical Christianity be explained?

Reasons for the Ambiguity. There is, I suspect, no single explanation for historical Christianity's silence and ambiguity concerning this world, but rather a number of factors combine to produce this result. First, while it cannot legitimately be claimed that Christian faith has to do exclusively with the individual person ("the relation between a man and his God," as it frequently used to be stated), it is true that from the outset the Christian faith response was typified by an intensely personal form of commitment. Jesus' ministry as it is depicted in the Synoptic Gospels is not only toward individuals; yet by comparison with the Hebraic scriptures, individual encounter and transformation (*metanoia*) does play a very central role in the New Testament's story. Even the important place of the church in the Gospels and Epistles does not displace this emphasis on personal faith. In fact, the most characteristic problem addressed by the New Testament in connection with its evolving conception of the *ekklesia* is how to make good the corporate thrust of the Good News (the reconciliation of person to person) without in the process subverting its concern for the individual man, woman, and child. Paul's metaphor of "the body," with its many and unique members, was able to endure partly, one supposes, because it provided a creative symbolic solution to this question.

Secondly, when this emphasis on the personal is combined with the recognition that the earliest Christian fellowships were small, politically insignificant groupings in the midst of a powerful—if increasingly decadent—society, it is not surprising that they concentrated on the internal life of self and *koinonia*. And if— thirdly—it is remembered that at first they expected the early "return of the Lord" and the consummation of the kingdom, their injunctions to concentrate on God and "things eternal" and not to become enmeshed in the life of "this present age" are at least more understandable (see Acts 2:40–47; I Cor. 7:29–33; Mk. 13, etc.).

A fourth reason for Christian ambiguity about the world—and one of a quite different magnitude—stems from the influences coming into early Christianity from the Hellenistic culture. As C. R. North has expressed it,

> . . . a strain of pessimism was always latent in the Greek attitude toward the world. Each successive emanation meant one farther remove or declension from the source of being. Thus there emerged a kind of dualism: the material world, if not actually evil, was an obstruction to the soul (*psyche*) or mind (*nous*) by which man was related to the divine. Redemption came to be conceived as a release from matter (*hulē*) or the body (*sōma*). . . . This pessi-

mism, and its consequent attitude of world-negation, was deepened with the decline of the polis and the political insecurities of the Hellenistic period.[27]

Although the influence of Hellenistic religion and culture on Christianity has been documented by many scholars for more than a century, the extent of this influence is still to be grasped by most Christians. This is largely, in my view, because the real differences between "Jerusalem and Athens" can only be imaginatively appreciated by Christians when they have recaptured something of the Hebraic milieu away from which Christianity moved so long ago. Christian self-discovery, prompted by a combination of biblical scholarship[28] and the shock of Christian guilt in connection with the Holocaust,[29] has caused a significant minority in the churches to rethink and renew our origins as a Jewish offshoot, that is, "a movement of renewal within Judaism."[30] When such thinking is pursued studiously, nothing is more prominent in it than the distinction between Hellenistic world-negation and Hebraic world-orientation.[31]

A fifth source of Christian ambiguity concerning the world is suggested by an insight of Professor Berkhof. While the pre-Constantinian church tended to separate itself from its host culture, concentrating on its own internal life, the Constantinian adoption of the Christian religion as the primary (and later, under Theodosius, the exclusive) religion of the empire prompted the church to accept too easily its new status as being of the will of God. While under these sociological conditions the church was certainly no longer nonworldly, its attitude toward its world was now one of conformity to the status quo. It did not seek to change the world, to transform it according to the standards of "the kingdom" taught by its Lord; rather, it accepted the existing order, "exploiting it for its own benefit."[32] "That is the reason," concludes Berkhof, "why Christian Europe was for at least a thousand years barren soil in which the seeds of a vision of the world renewed could not germinate."[33] With the establishment of Christianity, "the world" enters into Christian thought and history in a different way; but the world's fate is no more the ultimate concern of the church after its marriage to empire than it was before. There are, of course, exceptions to this rule throughout Christian history;[34] but the broad pattern of dominant Christianity is not greatly altered by them.

Sixth, and finally, a significant reason for Christian ambiguity about the world must be traced to linguistic confusion (though it goes without saying that such misunderstandings are never just semantic). There are three Greek words (*oikoumenē, aiōn,* and *kosmos*) that are all translated "world" in most English versions of the New Testament. Important shadings of difference pertain between these three terms, and though they are not used with entire consistency in the scriptural writings, differences are rather significant. Thus *aiōn* means "age" or "epoch," and when Paul writes to the church at Rome that it should not be "conformed to this world" (12:1) he is obviously saying that Christians should not emulate the trends, goals, and values of their society but should allow themselves to be shaped instead by their new identity "in Christ." Again, when he writes to the Ephesians (6:12) that "we wrestle . . . against principalities, against powers, against the rulers of the darkness of this world," it is not the creation as such that he claims is under the sway of the evil forces but the "aeon" — that is, the old dispensation of sin, introduced by the Fall, which is being displaced by the new aeon inaugurated by Christ. *Aiōn* thus lends itself to thought about the world that implies a questionable dimension of creaturely existence without suggesting (with Gnosticism, for example) that creation as such is questionable. *Kosmos,* the more prominent New Testament term for the world, is axiologically more neutral. It can be the vehicle for either positive or negative statements. An example of the latter would be the Synoptic admonition, "For what will it profit anyone to gain the whole world and lose his life?" (Mt. 16:26, par.) On the other hand, it would be hard to find a more positive connotation for *kosmos* than that suggested by the familiar declaration of John 3:16, or Paul's summary statement in II Corinthians 5:19: "God was in Christ reconciling the *kosmon* to himself." The third term for world, *oikoumenē,* means literally "the inhabited earth," and in Greek it originally designated the Greek (i.e., civilized) world as distinct from barbarian lands.

The main point to be made here is that this variety of New Testament terms and the differing ways in which each of them can be employed suggest theological nuances that are not readily captured by the single English word "world." Combined with the other five factors that we have treated, this linguistic confusion has made it all the more inevitable that an abiding ambiguity would surround the Christian apprehension of the world. And if the negative side of this ambiguity has been dominant in spite of some very positive sentiments respecting the world in biblical writings, this is at least in part due to the incapacity of our language to capture the nuances of the ancient distinctions.

Consequences of the Ambiguity. Ambiguity is not necessarily an undesirable or dangerous state. It can describe the tension of living between two polar tendencies with respect to a given reality, and to live within such tensions can be a source of creativity. It can also, alas, become a reason for passivity — a fence to sit on! My suspicion is that it is more consistently the latter.

For both R. Gregor Smith and John Macquarrie, Christian ambiguity about this world describes a creative tension. "The ambiguity of the concept of the 'world' in Christian thought," writes Smith in *A Dictionary of Christian Ethics*,[35] "is present from the beginning. In the New Testament the world is the world of men, in opposition to God, but it is also the world which God loves and which he has reconciled to himself in Christ." Smith continues: "The tension which has consequently been maintained has been immensely fruitful for all spheres of Christian thought and enterprise." Obviously reacting to the emergence of "worldly Christianity" stemming from Bonhoeffer's later writings and the "secular Christianity" of the 1960s, John Macquarrie again and again refers to "the ambiguity of the world" in his *Principles of Christian Theology*, and warns:

> We delude ourselves if we think that some ideal state of affairs is attainable on earth, or that the main business of Christianity is to establish a super welfare state. . . . Christianity is not a mere worldliness. . . . Precisely because of the current stress on worldly Christianity, it is necessary that some should witness to the transcendent element in faith and remind us of the need to maintain a dialectical attitude to the world.[36]

In my view, this argument does not address the real problem. The real problem is not that Christian faith is called to live in the tension between God's judgment of this world and God's love for it. That tension is in fact potentially a very creative one — indeed, it is the cornerstone of Christian ethics. For it combines a vision of what the world essentially is and could (under grace) become, with a zeal for naming and struggling against the things that prevent it from attaining its full glory as God's good and beloved creation. The real problem contemporary theology has to wrestle with is that historic Christianity has spurned living within precisely this tension. The real problem is that, instead of living *within* the tension, the majority

forms of the church have rejected the biblical duality of attitudes toward the world, have opted for the uncertainty principle contained
in their combination, and have in this way emerged with the kind
of ambiguity that fosters indecision, passivity, and "silence" (Berkhof), where it does not actually go over into withdrawal and
denigration. It is one thing to embrace a gospel that says two paradoxical things about the world: that it is loved absolutely and that
it is judged absolutely. That may be ambiguity of a kind, though it
is more accurately termed paradox. It is something else to say (or to
think without actually saying) that one cannot give oneself wholly
to the healing of the creation because one is not clear that divine
redemption implies such a thing. This is real ambiguity — the genuine article! And when Macquarrie worries that we should be careful
not to turn Christianity into "mere worldliness," and is at pains to
remind us "that the aim of Christianity is not just universal affluence
and enjoyment of life," it is real "ambiguity" (his word) that we are
hearing about, the very ambiguity that has such a long and impressive history in the Christian tradition concerning this world.

The Challenge to Transcend the Ambiguous State. Two things are
remarkable in recent Christianity. The first is that the most significant symbolic figures represent Christianity in this age — people
like Bonhoeffer, Thomas Merton, Martin Luther King, Mother
Theresa, Dom Helder Camara, Jean Vanier, and others — are almost
without exception individuals who have had what may be termed
a "conversion to the world."[37] The second is that these persons could
only achieve such a conversion through an often painful process of
detaching themselves from the powerful Christian conventions in
which they were reared and, very frequently, alienating themselves
from the guardians of those conventions.

Teilhard de Chardin, in a particularly poignant prayer, exem-
plifies both of these points:

> There is one thing more, Lord, just one thing, but it is the most
> difficult of all, and, what is more, it is a thing that you, perhaps,
> have condemned. It is this: if I am to have a share in your king-
> dom, I must on no account reject this radiant world in the ecstatic
> delight of which I opened my eyes.[38]

That Teilhard had to utter such a prayer, that he had to suppose that
God had perhaps "condemned" love for the world — this speaks
more affectingly of the power of the ambiguity we are tracing here
than any historical analysis could manage.

Not necessarily in all that they have said and done, but in their fundamental posture as people of faith, such symbolic figures are, I believe, forerunners of the coming church. Their conversion to the world is the form that must be taken by Christian *metanoia* in our time. This cannot be achieved without a break from the past, and we deceive ourselves if we think that past is without its vigilant and stalwart guardians still today. Ambiguity about the world is the one thing that unites all such guardians. Regardless of their style of churchmanship, theology, liturgy, and the rest, they all resist the radical reorientation of the faith toward this world. For once it is determined that the gospel is intended for the world and that the healing of the creation is its ultimate aim, the path of Christian obedience is perfectly clear: it must bring to bear all the considerable weight of the message of divine judgment and divine love on this world, its structures and infrastructures, its "principalities and powers," its economic injustices, its machinery of death, its "spiritual wickedness in high places" — all that threatens the life of the beloved *kosmos* must be named and rejected. All that makes for its well-being, including those who strive for its shalom under whatever banner, must then be consecrated and supported. It is not surprising, therefore, that there are strong vested interests in maintaining the theology of ambiguity in relation to this world. For it would be impossible, finally, for any theological community that had undergone such a conversion to the world to avoid becoming in the most rudimentary sense of the term a *political* theology.

The challenge to transcend the ambiguous state is issued, however, not only to churchfolk, activists, or doers of deeds. It is as much a conversion of the mind as of the heart and the hands. "We who live in the twentieth century," writes Hendrikus Berkhof, "can no longer, not in our study of the faith either, avoid the question concerning the world and its renewal."[39] Berkhof finds three reasons why our "silence" on this matter can no longer be permitted. The first is the rise of a militant form of humanism that has dared to take the destiny of this world into its own hands, to wit, secularism. Secularism is born with the decision, explicit or simply assumed, that if there is to be any meaning, it must be found and nurtured within the *saeculum*, and that humanity both can and must assume responsibility for its own destiny. Harvey Cox and others have demonstrated that secularism is a product of the Judaeo-Christian world view.[40] And while, in my opinion, John Cobb is correct in thinking that the secular mind does not provide "the focus for a long-term commitment to the healing of our natural environment,"[41] the active presence of this militantly human and worldly form of atheism[42] has, I believe, put to its parental cultus the challenge to declare itself either friendly or unfriendly toward this world. It demands, in other words, that the posture of ambiguity be dropped once and for all.

Berkhof's second reason for breaking our silence about the world is Marxism. Under the judgment against "religion" pronounced by Karl Marx (namely, that it functions as an "opiate"),[43] Christianity is reminded of the commitment of prophetic faith to the God who has what liberationists have called "a preferential option for the poor." It is reminded too of the social dimensions of its doctrine of sin: alienation and the evils of unchecked egoism, for instance in "ruthless capitalism" (Berkhof), even when, as John Kenneth Galbraith phrased it in a recent speech, "the trickle-down doctrine" serves as "the necessary cloak over avarice."[44] Berkhof writes:

> Only in recent times do we discover with and through Marx how much of an alienating effect the structures of our world can have with respect to the quality of human life as desired by God. As a result of that discovery, the theme "world" now presses itself upon our attention as never before. It is even difficult to indicate precisely what the difference between Marx and the gospel is on this point. For Marx, too, was concerned with man and his happiness and with trying to make the structures serve that purpose.[45]

Thirdly, Berkhof writes of the dynamic outlook produced by evolutionary thought. Traditional theology conceived of reality in static terms. Evolution has caused us to appreciate the dynamic nature of all life.[46] A changing human situation cannot be served by a religion in which nothing changes, which even depends on a commitment to changelessness. This, says Berkhof, "involves a challenge to theologians to broaden the belief in man's changeability (sanctification) so that it includes the sanctification of the world as well." And yet, he adds, "in spite of all that, in present-day dogmatics the problematic of the world is hardly discussed."[47]

To this list we should now add a fourth reason why late twentieth-century Christian thought cannot remain either silent or ambiguous concerning the world and its "fate" (Jonathan Schell). I call this "the omega factor." In multitudinous ways—not just in the threat of nuclear warfare—we are confronted now by the absolute vulnerability of the planet. Christians have always confessed creation's finitude, dependence (contingency), and limitations; but never before have Christians been faced with the prospect that this world might end, not as a consequence of divine decree (that is, in some meaningful sense) but through human accident or design.[48] Humanity now possesses the technology that is capable of terminating the life of a planet for which sufficient raison d'être cannot be found. And it is not sufficient reason-for-being simply to register a distaste for *not*-being! Ambiguity about the being of the world is almost an open invitation to the Destroyer.

Under these conditions (no longer merely physical, for they have acquired the status of the metaphysical), Christians, among others, are required to declare themselves with respect to this world. These circumstances constitute the final form of the question that has been put to Christendom in a great variety of ways throughout its history: Is this the world that God loves, the world reconciled to God through Christ, the world whose "life" was the object of the Incarnation and the Cross? Is this the world God wills to renew, fulfill, bring to completion, and are these the kingdoms that "have become the kingdom of our God and of his Christ"? Heretofore, it has been possible for the church to set aside the forerunners of this question, including the three factors named by Berkhof. Now, however, we face the question about the world in its final form, beyond which there are no more choices. Either we shall choose to embrace the life of this world, or we shall have chosen (or been chosen by) death — one of the many kinds of death, physical and spiritual, that are gathering themselves for the final attack on the edges and at the center of our corporate existence. "Perhaps," writes John Carmody, "that would be the ultimate impiety and sacrilege: to cause creation to die."[49]

We find ourselves, then, at one of the most decisive crossroads in the Christian pilgrimage through history. Carmody and others are correct in drawing our attention to the human attitude toward nature as the crux of the matter; they call for "a firm commitment to nature's preservation," insisting that "God has placed nature in our care, made nature subject to our responsible stewardship."[50] But there is a preliminary step that Christians must take before the commitment to the natural order can be anything more than an ethical imperative: it is the theological/ontological decision that the gospel of Jesus as the Christ implies a rudimentary indicative concerning this world, namely, that it is greatly loved, and that its mending is an immediate and vital dimension of the whole work of God. Only such an indicative (is) could sustain imperatives (ought to be) such as the command to tend the earth as nature's stewards.

Is such an indicative in fact present in the Christian gospel? For my part, I have determined that it is, that Christian belief and tradition does have within it the wherewithal for transcending its own record of ambiguity about the world. Were I not able to come to this conclusion, I should feel obliged at this time to renounce Christianity and find, if possible, a faith that is more worthy of the goodness of the world. Fortunately for my own integrity, I do not feel that it is necessary to take that drastic step. I believe that a word can be recovered underneath the rhetoric and the ruins of Christendom on the basis of which Christians not only may take to heart an ultimate concern for this world's destiny but must do so — unambiguously and joyfully. "Must" — not only because external circumstances are giving us this one last chance to come over to the side of the creation, but also because of strong and neglected currents within the tradition of Jerusalem itself. It is at least possible that, even apart from the historical circumstances that are driving all persons of good will toward stewardship of the earth today, Christians in our period would have unearthed some of the submerged but fundamental themes of our tradition that move in that direction. But the gravity of the world situation has certainly expedited this discovery, so that it is not surprising to find ecclesiastical bodies insisting that, for example, peacekeeping is now to be regarded as a matter of *status confessionis*,[51] or to hear the World Council of Churches announcing that "Jesus Christ is the Life of the World."[52]

This does not imply that Christians are called to endorse a theology that ties the victory of God in Christ to the survival of some particular kind of society. A global theology today (and there can be no responsible theology now that is not global in its perspective[53]) must not only transcend the church's general ambiguity about the world, but it must transcend every ideology that construes the world in restrictive and chauvinistic terms. I suspect that we may not yet say (perhaps a future generation of Christians will be permitted to do so again) what the best form of society in a world that had come to terms with "the omega factor" would be — whether, for instance, it is desirable still to encourage and support the sovereignty of individual states. For the present, our mandate is only to move past the threshold of ambiguity and decide for the world, its survival, its life, its shalom, its salvation.

In doing so, we shall need to exercise the modesty that belongs to faith in Jesus Christ. The Christian church cannot ensure the world's healing all by itself. Such triumphalistic pretentions were denied us long ago. If we are cognizant of the signs of the times, we have also noticed that there are stirrings of world-orientation within many other religious traditions today. In all of the historic religions, as well as in many newer religious and semireligous groupings, sensitive believers have been moved, as have many Christians, to search their traditions for ontological foundations that can undergird the need to affirm the life of the biosphere at this critical juncture in world history. It may be that what brings all sincere religious faiths into genuine dialogue at last will be their common search for an ethic that embraces the earth. We are not alone. Yet an unambiguous act of world-affirmation on the part of the church catholic would certainly not be insignificant. Given our hesitant and indecisive past, in fact, such a movement toward the world on the part of Christians everywhere would be nothing short of momentous. It could alter the destiny of earth if the behavior of Christians universally began to reflect concretely the prayer they utter millions of times daily, that God's kingdom should come "on earth, as it is in heaven."

IV. DIVINE GRACE AND THE HUMAN WILL

"The earth," wrote Joseph Sitler, "is not merely a negative illustration of the desirability of heaven."[54] Heaven—that difficult and much-misunderstood scriptural term—certainly connotes a reality more inclusive than earth. But the heaven that is regularly offered by the hucksters of simplistic religion as an alternative to earth is not, surely, the abode of that "Father in heaven" to whom Jesus instructed his disciples to address their prayers. Whatever else it may designate, Jesus' heaven encompasses earth—or would do so if only earthlings would stop denigrating their God-made habitat and desiring to exchange it for some heaven!

If we have established the point that the fate of the earth is at the core of the gospel concerning the advent of God's kingdom, we may move to the second major problematical area of Christian belief as it relates to the search for a better theology of humanity's relationship to the natural order. Our question here can be stated along the following lines: If the destiny of this world is a matter of ultimate concern to Christian faith, is the governance of the world in any sense a human responsibility, or is it entirely a divine prerogative? This question must be addressed before we can move to the third area of investigation and the major concern of this study, namely, the character of the relationship between human and non-human nature. For it will be our assumption there that human beings have a certain responsibility (*Verantwortlichkeit*) within the natural sphere. Precisely this, however, cannot be assumed. If we are to propose such a thing, we must lay a reflective foundation for it, and that can be done only by making our way quite deliberately through a very confusing doctrinal past.

The past in question has to do with the juxtaposition of the two terms in the above subheading: divine grace/human will. Christian understanding teeters between an emphasis on divine sovereign grace that leaves little or no room for human responsibility and, on the other hand, a call to human responsibility that seems in effect to preclude any lively belief in the transcendent ordering of the world. An imaginary visitor from outer space, observing the teaching and activity of Christians, might well ask: "Who is in charge here?"

Alternative Routes. Two responses would have to be given to such a question, for they have vied with each other throughout Christian history and have seldom achieved anything like mutuality.

(a) The first — and historically the more vigorous of the two — accentuates divine sovereignty, omnipotence, and providence. Augustine gave classical expression to this position,[55] and in the Protestant camp John Calvin made the sovereignty of God alone his primary theological theme[56] — to the point that he found himself, at last, having to embrace the "horrible decree" of double predestination: for if God alone determines the fate of all things, human failure to respond positively to the saving grace of God in Christ must finally be attributed to divine determination.[57]

Within this tradition, the characteristic attributes of the divine being have quite naturally revolved around the idea of power: God is the omnipotent, omniscient, omnipresent One whose will shapes everything that occurs. The vocation of believers is not to initiate but to "obey" (the characteristic term of all ethical teaching stemming from this source). Historically, in fact, this position in its most influential articulations has evolved in reaction to Christians and others who insisted on the possibility and necessity of human initiative. In the case of Augustine, the emphasis on divine sovereignty came to fruition in his struggle against Pelagianism; and Calvin hardened his theology of divine determination in reaction to the teaching of Arminius and others.

Implied in all expressions of this convention is a strong distrust of human wisdom, goodness, and ability. Theocratic conceptions of world governance are embraced, in other words, not only for the positive reason that they assume a "high" theology (doctrine of God) but also for the negative reason that their anthropological presuppositions are correspondingly "low." The human creature is so limited, so sinful, so egocentric, so "depraved" that it cannot be trusted to initiate — or even possibly to execute — correct decisions. Even the regenerate, "the elect," must be wary of the dangers of an ongoing human willfulness: their discipleship is a matter of following, not of initiating. Their task is to submit in all things to the divine will; and it is indicative of this convention's power that the confession of sin in circles of belief it has shaped almost invariably consists in the acknowledgment of failure to achieve a total "submission" to God's will.

(b) The second response to the question of world governance, conversely, stresses human responsibility. This in part represents a reaction against the more stringent conceptions of divine rule we have just been discussing (a process of what is now called "polarization" can be observed in this whole discussion throughout the history of Christian thought). But it is also in part a reflection, in Christian circles, of the modern sense of human autonomy. To employ the nomenclature of Paul Tillich and others,[58] modernity replaced heteronomous conceptions of the determination of the world with an autonomous conception. That is, the *nomos* (law or ordering) of existence is not from beyond (*heteros:* other) but from within (*autos:* self). In Christian terms, as this spirit of autonomy was taken up by liberal and modernist schools of theology, it was translated into a language that still retained — at least in principle — the idea of divine intentionality but identified it more explicitly with human historical potentiality. The human being has been created by God with intrinsic capacities of rationality, freedom, and dignity. Although these may be found in a weakened state in existing persons and societies, they are continuously reactivated and enhanced by the divine Spirit permeating all life. Thus human beings generally, and in particular those who are consciously influenced by the Spirit of Jesus, are capable not only of initiating change but of participating in the gradual transformation of the world into the divine kingdom. The extent to which this message implied *extraordinary* as distinct from *common* grace, thus retaining a dimension of heteronomy, depended naturally on the degree to which one moved from transcendental to immanental assumptions concerning the deity in one's doctrine of God. The following statement by Walter Rauschenbusch typifies the tendency of liberalism to accentuate the latter propensity:

> When he [God] was far above, he needed vice-generals to rule for him, popes by divine institution. . . . If he lives and moves *in the life of mankind,* he can act directly in the masses of men. A God who strives within our striving, who kindles his flame in our intellect, sends the impact of his energy to make our will restless for righteousness . . . and always urges the race toward a higher combination of freedom and solidarity . . . etc.[59]

Between these two polar conceptions of the determination of the world, the one stressing divine and the other human governance, one can, of course, detect a whole spectrum. It is difficult to find either position embraced at the practical level in its pure theoretical state. Fortunately, human beings are usually less consistent than some of their more one-sided pronouncements indicate. But it is obvious that as theories they contain antithetical elements. While creative individuals like Schleiermacher and Reinhold Niebuhr managed to forge their answers to this question by drawing on aspects of both positions, a conspicuous confusion informs the general spirit of Christendom here. Stated in terms that are no doubt oversimple, the spirit of modernity that informs the thought of most Christians within the older denominations of the church assumes that human beings may and must take charge of their world, while the residue of "orthodoxy" in the same Christians continues to insist that God alone is sovereign Lord, and that the spirit of human autonomy may just possibly, therefore, be blasphemous.

Dangers in Both Positions. This state of confusion is far from being a harmless theoretical problem. Together with the ambiguity about the world that we have discussed, it constitutes the kind of theological mystification that leads unerringly to an ethical hiatus. Given our present historical situation, such an impasse must be regarded as dangerous. There are perils in both of the positions described, as well as in their confused combination.

(a) The danger of the first alternative (overemphasizing divine sovereignty) is that it identifies the actual course of historical events with heavenly intention. Thus it provides the ultimate conceivable sanction for the status quo: what is, is what God wills. Does a tyrant assume the throne? It cannot be pure chance or human ambition only. Do the nations rage against one another and pursue "mutually assured destruction"? God, who makes human wrath the vehicle for divine providence, is accomplishing his "unfolding purpose."

European, and especially Germanic, history in this century has demonstrated graphically and tragically the consequences of such an interpretation of the determination of the world. It has also demonstrated that these events cannot be divorced from the Reformation's emphasis on divine sovereignty and the priority of prevenient and irresistible grace, which in Lutheran lands particularly worked itself out in a theory of the divine election of political authorities (the "two realms" concept).

A rather different—and more complex—illustration of the danger in this position has manifested itself in North American experience. Here, especially in the United States, the combination of Enlightenment idealism and Calvinistic providentialism produced what George Grant has called our primary religion—"the religion of Progress."[60] The modern assumption that redemption is built into the historical process as such, mingled with the Reformed belief in the *providentia Dei*, has issued in a spirit of what may be called happy determinism. The determinism was happy, unlike the darker religious and philosophical forms of determinism prevalent in the Old World, because while with the latter it embraced the sense that whatever would be would be, it was sufficiently modern to think that whatever would be would be good. Good at least for us, a favored people—the new Eden for the new Adam.[61] As Reinhold Niebuhr has pointed out, this happy determinism was never wholly compatible with our New World brand of voluntarism (America as the "can do" society), a mood that at the rhetorical level has probably been more conspicuous.[62] In fact, as a people we seem never to have been able to make up our minds whether we were meant to achieve greatness (through will and effort), or simply have had greatness "thrust upon us," as Malvoleo puts it in Shakespeare's *Twelfth Night*. The one thing we have agreed on is that greatness has been our destiny.

In these latter days, however, it is precisely this assumption that has become our almost universal point of uncertainty. If we as a people suffer from "future shock" (Toffler), "narcissism" (Lasch), "psychic numbing" (Lifton), and so forth, it is surely because, having believed ourselves to be the favored children of a beneficent historical providence, and having lost touch with older spiritual and intellectual resources for the experience of negation and failure, we now find that we are confronted by a horizon that does not confirm our happy prospectus but on the contrary threatens what popular magazines insist on calling the "unthinkable" (unthinkable because we have been conditioned to think only positive thoughts).

Contemplating a future that does not ratify our expectations, those among us who do not resort to hedonistic forms of escape are often driven back into the old deterministic mindset that is the ontic basis of our New World optimism. "Christianity" again becomes important in our situation, therefore, for it was a species of Christianity — the providentialism of later Calvinism — that provided the necessary cultic foundation for our cultural positivism. In some quarters today, increasingly simplistic versions of this providentialism are able to sustain the belief that God still intends "America" for greatness, and thus "Christianity" becomes an indispensable factor in the military build-up of the United States and its allies. In other quarters, the "blessed assurance" that comes with belief in the direct divine determination of the world translates itself into apocalyptic forms of hope. A happy fate having been denied us as our national heritage, we transfer to the "next world" the great expectations that have been thwarted by this one.

(b) If the hazard of an undialectical providentialism is that it leads to fatalistic withdrawal from responsibility for earth's destiny, the danger of accentuating the human governance of the world is that it produces an exaggerated estimate of human wisdom, freedom, and goodness. As our own recent history has shown, the apotheosis of the human is not likely to occur without a corresponding denigration of nonhuman species. For when human autonomy is unchecked by a sense of the human creature's accountability to what transcends it, what is to prevent us humans from doing with nature whatever we will? Thus, as John Cobb has said, the human quest for dominion has led inevitably to the conclusion that nature's "value lies entirely in its usefulness to man. Only man has intrinsic worth. The value of the subhuman world is purely instrumental."[63]

As with the previous consideration (the overaccentuation of divine determination), so in the present instance, the problematical character of an exaggerated emphasis on the human cannot be divorced from Christian influence, and from the general confusion surrounding this whole subject in Christian history. Cobb is right, in my opinion, when he accepts Lynn White's charge that the Judaeo-Christian tradition bears considerable responsibility for the crisis of nature. He is even more justified in his opinion that "since the attitude that is responsible for our difficulties is a religious or theological one, the change that is required must be at that level."[64]

The question is, what precisely is the "religious or theological" source of this attitude? How could religion—in particular the Christian religion—have fostered an image of the human that elevated *Homo sapiens* so unqualifiedly, and at the expense of the other creatures of God? My own thesis is that Christianity could have permitted this to occur only at a point in its evolution where it had lost touch with any operative sense of the transcendent. Liberalism, which was correct over against the older orthodoxies in claiming human responsibility for the world, nevertheless so unambiguously identified the transcendent with what it fancied were the best impulses within the human spirit that it robbed the faith of any effective basis for a prophetic critique of human initiative.

Neither the elevation of the human nor the "thingification" of extrahuman nature is warranted by the biblical tradition. It is true that the tradition of Jerusalem does not attribute divinity to the creation itself. Christianity always managed to resist its own pantheistic tendencies—as in Origen or Eckhart. But as the recurrent mysticism of Catholic, Protestant, and Jewish (e.g., Hasidic) religious traditions amply testifies, refusal to consider the world divine does not necessitate ignoring or rejecting its sacredness. Earth and its manifold creatures are not emanations from God: they are "made, not begotten." But as God's good (Gen. 1), wondrous (Ps. 8) and awesome (Ps. 104) work, creation itself contains an ineffable depth that is as much the source of faith's sense of transcendence as is the height of its Maker. Is it not in fact impossible, within the framework of biblical religion, to separate wonder about the creation and adoration of the Creator? It is not doubted that "the earth is the Lord's, and the fullness thereof" (Ps. 24:1), and therefore not to be worshipped. But the God who addresses Job out of the whirlwind recites at length the wonders of creation, for "the things that are made" bear the mark of the glory of their maker (Rom. 1:20). As a modern writer phrases it, God is also "the mystery of the world."[65]

It is only with the disappearance of this sense of the sacred inhabiting the secular that a species of human autonomy could arise that ceased to recognize in the inarticulate creation traces of its wondrous origins and governance. Sheer, unabashed images of human mastery cannot form themselves in the minds of human beings who still acknowledge their creaturehood in an immediate and simply axiomatic way—that is, who still recognize the *dominium* of the Lord.

The most that may come of a religious faith that confesses human creaturehood, divine sovereignty, and the mystery of life is the penultimate dominion of the human, that is, a form of governance that in the very act of taking initiative within the natural order knows that it is accountable to the ultimate.

The more precise word for such dominion is *stewardship*. Neither the concept of possession nor that of mastery is appropriate to this mindset. As John Wycliffe saw very clearly at the waning of the Middle Ages, both mastery and the assumption of property defy the sole *dominium* of God.[66] It is not accidental that Wycliffe developed a lively theology of human stewardship. He is one of the few important historical theologians to have done so, and his sensitivity in this respect is related to the emergence, in his time, of a new spirit of prometheanism. His attempt to recall his contemporaries to a radical sense of their tenancy of earth failed. And unfortunately, it was not picked up by the major reformers of the next century, though it can be detected among some of the writings of the Reformation's "left wing." With the advent of the modern *imago*, the human creature, trained by scholasticism to regard itself as the only "rational" animal but now set free from direct answerability to the Source of its rationality, could think itself in charge of nature, the maker of history, the determiner of the fate of the earth.

The Corrective. We thus find ourselves, both as citizens of First World societies and as Christians, heirs of a long-standing confusion concerning the governance of the world. A prominent strain in our religious heritage (especially strong in North America because of the Calvinist influence) promotes the primacy of divine sovereignty. For the majority this concept seems more rhetorical than real ("In God We Trust"); but for a vociferous and even aggressive minority it is their fundamental credo. Combining the sovereignty of a well-defined and exclusively "Christian" God with equally restrictive renditions of such biblical ideas as divine election, the just or holy war, and the *parousia*, this powerful minority provides cultic sanction for the most militant political elements within our nations. It does not fear Armageddon. Why should it do so, when God is clearly in charge and has already announced that final battle as the goal of "His" strategem?

A second strain in our heritage, which can draw upon both religious and philosophical roots, insists that human beings have both the capacity and the responsibility to shape the future. This too has a powerful rhetorical appeal for the majority, for it belongs to the whole *mythos* of the New World. Yet it seems increasingly to inspire only minorities—"activists." (One might well ask why, in a society whose mythology abounds in tales of overcoming obstacles, human ingenuity, initiative, and know-how, the term "activist" has almost become one of derision.)

Between these two possibilities, the vast majority of our populace appears to drift to and fro on the misty flats. People vacillate between the frustrated feeling that "*we* ought to do something" and the half-belief that "*He's* got the whole world in his hands." If the world is endangered on the one hand by the self-righteousness of those who think they are on the side of a sovereign and omnipotent deity, and on the other by those whose belief in human mastery has blinded them to the traditions of human accountability, it is most endangered, I suspect, by those who are reduced to moral passivity because of their confusion—for they are the majority. Christianity is at least partially to blame for this confusion.

For serious faith, therefore, this situation raises the question: Is it possible to elaborate an understanding of the divine governance of the world that does not *a priori* negate but positively establishes the necessity for human responsibility within the world? How can we speak about God's sovereignty without undermining human accountability? Or to pose the question from the other side of this tension: How shall we think of human responsibility without betraying a covert atheism in the process?

As with Christian ambiguity concerning the fate of the world, so with the question of the world's governance, Christians are challenged by the crisis of planetary existence to come to terms with this ancient, unresolved problem of belief. We have never satisfactorily articulated for ourselves the biblical tension between divine grace and human freedom, gospel and law, indicative and imperative. That is partly true because we have never before been forced to do so by the actual circumstances of history. Time has permitted us the luxury of theological debate and the formation of parties. We have had a party of grace and a party of freedom, a party of gospel and a party of law. We have known the argument from divine sovereignty and the argument from human initiative, heteronomy and autonomy. Here and there, individuals and minorities have transcended this historic debate and learned how to live within the tension posed by its two polar categories. But today the whole church is confronted by the need, unprecedented in history, to develop a theological praxis enabling it to bring to bear on a threatened globe not only its own undivided service but also a wisdom that is sorely needed within society at large.

That wisdom is obscured by the separation of the two factors in this discussion. It is in their juxtaposition — and the creative tension posed by it — that we may find our way toward a responsible exercise of Christian discipleship in this critical hour of world history.

Since I have already introduced Paul Tillich's two terms for the polarities of the question (heteronomy/autonomy), it will be useful to employ his third term to explicate what is meant by the juxtaposition of the two: *theonomy*. Theonomy is Tillich's linguistic device for the situation in which the *nomos* (law, determination, ordering) of being contains an external (heteronomous) dimension that is not in conflict but rather in a creative tension with the internal (autonomous) dimension: that is, in such a way as to elicit from the self (*autos*) or the human being its full potentiality for self-expression.[67]

Translating this into the terms of the present discussion, we might state the matter as follows: The ordering or governance of the world implies an initiating presence (God's), which is indeed external to it (*heteros*: other) but which, rather than imposing demands on it that are contrary to its nature and destiny, elicits from it — autonomously, through its own conscious, willing creatures — the "good" that is inherent in it as potentiality, thus enabling it to become what it (essentially) is. In other words, divine grace and sovereignty, while certainly "other," work in and through human freedom and responsibility to achieve the fullness of being for which the created order already possesses potentiality. Thus it is not a case of either/or: either divine sovereignty or human willing, either grace or freedom, gospel or law, faith or works. It is a matter of both/and: namely, a sovereign grace that grasps the human subject and evokes from it the creaturely responsibility for which it has a capacity but which, on account of false pride and sloth, it fails to make good. In other words, it is a gospel that frees us from self-preoccupation in order for us to become responsive to the Torah of conscious, deliberate, and joyful participation in the divine governance of creation.

Such an articulation of the determination of the world guards against all three dangers discussed in the foregoing: a) The danger of a providentialism, which flees an "unsavable" world in favor of otherworldly bliss or courts oblivion by cultically undergirding political imperialism; this approach instills the courage to believe that the world is indeed "renewable" (Berkhof), that its "leaderless" (Buber) forces can be confronted and directed, that it can be "changed" (Marx), that human hope and work are not vain because they can both reflect and effect God's own transforming grace. b) The danger of an autonomous mastery that threatens to impose oppressive technocratic structures on the world of both nonhuman and human being, reducing to predictability the rich profusion of creaturely life; such an articulation of the determination of the world places important restraints on human autonomy: there is a *nomos* within which our human ordering must take place; there are limits, coming both from the side of the Creator and that of the creature, beyond which our trespassing can only result in universal suffering. c) Finally, the danger of a religion that cannot act because it either fears there is no way out of the confusion of conflicting traditions or (what is more probable) because it finds psychic refuge in that confusion; this understanding of the governance of the world insists that confusion is by no means the inevitable consequence of a religious tradition that emphasizes both divine grace and human freedom. Of course, there is a tension implicit in the confession that God is sovereign Lord and that we ourselves are fully responsible for our world. But it is possible to live within this tension. That is, it is possible to believe simultaneously in the entire indispensability of grace and the absolute necessity of the most mature human thought, word, and deed.

Is it not true that living within precisely this tension is the only really creative basis for Christian ethics? Just this tension would seem to be the evangelical foundation of the Christian ethic. For the gospel is nothing more or less than the coalescence of authentic deity and authentic humanity (*vere Deus* and *vere Homo*). True God, though "other" and even "wholly other" (*totaliter alliter*), here declares the destiny of the earth, its redemption, to be the object of divine sovereignty; and true humanity here demonstrates its willingness to sacrifice what is exclusively human to a larger cause that embraces both the will of the Creator and the care of the creation. This coalescence is not, of course, achieved without pain. After all, we are speaking of Jesus Christ, of Gethsemane and of the Cross. To be the church is to be taken up into the pain of this coalescence, to experience the "otherness" (heteronomy) of what is required of those so taken up, to suffer the loss of self and self-will (autonomy), and to discover a harmony in the ordering of life (theonomy) only in a measure, and only in the crucible of this relationship—but nonetheless as real possibility. Here and there, now and then, faith knows that divine dominion and human stewardship are part and parcel of the same providential process.

V. RELATIONS BETWEEN HUMAN AND EXTRAHUMAN NATURE

If we have suggested a way in which the determination of the world may be said to involve both a strong doctrine of grace and an equally strong sense of responsible human willing, then we are in a position to move to the third and final problematical area of Christian doctrine as it pertains to the quest for a better understanding of the human role in the natural order. This is the question that belongs most immediately to that quest, and as such it will become the subject of everything that follows. Here we merely introduce the question in order to show its continuity with the two preliminary concerns (subheadings 3 and 4), and to anticipate somewhat more precisely the kind of question that it is.

We may state the present concern in regard to the two previous areas of consideration as follows: If the fate of the world *is* a matter of ultimate concern to Christians (3); and if the governance of the world *does* involve human participation indispensably (4); then what does this imply concerning the relationship between the human being and the rest of the created order?

Conventional Christian Anthropology. Behind this general question — but lurking very near the surface of it — is the more direct and confrontational query, which one may encounter everywhere in environmentalist circles today: Precisely what, if anything, is distinctive about the human being, and what, if anything, should be his and her special role in the biosphere? This question, which is not always stated in such a polite form, is a direct consequence of the centuries-long tendency of conventional Christian and notably Western Christian anthropology to accentuate the centrality of the human being in the scheme of things. While biblical — and especially Old Testament — faith obviously knows how to speak graphically about the solidarity of humankind with all other created beings and things, the clear tendency within historic Christianity has been to emphasize their difference. With almost dismal regularity (as we shall see concretely in our later discussion of the *imago Dei* symbol), the uniqueness of the human has been expressed in terms of its distinction from and superiority to all other creatures. This practice has characteristically taken the form of a concentration on the "spiritual" dimension of the human, whether in terms of human rationality, human volition, or a more mystical conception of the unique relatedness of the human and the divine.

Such an identification of the essentially human with spirit (soul, mind), where it has not explicitly stated it, has nonetheless consistently implied a concomitant denigration of the body (flesh, matter). Since the human body is the most obvious link with other creatures, its relegation to the status of the inessential or — as frequently happened — to a position actually detrimental to the attainment of "righteousness" has robbed theological anthropology of its potential for affirming material creation and for pursuing in a positive way the link between the human species and the myriad other creatures of earth. Darwin's hypothesis shocked so many good Christians not because it challenged their belief in Scripture (few of them were in any case deeply committed to biblical literalism) but because it made them embarrassingly conscious of the very thing their whole social apparatus was constructed over against: their obvious physical relatedness to the so-called higher mammals. Being insulated by "civilization," with its elaborate Victorian and Wilhelmian manners, from their own bodies, and spurred on by their religious sense of high calling, our forebears could regard themselves as bearing no kinship whatsoever to "dumb creatures." Clothed in their hoops and stays and petticoats and wigs — and their even more impenetrable self-estimate — they believed themselves infinitely above "the brutes," and, as we know from the shameful history of slavery, imperialism, racism, and genocide, above those human beings who in the eyes of the "civilized" seemed to approximate much too obviously the features of the animal kingdom. Christian missionaries openly referred to those whom they deigned to enlighten with "wisdom from on high" as "the lower races" — and this well into our own epoch. What they especially deplored in these races was, quite predictably, their apparently happy unawareness of "the sins of the flesh."

Not only did the church at large fail to critique this image of the human, but it provided the primary cultic substructure for the whole construct. In its basic source, Scripture, as well as in important minority traditions throughout its history, the Christian church had access to powerful spiritual and intellectual tools for correcting this exaggerated image of the human in relation to other species. First, it could have drawn on the biblical confession of human creaturehood as a condition humanity shares with all other finite beings—a confession beautifully and concretely expressed in the second (and older) saga of creation (Gen. 2). Instead, it preferred the hierarchic structuring of creation, with *Homo sapiens* at the top, "a little lower than the angels" (Ps. 8). This position is more conveniently maintained on the basis of the first, or Priestly, account of creation in the first chapter of Genesis; and, in this connection (as we shall see in greater detail presently), the evolving dogma of Christendom singled out and made into *doctrina* the *imago Dei* symbol, causing it in the process to bear a great weight of anthropocentric glory commensurate with these hierarchic presuppositions.

Second, the church of the centuries could have stressed (with its scriptures) a very positive and appreciative sense of creation: its essential goodness (Gen. 1); the wondrous variety of its creatures (Job, Ps. 104, etc.); the divine compassion for "dumb" animals (Deuteronomy, Jonah, etc.); the prophetic recognition (as in the Isaiah passage at the head of this chapter) that the earth itself has its own "covenant" with its Maker, and that when its inherent laws are broken, their abrogation redounds on earth's human inhabitants; Jesus' use of natural phenomena to demonstrate the character of authentic human behavior in the Sermon on the Mount, and so forth. Instead of promoting a sense of the wonder of nature based on such biblical evidence, however, the church permitted and encouraged an objectification of nonhuman nature—a process that came to fruition in the modern period. So successful was Christian education in objectifying the natural order that students of theology, charmed though they may be by Martin Buber's *I and Thou* as a way of discussing divine-human and human-human relationships, are invariably amused to find Buber insisting that it is possible to have an I-Thou relationship with a tree and a cat:

> It can, however, also come about, if I have both will and grace, that in considering the tree I become bound up in relation to it. The tree is now no longer It.[68]

Third, the church could have invoked—over against human hubris and egocentrism—the strong biblical and Reformation understanding of humankind's existential distortion of its creaturely essence, its sin. Of course, Christians did pay attention to sin—almost too much attention! But what sin? Clearly, the sins on which ecclesiastical consciousness fastened and for which the church is famous to this day—other than sins against property—are all of them the so-called sins of the flesh. Thus by way of negation it is confirmed in the minds of all who have come under Western ecclesiastical influence (what the church established *via positiva* in its creation theology), namely, that our essential ("higher") nature is spiritual while the physical ("lower," "animal") nature is the source of our degradation.[69] In opposition to this influence, in the Bible as well as in the more considered doctrinal traditions, sin is primarily a spiritual reality.[70] Moreover, it is manifested in two interrelated psychic states that have precisely to do with the subject under discussion: *pride*, which incites us to attempt a status above our creaturely condition, that is, our solidarity with all the other created beings; and *sloth*, which prompts us to slink out from underneath our particular creaturely vocation, that is, our responsibility for the other creatures.

It is neither necessary nor justifiable to claim that these three biblical emphases were entirely lost to Christendom, to be discovered only by our generation. The Bible itself was never lost, and throughout Christian history there have been persons and movements that have recalled triumphalist Christendom to its more humble origins and destiny. But the cumulative effect of the conventional anthropological doctrine of the Christian religion has been to foster in the dominant societies of the Western world an unwarranted discontinuity between human and nonhuman nature, and to encourage humanity to regard itself as being not only above nature but masters over it.

The Romantic Reaction: Return to Nature. Beginning with what Sir Kenneth Clark has called "The Romantic Rebellion,"[71] that is, the revolt of a more meditative form of rationality against restrictive functionalist definitions of reason, the last two centuries have seen the emergence of a countercultural reaction to the humanity-above-nature syndrome whose genesis and character we have sketched. Since the beginning, sometime in the 1960s, of a more widespread awareness of the environmental crisis that has been brought on by human technical mastery,[72] this reaction has rather quickly worked itself out in a movement whose primary philosophical point is the reestablishment in human society of the continuity principle between humankind and "otherkind." To speak of this as *a* movement is certainly imprecise. What has come to be is not a single, clearly articulated program but a broad and even amorphous trend that has expressed itself in some quarters politically (the various "Green" parties), in some through direct action ("Greenpeace" and other organizations aimed at the conservation of nature), but more frequently and perhaps more effectively in the creation of a new consciousness of the uniqueness, beauty, and indispensability of nature.[73]

In its more doctrinaire articulations, this movement has all the earmarks of a reaction. Against the humanity-above-nature concept prevailing in the dominant industrial culture, it insists that humanity is simply one of nature's many species. In opposition to the technocratic exploitation and manipulation of the natural world, it believes that humanity must conduct its life in complete harmony with the rest of nature, must have done with its aggressive ways with the other species, and must if necessary sacrifice its own perceived well-being for the preservation of other forms of life. This movement inspires in some of our contemporaries the sentiment that if anxious, grasping *Homo sapiens* is ever to find its way back to sanity and wholeness, it will have to rediscover its essential unity with "things":

> Civilized, trying how to be human again; this will
>   tell you how.
> Turn outward, love things, not men, turn right away
>   from humanity,
> Let that doll lie. Consider if you like how lilies grow.[74]

No one who has witnessed the industrial pollution of the Great Lakes, the massive and reckless destruction of Canadian forests,[75] the subtle but entirely effective poisoning of vegetation and the erosion of ancient monuments by acid rain; no one who has lived through a decade during which the disappearance of species has accelerated madly; no one who watches with a sense of helplessness as superpowers stockpile arms that could end all life on earth — no one who has witnessed these things will wish to be found on the side of those who ridicule this attempt to bring humanity "back to nature." If human beings in their arrogance have made themselves fearsome lords of the earth, then they must be taught that they are in fact not lords but only mortal beings, whose greatest wisdom can (as Paul knew) lead to the greatest folly, and whose best deeds are tainted by inordinate self-interest. Biblical religion would be the last voice to decry a philosophy that counsels human beings who have lost touch with their true, biological base to "consider . . . how the lilies grow."

Yet the romantic reaction against the spirit of technocratic mastery cannot be a permanently responsible answer to the exaggerated anthropocentrism of the Western world. As a reaction, it is entirely understandable; and as a strategy it may be effective for certain problems among certain peoples. For the peoples of "developed" societies, the rediscovery of their strict continuity with the natural world and their dependence on it can help create a new self- and society-awareness, a sense of belonging and compassion, that could become a stage on the way to a more responsible kind of global behavior. But if the return to nature is regarded as a way of solving the great problems of the earth, it is naive and self-defeating. For one thing, it makes little sense to urge human beings to dispense with their human capacities for reasoning, willing, and transforming in order to discover the "peace" that seems (to some) to belong to species that do not possess these capacities. It is even more ludicrous to urge such a *modus operandi* through the production of books, films, conferences, and other appeals to the very human uniqueness that people are being asked to relinquish in these same books, and so forth. More important, while middle-class North Americans and others may derive a certain euphoria from "nature" in the form of the summer cottage experience, this is hardly adequate counsel for Ethiopians and others among the two-thirds in the world who have not been given the choice whether they would return to nature, but have had nature thrust at them in its cruelest aspect.

In short, the return to nature is not only an idea that is impractical and romantic (in its pejorative sense), capable of being entertained only by the already affluent who have little awareness of the "dirty" side of nature; it is quite possibly a frivolous and even dangerous alternative to humanity-above-nature. For what it does in effect is remove from the ranks of the thoughtful within First World societies many people who might otherwise achieve a greater social consciousness. Through their "option out" of the technological society such persons may indeed find personal peace. Certain very important lessons can be learned by all of us who dwell in these urbanized cultures through a serious return to our roots in the natural world. But responsibility is not, I think, one of these lessons. We shall not learn accountability for our co-creatures, human and non-human, by substituting passivity for action, experiencing for reasoning, feeling for thinking, body-celebration for honing the mind and chastening the will. The answer to a world "suffering under its inhabitants" (Isaiah) is not the effective demise, whether literally or through the deliberate renunciation of human aspirations, of the capacities for thinking, willing, making, judging, and changing.

The only answer to such a suffering world is to redefine and redirect what *is* distinctively human so as to bring about a different effect within the natural order.

VI. CONCLUSION AND TRANSITION

We have now prepared the way for an attempt, on the level of theological reflection, at just that: a redefinition and redirection of what is distinctively human. The preliminary questions that had to be addressed before we could turn our attention to the details of this task have at least been acknowledged. We have established that Christian faith implies a decisive orientation toward this world, which makes the question of "the fate of the earth" a matter of ultimate concern for Christians. We have also established the principle that while the determination of this world's course is — for Christians — in the hands of the Lord of history, to be a recipient of divine grace is to know oneself, as human being, to be participant in the gracious governance of the world toward its envisioned *telos*, the kingdom that is to come "on earth as it is in heaven." This in turn led us to the question of whether human participation in the divine governance of the world implies a conception of the human that places the human species in a category entirely discontinuous with the other species; and with that question, and some preliminary reflections on it, we have set the stage for the remainder of the inquiry.

What we have so far established in relation to the latter question are two negatives: We have rejected the common assumption of conventional Western Christendom that humanity is "above" nature; and we have also rejected the romantic reaction to that convention that wants to put humankind "back into" nature. We are thus left with a human creature who is neither strictly discontinuous with the other creatures nor strictly continuous with them: he/she is not merely "natural" as the other creatures are natural; yet neither is he/she "unnatural," whether sub- or supernatural.

The question is: How can we describe this creature positively? And not only positively, but in such a way as to counter — if not to resolve — the typical anthropological problems that have confused the history of our religious tradition and contributed to the crisis of nature.

Such a positive rethinking of human nature and vocation, when true to the rudiments of Christianity as we have already sketched them, 1) could never embrace an image of the human being in which that being and the destiny of that being is unconnected with the destiny of its home, the earth; 2) could never envision the human being as having no active part in the governance of the world; and 3) could never regard humans as being so far above nature as to acknowledge no limits to their mastery, or so thoroughly within nature as to bear no special responsibility for it.

As I intimated in the Introduction, I shall attempt this positive rethinking of the human by taking as my primary theological device the biblical symbol *imago Dei*. Through this symbol we shall be led to a reconsideration of the nature of being itself, as it appears in the tradition of Jerusalem. And this will in turn help us establish a conception of the relationship between human and extrahuman being that can become the ontological basis for an ethic of human stewardship.

In commencing with the *imago Dei* symbol, I am conscious of the fact that it is precisely this device that the most triumphalist anthropologies of Christendom settled on. It is my conviction, however, that a rethinking of just this symbol can provide the church with one of the best and most provocative foundations for the human stewarding of nature. For one thing, if it is possible to redeem this "dogma" from its misleading usages in the church, we shall have gone a long way toward redirecting Christian thought concerning the character and role of the human within the natural order. My thesis, stated in the most rudimentary manner, is that the vocation of the human being within creation is to image God, and that the imaging of the God (*Dominus*) described in the tradition of Jerusalem would mean exercising the dominion of stewardship.

CHAPTER TWO

Imago Dei:
The Scriptural Background

I. INTRODUCTORY: BACK TO THE
SOURCES—WITH NEW QUESTIONS

Whenever throughout the centuries Christians have felt compelled by historical circumstances to return to their basic sources with new questions about the human condition, they have had to deal with this little term, traditionally rendered in Latin, *imago Dei*. This is not accidental, for very early in its history — already in the writings of the New Testament, in fact—this term, coming from the Hebrew scriptures, began to take on a technical, theo-anthropological mean-ing for the faith of the church. It became, so to speak, an abbreviated way of referring to what Christians considered the original status and vocation of the human creature. In the Introduction I drew attention to Segundo's sentence, "The world is not the way that it should be." *Imago Dei* came to stand for what Christians believed should be so far as the human being is concerned. Humanity in the intention of God — genuine, authentic, "true" humanity (*vere Homo*) — is humanity "in the image of God." To use the more philosophical language with which the term eventually became associated, *essential* as distinct from *existential* humanity is humanity imaging God.

Once more, historical circumstances require us to rethink the fundamentals of our tradition. As we have reminded ourselves in the foregoing, a particularly problematical aspect of these circumstances is the spoliation of our natural habitat by a rampant technological society that seems to have lost its human identity. Therefore, since it is the character of *Homo sapiens* that concerns us, we in our turn are driven back to this doctrinal symbol to ask of it, and of the long tradition surrounding it, whether it holds some wisdom useful to our situation.

But can we expect so much of one symbol? Is it perhaps too restrictive for our purposes? Or too ancient? After all, we have to be conscious of a special dimension of human identity and vocation: the human relationship to nature. The ancients of Israel and the early church were not confronted by an environmental crisis. Besides, as we have already noted in passing, just this little term seems to have served in the Christian and Western past to symbolize a conception of the human that not only did not make much room for a positive and sympathetic understanding of the nonhuman but tended to aggravate the alienation between humanity and nature by exaggerating human worth over against the other creatures. Even today, when people want to emphasize the allegedly high and noble nature of our species, they frequently employ this same symbol. "Man," they will affirm (and one remarks how consistently sexist language still accompanies the statement) — "Man, unlike the animals, is created in the image of God."

There are two interrelated problems here. One has to do with the symbol itself, namely, whether it is sufficiently inclusive to incorporate the specific concerns of humanity in relationship with the natural order. The other relates to the traditional usage of the term and asks whether that usage has not rendered this symbol inappropriate for our present purposes. The only way it will be possible to answer these questions is by putting the symbol to the test, which is the greater task of this study. But it will save simply begging these questions if we respond to them at least cursorily before we engage in the more detailed exposition of the symbol.

Whether the Symbol is Sufficiently Inclusive. In order to propose an answer to this question, it will be helpful to distinguish between symbol, doctrine, and sign. Tillich's differentiation of sign from symbol is instructive,[1] despite the weaknesses John Macquarrie alleges.[2] Symbols, Tillich claims, both point to and participate in the realities they symbolize. Unlike signs, symbols are not arbitrarily chosen; they come to be "when the time is right for them," and they cease to be lively symbols when they no longer function to put people in touch with the transcendent realities to which they are pointers. Thus symbols are not strictly the products of human ingenuity and rationality, after the manner of dogmas, formulae, or ethical precepts. The church does not set out deliberately to devise a symbol, as in the first centuries of its life it was compelled to make certain definite decisions concerning the nature of the Godhead. Rather, it simply "finds" symbols that are already there and seeks to relate itself and its message to them. Something is "there" (the term *logos*, for example, was present in the cultural atmosphere in which the Gospel of John was written), and the community of faith reflects on it. As it does so, the symbol takes on other dimensions while retaining its original connotation. It becomes a way both of communicating with those outside the community of belief and of acquiring greater depth of understanding within the community. Yet, while revealing it still conceals. It provides a clue, but the clue to a mystery that remains mystery; it is a doorway, but the doorway into a room that is only partly illuminated and still holds many surprises. While the doctrine attempts to capture the essence and set the boundaries of the thing in question, the symbol withholds fullness of comprehension in favor of ongoing discovery.

It was just this flexibility of the *imago Dei* symbol—its openness to discovery—that rendered it accessible and meaningful to New Testament and subsequent Christian writers. Paul could employ it as a way of speaking about Christ and those who are "being conformed to" his image; and even though such a connotation is obviously not present in the original Priestly writer's usage of the term, Paul's use of the Genesis symbol does not violate its original meaning. At the same time, it achieves a linkage between the Hebraic background and the explicitly Christian message, in the process suggesting dimensions of meaning hitherto unexplored.

Similarly, in the early church the *imago Dei* symbol could become a means of communication and interpretation in the face of new questions. Both Irenaeus and his near-contemporary Clement of Alexandria were able to discover in the *imago* concept definite support in their struggle against Gnosticism. Not only did its presence in both Testaments help them to resist the Gnostic rejection of the scriptures of Israel, but it provided them with a convenient device for battling the antimaterial bias of the Gnostics. According to Irenaeus, it is not only the soul but also the body that God intends to redeem— in short the whole person. For the human being in its totality is created in God's image.[3] Augustine and later thinkers would also discover in the *imago* possibilities of comprehension and communication appropriate to the issues of their times.

This potential of symbols for incorporating new experiences

and addressing emergent problems is what gives to the symbol of the *imago Dei* its positive usefulness for our present purposes. It is true that it has not heretofore been explored for its potential to include the human relationship with nature—at least not with any consistency. On the contrary, as we have noted, its conventional usage constitutes something of a detriment to that exploration. Nevertheless, just as this symbol has lent itself in the past to new discovery, so today it can become a linguistic vehicle for the perception and articulation of yet unexamined dimensions of the creature made "in God's image." As Paul Ricoeur has said, the theologians of the past "did not master all at once" the "wealth of meaning" contained in this symbol. "Each century has the task of elaborating its thought ever anew on the basis of that indestructible symbol. . . . "[4] If, in order to draw out its potential for our century, it is necessary for us to be critical of certain past expressions of the symbol, that by no means entirely disqualifies either the past or our perhaps "unprecedented" interpretations. It may be that in at least some of those past articulations truth was present then, even if it cannot serve as truth for us now. The advantage of a symbol, as opposed to a dogma or doctrine, is that it lends itself more readily to the contextualization that is a necessary dimension of theological thought. Without discounting the past—in fact, maintaining positive contact with the tradition—one can through the symbolic side of the Christian vocabulary do justice to the ongoing and always new circumstances to which the Christian witness must speak.

Whether Conventional Interpretations of the Symbol Preclude Its Use Today. We have established that a symbol is never wholly defined by its history but is an open, dynamic hermeneutical vehicle capable of incorporating new insights. But this does not deny the possibility that some symbols are handicapped, or even rendered unserviceable, by their past usage. Is this perhaps the case with the *imago Dei* symbol?

It could be said about every aspect of Christian theology that it is burdened by its own past. Everyone who works seriously in the discipline of systematic or dogmatic theology knows that the theological tradition is both a great gift and a great encumbrance. Without the tradition, theology would be at the mercy of immediate religious experience, and this would soon destroy whatever unity of truth practitioners of this discipline are allowed to glimpse. For that unity depends in large measure on a common tradition of reflection and experience. At the same time, the tradition is theology's burden because, human nature being what it is, the past continuously imposes itself on the present, discouraging the frail faith of the *koinonia* from venturing out into the unknown, and tempting it instead to remain within the familiar confines of past expressions of belief. It belongs to the ongoing task of theology in the life of the Christian community to wrestle with its own past articulations. Each generation must both learn from and struggle with what is "handed over" (*tradere*); for, unless it does so, it remains dependent in a false sense, that is, it fails to achieve theological maturity. Maturity in theology means accepting the past for the truth that it conveys, but also testing that truth in relation to present and impending realities that our mothers and fathers in the faith could not have anticipated—as we, in turn, shall not profoundly anticipate the realities and problems that future generations of Christians shall have to confront.

> New occasions teach new duties;
>   Time makes ancient good uncouth;
> They must upward still and onward
>   Who would keep abreast of truth.[5]

Much of what styles itself "conservative" Christianity in our time graphically illustrates how readily "ancient good" becomes "uncouth" when theological conventions are perpetuated beyond their day.

One way of avoiding this pitfall, of course, is to find new modes of expressing the faith. In the wake of the death-of-God controversy of the 1960s, some theologians suggested that the term "God" itself should not be used any longer, since it had become the bearer of theistic and other ideas inconsistent with biblical faith and could thus only be received as a stumbling block by our contemporaries. Others, however, proposed a different approach: use the word "God," but in "jarring" ways.[6] Subsequent developments, I believe, have demonstrated that the latter approach is the wiser of the two. The reason is not obscure: words like "God," "Cross," "Incarnation," "Kingdom," and so forth, are symbolic expressions, and therefore it seldom happens that restrictive or misleading usage alone can render them useless. Symbols do not die because they are badly handled; for they always contain suggestive depths that are not exhausted by the conventions that take them up. They resist circumscription.

It will be one of the most salient points of the present analysis that the dominant historical deployment of the *imago Dei* symbol is misleading and even—given our present socio-historical context— dangerous. But I do not think that this symbol has been so thoroughly spoiled by those conventions that it cannot open itself to the quest of our generation. Rather than dispensing with it, as some felt the church should call a moratorium on the term "God," we may learn to use *imago Dei* in "jarring" ways, reinterpreting it in the light of our contemporary needs. In doing so, we shall not have to eliminate the past (which in any case does not admit of elimination) but rather, driven back to our scriptural and traditional sources by our own existential questions as First World dwellers in the late twentieth century, we shall bring to bear upon that past new demands and perspectives that may elicit from it insights that were not needed, or could not be acquired, by our progenitors.

This, surely, is what genuine conservatism in theology and faith must mean: taking the past so seriously that one struggles with it for insights — "blessings." It will certainly not bless us easily. But if we persist, as Jacob persisted with the angel at the brook, it will eventually bless us, even if we must go away from the encounter limping! What we shall discover about the past surrounding this particular symbol, for instance, is that it is, after all, not as bound to its dominant conventions as at first appears. There are minority or submerged traditions with this bit of theo-anthropology as there are in almost every other aspect of Christian doctrine. Therefore, we need not find ourselves rootless, even if we must discover that it is necessary to dissociate ourselves from very prominent interpretations. In the search for a "usable past" (Martin Marty), theology has always been able to discover alternative lines of descent.

II. THE INSEPARABILITY OF THE COUNTERPARTS OF HUMAN RELATEDNESS

One final introductory comment must be made before we turn to the investigation of the scriptural background. We are to explore the *imago Dei* symbol for its potential to lead us toward a more appropriate way of conceiving the relation between the human creature and other created life. But part of discovering that potential will entail a rethinking of the other primary relationships in which, according to biblical faith, the human being stands: its relationship to God, and its relationship to other human beings. One reason why the *imago Dei* became a symbolic means for sharply distinguishing humankind from otherkind is that such thinking was founded on ontic and noetic assumptions that isolated the human creature from the complex web of its relatedness. This thinking inquired about "man-as-such." And of that practice Hendrikus Berkhof correctly says, "Not counting exceptions, [the anthropological traditions of the past] were all based on a static-idealist-individualistic conception of man. Man was regarded as an independent spiritual being." Since the contemporary discovery of humanity's "historicity" (*Geschichtlichkeit*), and since Marx, Darwin, and Freud, says Berkhof, we cannot approach the discussion of *anthropos* in that way any longer. "Humanness is now defined as fellow-humanness and viewed first of all as it is related to and differs from animal existence." Far from being a drawback, Berkhof believes, this contemporary necessity of regarding the human being relationally is in fact delivering us from our Christian bondage to "Greek" categories and opening our minds once more to the lost — or almost lost — biblical tradition.[7] It belongs to the biblical tradition (and we shall later attempt to elaborate on this claim) that the human creature is to be understood within the context of its manifold relatedness. One has this, for instance, in the Johannine insistence that if anyone says he/she loves God and hates his/her neighbor, that one is "a liar" (I Jn. 4:20). One has it also in Jesus' summation of the law, where the "second" commandment is "like unto" the first (Mt. 22:39, par.); or in Paul's even more pithy summation: "The commandments . . . are summed up in this sentence, 'You shall love your neighbor as yourself' " (Rom. 13:9). The point in all three references is, of course, that the love of God and love for the human counterpart are inseparable.

What I think we have to attempt to do in our own historical moment — which, in this respect at least, is different from both that of the early church and that of the Reformation (which as we shall see rediscovered some of the relational presuppositions of biblical anthropology) — is try to incorporate in our anthropology that dimension of human relatedness to which we have reference when we speak about humanity and "nature"; and to do so in a manner that can give to this dimension of our total human relatedness the depth and significance that belongs to the other two dimensions.

To be concrete: Can we — perhaps must we? — in order to be faithful to our fundamental biblical sources today, insist that there is a commandment to "love" the earth and all its creatures which is "like unto" the commandments to love God and the neighbor, and inseparably linked with them? Can we, if we are to do justice to the profundity of our tradition under the contextual circumstances in which we find ourselves, be just as bold as was the writer of St. John's

First Epistle and say, "He who says he loves God and hates the earth is a liar?"

The pursuit of this question will lead us, first, through a brief discussion of the biblical background of the *imago Dei* symbol to a broader discussion of basic biblical ontology. Our meditation on the meaning of being in Hebraic-Christian thought will in turn induce an examination of the three foci or counterparts of our human being: God, the other human person (neighbor), and nonhuman nature. Throughout, our aim is to see whether the human relatedness to the latter—to nature—should not be regarded as a central and integral dimension of our being itself, according to our primary sources. But to achieve this end we shall have to consider the total relatedness of human being; otherwise, we should only confirm the error that is at the bottom of our present cultural dilemma, namely, that the relationship to the natural order is indeed separable from our other primary relationships.

III. *IMAGO DEI* IN THE HEBREW SCRIPTURES

The origins of the *imago Dei* symbol are located in the book of Genesis. There are three explicit references, and they are all from the "P" (Priestly) document. Historically, by far the most important of the three is the first reference, which occurs in the Priestly writer's account of the creation of the world:

> Then God said, "Let us make man in our image (*tzelem*) after our likeness (*demuth*); and let them have dominion over the fish of the sea, and over the birds of the air, and over the cattle, and over all the earth, and over every creeping thing that creeps upon the earth." So God created man in his own image, in the image of God he created him, male and female he created them.
>
> (Gen. 1:26–27)

A subsequent reference draws a kind of parallel between God's creating and Adam's procreating:

> This is the book of the generations of Adam. When God created man, he made him in the likeness of God. Male and female he created them, and he blessed them and named them Man when they were created. When Adam had lived a hundred and thirty

years, he became the father of a son in his own likeness, after his image, and named him Seth.

(Gen. 5:1–3)

Finally, a reference following the saga of the Great Flood links the value of the life of the human being with its being *imago Dei*:

God said to Noah: "For your lifeblood I will surely require a reckoning; of every beast I will require it and of man; of every man's brother I will require the life of man. Whoever sheds the blood of man, by man shall his blood be shed; for God made man in his own image."

(Gen. 9:5–6)

It is not within the scope of our present purposes to engage in a detailed exegesis of these passages; such exegeses can be found in any good commentary on Genesis. Our discussion will be served best by making four general observations about these Scripture references.

Influences. Since all three references occur in the Priestly document, they date from the fifth century B.C.E. Some commentators[8] believe that this implies Hellenistic influence. Others (for example, von Rad and Eichrodt[9]) think that while the references to "image of God" do run contrary to the Hebraic insistence on the qualitative distinction between God and humanity, they are not to be thought of as contradicting the concept of the divine transcendence but as related to it dialectically. It is noted in this connection that, in contrast to the Priestly writer, the Jahwist (J-document) in his account of the creation of the world (Gen. 2) emphasizes humankind's affinity with "the dust"; whereas the tendency of the Priestly code appears to be to stress the human distinction from the basic "stuff" of creation. Although this creature is part of the creative process out of which all the creatures emerge, only this one—*ha Adam*—is "image of God." Of course, one may question whether this interpretation is true to the texts, or whether it reflects the bias of Christian interpreters who have been conditioned to think too uncritically in terms of human distinctiveness.

Image and Likeness. The history of doctrine, particularly as it relates to the first reference (Gen. 1:26–27), makes it necessary to observe that it does not appear legitimate to modern biblical interpreters to make any substantive distinction between the terms

"image" and "likeness" (*tzelem* and *demuth*, respectively). It belongs
to the theological tradition concerning this symbol that very early
in the thought of the developing church such a distinction became
a significant one; and its importance did not diminish until the
Reformers questioned it.[10] Thus Irenaeus,[11] for example, reading
that God had made the human creature "in our image, after our likeness," believed that the latter term referred to the human being's
"original righteousness" (*justitia originalis*) which, he said, was lost at
the Fall, whereas "image" in his view continues to exist as an effective element even in fallen humanity.

This idea persisted, and Thomas Aquinas gave it a place of
prominence in his thought.[12] St. Thomas, in fact, makes the distinction between image and likeness the ontic basis of his whole approach to the knowledge of God. The human being is still "in the
image of God," even if the closer relatedness to the divine suggested
by the word *demuth* (similitude) has been forfeited through original
sin. Therefore, while *anthropos* does not have immediate awareness
of God as was the case in the prelapsarian situation, human
rationality—that is, the primary manifestation for St. Thomas of the
imago Dei—is able to discern the divine indirectly.

The point that has to be made on the basis of Reformation and
later biblical scholarship is, of course, that the writer of the Genesis
passage intended no such distinction between the two terms. It is a
case, rather, of a Hebrew parallelism, that is, a poetic device (often
used in the Psalms, for example) whereby a second, matching phrase
echoes the basic thought of the first, but in different words.

Meaning of the Term. What meaning can be assigned to the term
as it is used within these texts? Needless to say, a great many sugges-
tions have been put forward. Indeed, as Berkhof observes, "By
studying how systematic theologies have poured meaning into Genesis 1:26, one could write a piece of Europe's cultural history."[13]

(a) It has been claimed, for example, that the concept implies
physical resemblance: the human creature "looks like" God just as
Seth "looked like" Adam his father. "In the mind of P, there can be
little doubt, bodily form was to some extent at any rate involved in
the idea of the divine image," writes Cuthbert A. Simpson in the *Interpreter's Bible*. But even if this is so, physical resemblance by no
means exhausts the meaning of the phrase, since the body in Hebraic
thought is "an outward manifestation of the reality of which it was
a part." Hence this observation necessitates further inquiry concerning that more inclusive reality.[14]

(b) Could it be connected, then, with the thought of the human creature's having dominion over the other creatures? This is an idea that is at least closely linked linguistically with the image concept as it is stated in Genesis 1:26: "Let us make man in our image, after our likeness, and let them have dominion over the fish of the sea. . . . "

Psalm 8 (vv. 4–8), which celebrates the wonder of the human creature despite its obvious smallness by comparison with "the heavens," appears to make the same connection:

> What is man that thou art mindful of him . . . ?
> Yet thou hast made him little less than God,
>   and dost crown him with glory and honor.
> Thou hast given him dominion over
>   the works of thy hands;
> thou hast put all things under his feet,
>   all sheep and oxen,
>   and also the beasts of the field,
>   the birds of the air, and the
>   fish of the sea,
>   whatever passes along the paths of the sea.

The interpretation of the *imago* as referring to human dominion over the other creatures was upheld by the Socinians, among others, and was given classical expression in the Racovian Catechism.[15] On the other hand, it has been criticized by many students of Scripture, who point out that while the *imago* appears in the Genesis passage in close proximity to *dominium*, the language does not warrant our equating the two concepts; and in Psalm 8 the *imago Dei* idea does not even appear.[16]

To this, in view of the present-day criticism of the dominion idea, it may be added that while the Creator obviously intends the human creature for a unique office in the midst of the creation, it is hardly warranted exegetically to suggest (as both defenders and critics of the idea have done) that God intends the human being to exercise absolute authority over all the other creatures—to "play God" in the creation, as it were.

All the same, it would appear irresponsible exegetically to dissociate the *imago Dei* entirely from the concept of human dominion. The basic clue to the solution of this thorny issue is surely what we presuppose about the God whom the human creature is to image. If we take it seriously that the God actually described for us in the continuity of the Testaments is a serving, loving, suffering God, and no potentate, then we might well reclaim a genuine and indeed an apologetically provocative ("jarring") connection between *imago* and *dominium*. If, for example, we would take it quite literally that "God is love" and that Jesus, whom we name *Dominus* (Lord), is the fullest exemplification of the sovereignty of divine love, then an entirely new and radical connotation would be accorded to the concept of human "dominion." But since this is close to our main hypothesis, we shall return to it later.

(c) Another theological-exegetical interpretation of the Genesis passage that holds interest to many in our time, and is also suggestive for our present purposes, is that of Karl Barth. Barth believed that the best interpretation of Genesis 1:26–27 is given, implicitly, within the passage itself: "in the image of God he created him, male and female he created them." "This," Barth writes, "is the interpretation immediately given to the sentence, 'God created man . . . ' ":

> As in this sense man is the first and only one to be created in genuine confrontation with God and as a genuine counterpart to his fellows, it is he first and alone who is created "in the image" and "after the likeness" of God. For an understanding of the general biblical use of this concept, it is advisable to keep as close as possible to the simple sense of the "Godlikeness" given in this passage. It is not a quality of man. Hence there is no point in asking in which of man's peculiar attributes and attitudes it consists. It does not consist in anything that man is or does. It consists as man himself consists as the creature of God. He would not be man if he were not the image of God.[17]

What God wills in the creation of the human, Barth insists, is "a being which in all its non-deity and therefore its differentiation can be a real partner." God's own being, continues Barth, contains relationship within itself: "In God's own being and sphere there is a counterpart." This fact, he believes, lies behind the plurality of the form of speech "Let *us* make . . . ," but for him, of course, it also contains trinitarian overtones. The human creature is therefore created imaging God inasmuch as its being is at once and fully a relational being, a partnership, a coexistence—"male and female." The human being is "the repetition of this divine form of life, its copy and reflection," first in that it is the "counterpart of God," and secondly in that, like God, its being itself involves coexistence, cooperation, being the counterpart of the other human being. The most immediate, con-

crete, and "original" form of this coexistence is the relationship between man and woman. "Man is no more solitary than God."[18]

Berkouwer finds that Barth's explanation "involves constructive interpretation": "He is right in pointing to the unique importance of the man-woman relation in creation; but he is wrong in further concluding that this relation is the specific content of the image
of God, and all the more so in that other Scriptural declarations concerning the image make no direct reference to this relation."[19]

In view of the interpretation that I shall bring out in the subsequent pages of this study, and in anticipation of that discussion, I
would simply remark at this point that while Barth's argument may
or may not be convincing exegeses of the passages under discussion
(Westermann thinks that it is, on the whole[20]), it seems to me to
move in the right direction theologically. For it turns away from the
tedious but entrenched practice of identifying the *imago* with some
"quality of man" and starts us thinking about human beings in relational terms. The following passage from the *Dogmatics* indicates that
Barth's analysis of the *imago Dei* contains a remarkable affinity to our
present project:

> It is striking, but incontestable, that in his description of the grace
> of God in this final and supreme act of creation, the biblical wit-
> ness makes no reference at all to the peculiar intellectual and moral
> talents and possibilities of man, to his reason and its determination
> and exercise. It is not in something which distinguishes him from
> the beasts, but in that which formally he has in common with
> them, viz. that God has created him male and female, that he is this
> being in differentiation and relationship, and therefore in natural
> fellowship with God.[21]

(d) A final observation about the meaning of the Genesis expression is provided by Claus Westermann, who makes the
obvious — but almost wholly overlooked — point that *imago Dei* is
not in the first place a statement about the human creature as such,
in its uniqueness and isolation, but about the act of creation:

> What does the phrase mean? It is not a declaration about man, but
> about the creation of man. The meaning can only be understood
> from what has preceded the creative act. The text is making a
> statement about an action of God who decides to create man in
> his image. The meaning must come from the Creation event.
> What God has decided to create must stand in a relationship to

him. The creation of man in God's image is directed to something happening between God and man. The creator created a creature that corresponds to him, to whom he can speak, and who can hear him. It must be noted that man in the Creation narrative is a collective. Creation in the image of God is not concerned with an individual, but with mankind, the species, man. The meaning is that mankind is created so that something can happen between God and man. Mankind is created to stand before God.[22]

This emphasis on the relational, the responsive, and the representative connotations of the *imago Dei* will become very important for our further development of the basic thesis of this study. It will be useful in that same connection to also cite Westermann's commentary on the historical fate of the *imago* symbol, following immediately on the above explication of the meaning of the term:

From the period of late Judaism and the fathers of the Church, the phrase has roused such a lively interest that one can scarcely control the literature. But the problem is almost always determined by a question that must necessarily lead to an incorrect understanding. It was thought that we have here a declaration about man as such, as an individual. Consequently one looked for a special quality which had been given to man as the image and likeness of God. The point was missed from the very start, that the Creation narrative was not saying anything about man as such by using the phrase in this context, but was speaking of a Creation event. Man in the image and likeness of God had been cut off from the Creation event and had become the object of endless speculation about the alleged quality which he is supposed to have received. And this quality has always been explained in the light of the contemporary ideological viewpoint. When one glances at the history of the exegesis of the sentence (cf. *Biblischer Kommentar*, I, 3, pp. 203–14), one is deeply convinced that biblical exegesis is very time-conditioned.[23]

The reader will wish to recall this statement concerning the history of exegesis when we turn, in the next chapter, to a discussion of the development of the doctrinal tradition of the *imago Dei*.

Regarding the Paucity of the References. It may be thought that, given the importance of the symbol in the history of Christian doctrine, its scriptural base seems particularly narrow: three direct references, all found in one original source.

I must give two responses. First, while the term as such is indeed rare in the Old Testament, the sentiment for which it would seem to stand—not its precise meaning necessarily, but its underlying affirmation—is by no means unique. Although, as has often been pointed out, the Old Testament does not provide an explicit anthropology, the presupposition of its whole witness, including its description of God, is that the human creature, though undoubtedly creation's greatest troublemaker, stands in a relationship with God and with the rest of creation that is both unique and central. There is no independent interest in God in this collection of sacred writings. God is already oriented toward "the world" from the first line of Genesis, and within that world it is assumed that the human creature constitutes a special point of reference. At its most general, the Priestly writer's ingenious turn of phrase simply confirms this significance and encapsulates it. From this point of view, therefore, it is neither unusual nor reprehensible that Christians from Paul, Irenaeus, and Origen onward have latched onto this phrase.

Secondly, however, we must acknowledge that the Christians had their own reasons for fascination with the *imago Dei* of Genesis, and that the phrase suited them so perfectly that the paucity of its appearance probably never occurred to them. Those reasons center on the fact that the Christians, rightly or wrongly, believed that in the man Jesus of Nazareth they had been given a decisive glimpse of true humanity. The Formula of Chalcedon later was to make this explicit: this one human being is not only "true God" (*vere Deus*) but also "true human being" (*vere homo*). Their faith in this revelation of human authenticity in the midst of history caused them, quite naturally, to turn again to the question of origins, hence to "the first man." If God now manifests the divine intention for humanity in a "second Adam," we should not wonder that a new and existential interest was engendered in the "first Adam." The connection could hardly be missed; and it was not missed, even from the outset of the Christian movement (see, e.g., Rom. 5). From Genesis, Christians learned to think of the initial pair as being "image and likeness of God." It is not surprising, then, that when the New Testament picks up this term, it applies it principally to Christ, namely the "second"—and true—Adam.

IV. THE NEW TESTAMENT'S APPLICATION OF THE *IMAGO* SYMBOL

The explicitly Christian references to the *imago* symbol can be summarized succinctly in two interrelated ideas.[24] First, they affirm that Jesus as Christ is himself the image of God. Second, they affirm that those who through hearing, baptism, and the work of the divine Spirit are being incorporated into the life of the Christ—that is, believers—are being conformed to the image as revealed and embodied in Christ, and thus renewed according to the original intention of the Creator. There are fewer than a dozen explicit references, and with the exception of an oblique reference in James (3:9), they are all located in the writings of the Pauline school.[25] While the foundational concept is, as one would expect, the christological usage (i.e., that Jesus is the image), the (dependent) ecclesiological usage is the more frequently discussed of the two.

Christ as the Imago Dei. Since the two concepts are obviously very closely related, it is difficult to single out texts as having to do exclusively with one or the other; however, three of the relevant passages are clearly most concerned with the christological equation: Christ is the *imago Dei*. Perhaps the most important of these is Colossians 1:15: "He is the image of the invisible God (*eikōn tou theou tou aoratou*)." This is indeed one of the most christocentric statements of the New Testament as a whole. The christological declarations of the entire context of this equation are exalted, to say the least. C. F. D. Moule summarizes the claims made for the Christ by the Colossians author in the following way:

> Nowhere in the Pauline epistles is there a richer and more exalted estimate of the position of Christ than here. His work is related not only to the rescue of mankind from sin, but also (perhaps with special reference to current false teaching . . .) to the creation of the universe. He is associated both with the creation of the world and with God's "new creation", the church: He is both "the first born of all creation" (15) and "the first born from the dead" (18). He is the goal of the creation (16, "all things were created . . . for him . . . ") and "the head of the body, the church" (18). In Him, "all the fulness (*plērōma*) of God was pleased to dwell. . . . "[26]

Such exaltation could readily be misunderstood along the lines of a *christologia gloriae* were it not for two factors: that it is said over against "the Colossian Error," and that it presupposes a Pauline theology of the cross.

The Colossian Error, which is addressed by the author of the letter directly in 2:16–23, involves certain ritual acts connected with "a new moon or a sabbath," "self-abasement," "the worship of angels," subjection to "elemental spirits of the universe," and so forth. Evidently something like a pre-Gnostic message was being promulgated among the Colossian Christians. There is evidence in the author's injunctions against this *philosophia* that it conceived of the world in basically dualistic terms: matter is evil, spirit is good. The various rituals and abasements are designed to minimize the evil influences of the flesh and placate the powers and principalities that rule the universe. Such ideas, which are by no means unique to the ancient church at Colossae, attracted some Christians, for

> a Christian might have supposed that he had not (or not sufficiently) received [protection from cosmic powers] in the Christian proclamation and in the pronouncement of the forgiveness of sins. In addition, adherents of this teaching . . . presumably supposed that this "philosophy" could very easily be united with Christian faith.[27]

Against this error the letter to the Colossian Christians intends throughout to convey the message: the gospel of the Christ is sufficient. One need not supplement it, because Jesus Christ fully and finally represents God's whole "word of truth" (1:5). He is the *plērōma* — "in him the whole fulness of deity dwells bodily" (2:9); he is (in other, older words) the very image of the invisible God (1:15). If one wishes to discern and adhere to what is ultimate, then one is to know that this one, who lived among us some thirty years ago, perfectly images that ultimate.

And who, precisely, is this one? What sort of being was it who thus represented the fullness of deity? Here, in a characteristic Pauline twist, the tables are turned on those in the midst of the Colossian congregation who are enticed by a high *philosophia* of deity — deity based on power, deity that must be placated and groveled before, deity that can only despise the flesh. For this one in whom all of God invisible is made visible is none other than the Man of the Cross. It is a theology of glory that tempts the Colossians — almost, it would seem, a classic case of it, complete with omnipotent and unforgiving godhead, rejection of the material creation, and justification by works. Paul offers in its place the *theologia crucis*: "And you, who once were estranged and hostile in mind, doing evil deeds, he has now reconciled in his body of flesh by his death, in order to present you holy and blameless and irreproachable before him. . . . You were buried with him in baptism, in which you were also raised with him through faith in the working of God. . . . And you, who were dead in trespasses and the uncircumcision of your flesh, God made alive together with him, having forgiven us all our trespasses, having canceled the bond which stood against us with its legal demands; this he set aside, nailing it to the cross" (1:21–22; 2:12–14).

With such a testimony, it begins to appear that the imaging of God as it is shaped within this christological crucible is very different from what is often conjured up on purely theistic grounds. If Jesus reflects the fullness of deity—if Jesus is the image of God—then it will no longer suffice to put forward the most noble and exalted of human capacities and call them *imago Dei*. For the one who is exalted here is the one who was brought low, whose glory is inseparable from his "afflictions" (Col. 1:24), and whose "body," the church, is called to live a life of "compassion, kindness, lowliness, meekness, and patience, forbearing one another, and . . . forgiving" (3:12 f.)—and suffering (1:24).

There are more than casual overtones of this same Pauline "twist" in the second major passage that gives the christological definition of the *imago*. This is II Corinthians 4:4, where we find a literal repetition (in Greek) of the Hebrew term. Paul is speaking of those who do not believe—persons, he says, whom the god of this world has blinded "to keep them from seeing the light of the glory of Christ, who is the *eikōn theou*." The larger context of the reference, however, is a discussion of the hiddenness of God (the "veiled" gospel), and the *ecclesia crucis*, both themes vitally related to what Luther termed the theology of the cross. The "unbelievers" are prevented from seeing what faith sees in the "face of Christ" (4:6)—namely, "the light of the knowledge of the glory of God"—because they are looking for something quite different. The "god of this world" has conditioned them to expect of the divine a very different kind of glory. What they encounter in the representatives of the gospel, in Paul himself, is not impressive in the least. To Paul, it is precisely the unimpressiveness—the weakness, the foolishness—that authenticates the glory to which his gospel bears witness; for it is not personal glorification or self-aggrandizement that he is about:

> . . . what we preach is not ourselves, but Jesus Christ as Lord, with ourselves as your servants for Jesus' sake (4:5).

The "likeness" (*eikōna*) of the Lord in conformity with which, he says, we "are being changed from one degree of glory to another" (3:18) is after all the image of one who was crucified — who "though he was rich, became poor" (8:8), who was "made to be sin, though he knew no sin" (5:21). It follows then that identification with Christ (the second theme in the New Testament discussion of the *imago*) necessarily involves the suffering of the church: "We are afflicted . . . perplexed . . . struck down . . . always carrying in the body the death of Jesus, so that the life of Jesus may also be manifested in our bodies" (4:7 ff.).

Jean Héring suggests that the well-known *kenosis* hymn of Philippians 2:5 ff. contains essentially the same thought as does II Corinthians 4:4, and in a similar context, except that in the former text the term employed is not *eikōn* but *morphē*:[28]

> Have this mind among yourselves, which is yours in Christ Jesus, who, though he was in the form of God (*morphē theou*), did not count equality with God a thing to be grasped, but emptied himself, taking the form of a servant (*morphēn doulou*), being born in the likeness of men. And being found in human form he humbled himself and became obedient unto death, even death on a cross.
> (Phil. 2:5–8)

The juxtaposition of the two phrases "form of God" and "form of a servant" (literally, "slave") is highly provocative in the context of our present discussion and must be recalled especially in connection with the later treatment of the relationship between dominion and stewardship. Jesus' perfection as the divine *imago*, which is at the same time perfect humanity, is embodied in a lordship that serves.

The third major reference to Jesus as the divine image, Hebrews 1:3, makes use of yet another Greek term: *charaktēr*. "He reflects the glory of God and bears the very stamp of his nature (*charaktēr tēs hupostaseōs autou*)." (The KJV and older translations render *charaktēr* simply as "image": "Who being the brightness of his glory, and the express image of his person. . . . ") Of this Calvin writes that "*charaktēr* means the living form of a hidden substance," and he goes on to remark that this term

> reminds us that God is known truly and firmly only in Christ. His likeness is not just veiled and concealed, but is an express image which represents God Himself, just as a coin bears the image of the die-stamp from which it is struck. Indeed the apostle goes

even further and says that the substance of the Father is in some
way engraven on Christ.[29]

It must therefore be taken all the more seriously that the glory
"reflected" by Christ—the very "effulgence of God's splendour"
(NEB)—is a glory that he may claim only by virtue of his humility
and his humiliation. Commenting on the Hebrew hymn that, as we
saw earlier, celebrates human "dominion" (Psalm 8), the author of
Hebrews notes that in fact "we do not yet see everything in subjection" to the one who can legitimately claim this dominion, whom
we honor with the name *Dominus*; we only see Jesus, "who for a little
while was made lower than the angels, crowned with glory and
honor because of the suffering of death, so that by the grace of God
he might taste death for every one." "For," he continues, "it was
fitting that he, for whom and by whom all things exist . . . should
make the pioneer of their salvation perfect through suffering." (Heb.
2:9–10). The divine glory is rightly manifested only through the humility of obedience: "Although he was a Son, he learned obedience
through what he suffered . . . " (5:8); and the divine sovereignty
is manifested in one who, far from being above our human vulnerability, is able "to sympathize with our weakness," being "in every respect tempted as we are" (4:15).

In short, we are once more unable to pursue this equation of
Jesus with the *imago Dei* without undergoing a transmutation of our
ordinary human and "religious" presuppositions: expecting glory,
we are shown humiliation; expecting the power of deity, we are
shown a suffering Son; expecting transcendence, we are shown
service and compassion. But how could it be otherwise if the one
whom faith singles out as most perfectly imaging God is "Jesus
Christ, and him crucified"?

Conformed to his Image. The second important usage of the *imago
Dei* in the New Testament presupposes and extends this explicitly
christological assertion so that it issues in a consequent ecclesiological claim: those who are being incorporated into the *soma Christou* are
being brought to live the image embodied in and exemplified by the
Christ, and in this way they are being restored to the creaturely status intended for them as human beings.

The importance of this exposition of the *imago* symbol is ex-
tensive. For one thing, it contains the assumption—central to the
thought of the Protestant Reformers—that, contrary to Scholastic
interpretations, the image of God is not something that humanity in

its "fallen" condition still retains. It has been "lost"; it must be "restored." Christ is redeemer also in this, that he restores us to the original status of those who image God. As we shall see later, behind this insistence on the "lostness" of the image in postlapsarian humanity we must detect (what the Reformers themselves did not always recognize) a mode of reflection altogether different from the prevailing substantialism of the *imago*-theology. The truth is, the Reformers were not thinking of the *imago Dei* in the first place as a substance, something that could be altered but not lost. For them, the imaging of God presupposes a relationship with God. Relationships can be broken. For this mode of theological reflection the restoration of the "lost" *imago* is nothing more or less than the restoration of our human relationship with God, broken through sin.

It is therefore a process — and not an easy one! Romans 8:28–30 is one of the most significant references for this second, ecclesiological understanding of the *imago Dei*. In its context, it could be regarded as a description of the difficult process of God's restoration of the *imago Dei* within the Christian life. That life is a life of struggle and hope, of suffering and rejoicing — inseparably linked. The divine Spirit must wrestle with our reluctant spirits, causing us to know against self-doubt that we are "heirs of God and fellow heirs with Christ" — with the proviso that "we suffer with him" (Rom. 8:17). Thus it is a life of waiting, of participation in the travail of the whole creation, which also waits in hope. As persons "baptized into the death of the Christ" (Rom. 6:3f.), we "groan inwardly"; yet our groaning is also the sighing of the Spirit within us, and our suffering is the external sign of our conformity to Christ (*conformitas Christi*).

God is at work in this unfinished history of ours. We are part of a great process of restoration and redemption: the liberation of the creation from its "bondage to decay" (8:21). God is working "for good with those who love him, who are called according to his purpose. For those whom he foreknew he also predestined to be conformed to the image of his son (*eikonos tou huiou autou*), in order that he might be the firstborn among many brethren" (8:28–30). This vast renewal of creation requires that Christians, like and "in" Christ, enter into the depths of the "decay" and "death" that holds creation in bondage. Therefore, those "who are called" are called to be "conformed to the image of his Son; and the image to which they are conformed is the death of Jesus. . . . Under this image, under this incognito, the Son of God came into the world."[30] When they suffer, therefore, the called know that they are being given a share in Christ's struggle for the liberation of the world; so that "tribulation, distress, persecution, famine, nakedness, peril, sword" (Rom. 8:35), far from causing them despair, cause them to hope and even to rejoice. For the suffering of the church is the mode of its conformity to the image of the Crucified.

In Colossians 3:9–10 we again encounter the *imago* symbol as it applies to the Christian life: "Do not lie to one another, seeing that you have put off the old nature with its practices and have put on the new nature, which is being renewed in knowledge after the image of its creator." Here the link is made between the image as Christ, who is the source of the Christian's "new nature," and the *imago Dei* as a category of creation. The new being made possible through identification with the dying and rising Christ (3:1–4) is a "renewal" (10) of human creaturehood as it was intended from the outset. In this reference too, as Eduard Lohse notes, there is a greater sense of the present realization of the Christian's conformity to the image than in Romans 8:29. But he adds:

> Nevertheless this image of God has not been given as a secure piece of property to the person baptized into Christ. Rather it places him under the imperative to prove in his conduct his confession of Christ as the "image of God." The participle "being renewed" . . . lays stress on the exhortation. Just as the old man together with his practices has to be removed, so too must the new man be renewed in fulfillment of the duty of obedience laid upon him. The "knowledge" (*epignōsis*) which the new man has attained means the ability to recognize God's will and command. . . . The old man did not possess this knowledge. The new man, however, should conduct his life in conformity to the creator's will.[31]

The imaging of God thus contains a decisive ethical thrust, and there is no cause for complacency. The process is an eschatological one, that is, the gift of new being has been given, but it is not to be regarded as a possession. Rather, it is an identity into which we are beckoned.

Finally, we may consider I Corinthians 15:49 in this connection. This statement also expresses the dynamic character of the process whereby Christians are being conformed to the image of God, which is Christ. "The first man," Paul declares, "was from earth, a man of dust; the second man is from heaven. As was the man of dust, so are those who are of the dust; and as is the man of heaven, so are those who are of heaven. Just as we have borne the image of the man of dust, so we shall bear the image of the man of heaven" (15:47–49). The emphasis falls here on the future dimension: "we shall bear." The process is by no means completed. Yet it has definitely begun, and the "shall" in this context, while guarding against presumption in a characteristically Pauline fashion, also contains a definite note of confidence:

> Is it only after the resurrection that we shall bear this image in us? If we read the future indicative *"phoresomen"* = "we shall bear," we must answer in the affirmative; but the best manuscripts, P 46 and B among others, give the subjunctive. We suppose that this image may be already in us here below. It is a question of not refusing to accept it and of not falling back under the dominion of the *"sarx"*, which will not inherit the Kingdom of God.[32]

In a similar vein, Calvin comments:

> . . . we now begin to bear the image of Christ, and we are daily being transformed into it more and more; but that image depends upon spiritual regeneration. But then, it will be restored to fulness, in our body as well as our soul; what has now begun will be brought to completion, and we will obtain in reality what as yet we are only hoping for.[33]

Implications of the New Testament Teaching. According to the New Testament's usage of the *imago* symbol, then, and in keeping with other aspects of its teaching, we may conclude that only Jesus could be said without qualification to be or to embody the divine image. It is for this reason that when they seek to describe human authenticity, Christians point—as does Pontius Pilate in the Gospels—to this particular human being: *Ecce homo!* This man, as the Formula of Chalcedon stated the matter, this man alone is *vere Homo*, authentically human.

At the same time, these scriptural writings also boldly assert that those who are being incorporated into the life of the Christ through the hearing of the Word, through baptism and eucharist, and in all of this through the insistent struggle of the Spirit with their spirits (Romans 8)—in short that Christians too are being caused in a special way to share the image that is incarnate in Christ.

Not that they already live within the terms of the *imago*, not that they "have" it: there is a strong implication in all of these passages that the image of God is not, in any case, something to be "had." The language of possession is not the language of faith generally, and not here either. Rather, the *imago* stands for a life into which they are being called, a way of being that is already (proleptically) made available to them, but which in the meantime struggles with the old way of being, the way that belongs to "the man of dust." The new life that is offered to them as persons being shaped according to the image of their Creator is one that reflects the remembered life of the Christ. The *imago* is not, therefore, a vague and merely mystical thing, but it implies a rather precise ethic, one whose foundation and goal is just what we should expect it to be: love.

> . . . you have put off the old nature with its practices, and have put on the new nature, which is being renewed in knowledge after the image of its creator. Here there cannot be Greek and Jew, circumcised and uncircumcised, barbarian, Scythian, slave, free man, but Christ is all, and in all.
>
> Put on, then, as God's chosen ones, holy and beloved, compassion, kindness, lowliness, meekness, and patience, forbearing one another and, if one has a complaint against another, forgiving each other; as the Lord has forgiven you, so you also must forgive. And above all these things put on love, which binds everything together in perfect harmony.
>
> (Col. 3:9–14)

Implicit in these Pauline reflections is the assumption that authentic humanity is not only the humanity that expressed itself supremely in Jesus himself but the humanity into which we as "members of his body" feel ourselves strongly beckoned. The "essential manhood" (Tillich) that is the anthropological norm in relation to which we assess our present, "existential" state, is not some distant ideal. It is not derived through speculative contemplation of Adam and Eve before the Fall. It is not even—in any straightforward historical sense—the remembered humanity of Jesus; that is, it cannot be sustained by an attempt to keep "the historical Jesus" before one as paradigm and thus perhaps (with nineteenth-century liberalism) to make the effort to get behind the records and discover what Jesus "was really like." Nothing so remote as that! Essential humanity—the humanity for which Adam/Eve was indeed intended, the humanity which was indeed incarnate in the Christ—is the very humanity into which, through grace, we are being called. It is the "new humanity" that the writer of Colossians urges his readers to "put on."

This is a highly important epistemological point that needs to be emphasized in every discussion of humanity as intended by God: true humanity. For without this the whole discussion of what is essentially or authentically human deteriorates into speculation. The point is that when Christians reflect on humanity in God's intention they are not conjuring up an ideal or constructing out of fragments of a historical prototype some full-blown exemplar of human authenticity. Nor are they displaying an inordinate or esoteric awareness, as if—in the manner of the Gnostics—they had been vouchsafed extraordinary knowledge of the pre-Fall state, or of Jesus in his perfect manhood. Of course, the symbol of the pre-Fall first human pair, and to a greater extent still the New Testament's description of the second Adam, play their part in the Christian conception of humanity in God's intention—humanity imaging God. But our noetic entrée into the whole notion of essential humanity, and so into the distinction between "what is" and "what should be," lies much closer to us than either the mythic first parents or the historical Jesus. Authentic humanity for Christians means nothing more and nothing less than the humanity they themselves are being offered as a free gift: "new being" (Tillich) with a "new future" (Moltmann), a being and a future neither deserved by them nor commensurate with their own past. For Christians this new humanity is not merely a vision, a goal, an ideal; it is there for them (and not only for them) as real possibility, as a viable alternative to what is but "should not be."

It would be sheer arrogance, of course, on Christians' part if they translated this affirmation of the availability of renewed humanity into the assumption that one meets genuine humanhood in the church, while in the world at large one encounters only the distorted humanity of the "fallen." This is why the eschatological context and process character of conformity to the *imago Dei* is so important. The image of God, this symbol for humanity-as-God-wills-it, is not something that Christians have; it is a spiritual movement into which they are being initiated. It is a process and a struggle. For while they have a rather precise idea of what is involved in "putting on" that new being, they also know that they are at the same time—sinfully—putting it off. They do not already live the life into which they are beckoned; far from it! But they know, rather more explicitly than they should like to know, in fact, the character of the way they are invited to walk.

This being clearly understood, we repeat that the primary

source of the Christians' awareness of what should be, as distinct from what is, is their own corporate life: not the life they actually lead (which is, in fact, full of contradiction) but the life they are daily offered, the life that is already "tasted" (as in the Eucharist). If, then, we want to know what God intended as the Creator of creatures "in his image, after his likeness," we have only to ask what God *intends*, namely, as the One who through the Spirit seeks to bring us into ever closer proximity to that one human being, the only one, who is God's *imago*.

This, it seems to me, is the most significant implication of the New Testament's teaching concerning the theology of the *imago Dei*; and it is one that has too seldom been taken up by theologians. The usual practice in expositing the theology of the *imago* is to concentrate on the Genesis references, with some attention to that aspect of the New Testament teaching that finds in the Christ an embodiment of the *imago*. This approach tends to cast the entire discussion of the *imago Dei* in a speculative mode, artificially supported by biblical "evidence": "What must have been the character of pre-Fall Adam/Eve?" "What was Jesus really like?" But when the New Testament's discussion of the *imago* makes the ecclesiological link between the creational theology of this symbol and the redemptive process of "being conformed to" the image of God incarnated in the Christ, it translates the whole discussion into existential terms. Suddenly our primary orientation to the many questions surrounding this symbol is no longer theoretical and speculative ("What must have been . . . ?") and a matter for exegetical and historical research only; it becomes instead a matter of ultimate concern and immediacy. We are not only *permitted* to bring to this discussion our own personal and societal questions (as an afterthought); we are invited and commanded to do so. What, for example, is the implication of the New Testament's orientation toward the *imago Dei* for the contemporary question of the relationship between humankind and otherkind?

This does not imply that the past—the scriptural past and the traditions of theology—is excluded from our reflections on the meaning of the image of God. On the contrary, the past becomes all the more vital, since it now has to serve a reflective process in which our own involvement is more than merely theoretical. Our need for wisdom from the past becomes greater under these circumstances, not lesser. But if there is a genuine sense in which the new being we are getting clothed in is itself our primary spiritual and intellectual access to the understanding of what it means to be made "in God's image," if the *koinonia* as such is a foretaste of creation healed and human authenticity restored, then we are not confined to the past when we seek to know the import of this symbol for our context. We are urged by our own identity to search anew for the wealth of meaning that belongs to that "indestructible symbol."

CHAPTER THREE

Two Historical Conceptions of *Imago Dei*

I. INTRODUCTION: THE IMPORTANCE OF THE TRADITION

Having briefly traced the biblical background of the *imago Dei*, we turn now to an examination of its treatment in the history of Christian thought. At the very outset we notice the extraordinary significance of the symbol within evolving Christian doctrine. It is one instance (perhaps one among many, but a very important one) where the authority of the tradition has outshone biblical authority. The truth seems to be, in fact, that the biblical background of the symbol was not as significant for doctrinal development as was its sheer presence in the Bible, and particularly in the context of the creation narrative of the Priestly writer. The "image of God/likeness of God" reference in Genesis 1:26 especially became, one might say, almost a pretext for all sorts of speculation concerning the original condition of the human creature and its essential nature.

In a study devoted more exclusively to the historical evolution of the theology of the *imago*, it would be mandatory at this juncture to plot the development of the tradition chronologically through the ages—in itself a very demanding task.[1] Our purposes here are somewhat different. We are asking about the role of this doctrinal symbol in the formation of a problematical conception of the human within societies influenced by Christianity, and about its potential for the enucleating of a quite different *imago hominis*, especially regarding the relationship between humanity and nonhuman nature. Therefore, while we certainly need to know something about the historical evolution of the symbol, the more pointed requirement of our deliberations is to derive, on the basis of work that has already been done in the field of historical theology, a historical generalization that will permit us to reflect critically and constructively on that role and that potentiality.

The terminological basis for such a generalization has been proposed by Paul Ramsey in his *Basic Christian Ethics*.[2] Ramsey distinguishes between two primary interpretations of the *imago* concept, one he names the "substantialist or ontological" concept, the other the "relational" concept. Our purpose in this chapter will be, by using a modified version of this nomenclature, to develop the significance of the distinction it proposes and in this way to create a frame of reference for the next stage in the discussion, where we shall ask about the peculiar character of the biblical understanding of "being" that the historical distinction of the two types lays bare. (My modification of Ramsey's nomenclature for the distinction consists only in the fact that I shall not use his word "ontological," which he makes synonymous with "substantialist"—erroneously, in my opinion.)

II. THE SUBSTANTIALISTIC CONCEPTION OF THE IMAGE OF GOD

A long and influential tradition of Christian thought looks upon the *imago Dei* as referring to something inherent in *Homo sapiens*. Humankind in God's image, according to this view, means that as it was created by God, the human species possesses certain characteristics or qualities that render it similar to the divine being. These characteristics or qualities are built into *anthropos*; they are aspects of human nature as such. They are "capacities," "qualities," "original excellences," or "endowments" that inhere in our creaturely substance (hence the "substantialistic concept" of the *imago*). As Professor Ramsey has written, in this mode of thought the *imago Dei* refers to "something within the substantial form of human nature, some faculty or capacity man possesses" which distinguishes "man from nature and from other animals."[3]

The latter phrase is an important one because it is typical of authors whose basic orientation to this symbol is substantialistic (i.e., probably the majority of historic theologians[4]). It is almost the rule in articulations of the *imago Dei* according to this mode that part of the process of delineating what it means involves demonstrating that precisely this "image of God" in the human creature is what lifts it above the other creatures. In fact, it can readily appear—if one follows the history of the interpretation of this symbol closely—that the whole enterprise of defining the *imago Dei* in our Christian conventions centers on the apparent need to show that human beings are different from all the other creatures. Moreover, "different" almost invariably implies "higher," "nobler," "loftier," "better"; for it is hardly possible to adopt the kind of inherently comparative language involved in this approach without placing strong value judgments on the characteristics that are singled out as constituting the locus of the *imago* in the human creature.

As I have intimated above, as one reads the theology of the *imago Dei* in historical documents of doctrine, one gets the impression that one is witnessing the progress of a concerted polemic against the whole physical side of our human reality, as though we were corporately ashamed of being found "in the body," and were therefore determined to accentuate the fact that the really important (the really *real*) dimension of our being utterly transcends the physical. While we undoubtedly have bodies, and are in this way linked with "the brutes," our essential nature, guaranteed by the image of God in us, is spiritual. In short, the *imago* symbol seems to have been made to reflect our human determination to rise above our explicitly creaturely status as far as possible—which causes one to reconsider, as a corrective, the possibility that the Priestly writer may indeed have also had physical resemblance to the Deity in mind when chancing upon this expression.

It is certainly not the physical side of human being that most Christian commentators concentrate on in their interpretations of the image of God. Both in Catholic and in Protestant (especially neo-Protestant) doctrine, the obvious associations with the *imago Dei* are what would normally be identified as "spiritual" characteristics. This is what explains the nearly ubiquitous contrast with "all other creatures," the latter being assumed to be incapable of spirituality. Hence J. S. Whale writes in his well-read study *Christian Doctrine*: "Man is a creature divinely endowed with gifts which set him above all other creatures: he is made in the image of God."[5] One has no doubt that the "gifts" Whale had in mind are transphysical characteristics. Other writers do not leave this to the imagination. Harold DeWolf, for example, specifies precisely what he means by these endowments:

> . . . there are a number of observable human characteristics which mark man, in his concrete reality, as like God. Before elaborating them it must be emphasized . . . that to attribute these traits to human beings is not to deny that God himself is the source of them. Since man's very existence is due to God's creative and sustaining love it would be quite pointless to speculate on the question what attributes would belong to such a fictitious entity as "man alone" or "man apart from God." We are here concerned with man as he is sustained by God's power and love. That he is sinful we know all too well, but sinner though he is, he bears upon his person the stamp of his Maker.

This "stamp" (a typical substantialistic metaphor) is to be perceived, Professor DeWolf then informs his readers, "in four persistent qualities of human life . . . ": namely, 1) "spiritual being," 2) "the sense of moral obligation," 3) "longing for union with God," and 4) "aspiration to goodness."[6]

It is appropriate at this juncture to interject an observation from the side of critical theology. Throughout the history of theology there has been a conspicuous tendency to identify the "gifts" ("characteristics," "traits," etc.) that the *imago* is thought to stand for with values embraced by the particular cultures within which the theologians were doing their work. Professor DeWolf's "four persistent qualities" are, in fact, not very persistent. They reflect — and very conspicuously — values treasured by nineteenth- and early twentieth-century society, particularly as these values were cherished within liberal Christianity or broadly religious forms of humanism. Who, for instance, can read a phrase like "the sense of moral obligation" without hearing the voice of Immanuel Kant in the immediate cultural background? But in this respect DeWolf is by no means exceptional. It is, in fact, usual that when Christian thinkers throughout the centuries approached the discussion of the *imago* along these lines, they regularly named as the special characteristics of humankind in God's intention qualities that were highly valued in the societies to which they belonged, and even the classes to which they belonged. To reiterate Berkhof's telling observation: "By studying how systematic theologies have poured meaning into Genesis 1:26, one could write a piece of Europe's cultural history."[7]

Thus one of the hazards of identifying the *imago* with "endowments" supposedly inherent in the human character is the baptizing of qualities lauded by the dominant culture of one's society. This in turn leads to the prospect that the Christian community will have no distinctive image of the human by which to exercise a prophetic critique of existing social images. This was precisely, as we now know, the fate of theological liberalism. The society encountered by Martin Luther King, a favorite pupil of Harold DeWolf, was not one that manifested strong attachments to the four supposedly "persistent qualities of human life" named by his teacher!

Those aspects of human character that have been singled out in the traditional theologies as manifestations par excellence of the divine image have not, of course, been the four listed by DeWolf (all four of which reflect the modern era) but two still more "persistent qualities" — at least so far as Western civilization is concerned — namely, rationality and freedom of will.

Rationality. The notion that it is human reason that constitutes *Homo sapiens*, God's earthly *imago*, is so firmly entrenched in the conventions of Christendom that it is hardly possible for anyone who is part of the intellectual stream of our culture to read Genesis 1:26–27 without immediately and subconsciously assuming that the ancient Hebraic author's phrase "image of God" specifically referred to the rational capacities of the human creature. Yet it would not be difficult to demonstrate that rationality — at least the kind of rationality that Western humanity has evidently coveted — is far removed from anything the ancient author not only did think but anything he could have thought. At least until the Romantic rebellion against the spirit of rationalism (a rebellion with which North American technological society has still not come to terms), however, our civilization has been so persuaded that human rationality is humanity's absolutely highest good that we automatically assume this to be what the Hebrew writer must have had in mind. Unlike the other creatures, the human creature is rational — a "thinking animal" (Aristotle). Hence, we suppose, *imago Dei* obviously refers to our capacity to think — and (as modernity insisted) through thought to master our environment.

The explanation of this close association of the *imago Dei* with rationality is, of course, more far-reaching than the modern world's love affair with its own rational/technical capacities. The connection can be traced in Christian writers on the subject of the *imago* from very early times. According to David Cairns, in fact, "In all the Christian writers up to Aquinas we find the image of God conceived of as man's power of reason."[8] This includes Irenaeus, the first major theologian in the postbiblical period to discuss the *imago Dei*,[9] Clement of Alexandria,[10] Athanasius,[11] and Augustine.[12] Cairns attributes this (with considerable justification, I think) to the influence of Greek thought, which considered reason "the godlike element" in humanity, and to the fact that all these writers were "looking for some characteristic which was common to all humanity. . . . "

> If they read in Genesis that, after the creation of plants and animals, God created man in His own image, it was natural for them to ask, what is there in men that animals do not possess, and equally natural to answer, his reason.[13]

With Thomas Aquinas there are significant changes in the Christian understanding of what reason is and how it functions; but Thomas still assumes — and centrally so — that human rationality is the seat of the image of God. The great Dominican scholar believed that all creatures contain some evidence ("trace") of their Maker, but only "intellectual creatures" are "properly speaking . . . made to God's image."[14]

> Although in all creatures there is some kind of likeness to God, in the rational creature alone do we find a likeness of image . . . ; whereas in other creatures we find a likeness by way of a trace. Now the intellect or mind is that whereby the rational creature excels other creatures. Hence, this image of God is not found even in the rational creature except in the mind. . . . So we find in man a likeness to God by way of an image in his mind; but in the other parts of his being by way of a trace.[15]

(Note again the implicit downgrading of the body. Not only may it be separated from "the mind," at least for the purpose of this distinction, but it bears only a "trace" of its Maker — a thing that it shares with other material creatures.)

In the created, pre-Fall estate, the human creature (according to St. Thomas), while incapable of knowledge of the "essence" of God, "knew God with a more perfect knowledge than we do now." This, Thomas explains, is because

> God made man right (Eccles. vii. 30). And man was made right by God in this sense that in him the lower powers were subjected to the higher, and the higher nature was made so as not to be impeded by the lower. Hence the first man was not impeded by exterior things from a clear and steady contemplation of the intel-

ligible effects which he perceived by the radiation of the first truth, whether by a natural or by a gratuitous knowledge. Hence Augustine says that perhaps God used to speak to the first human beings as He speaks to the angels, by shedding on their mind a ray of the unchangeable truth, yet without bestowing on them the experience of which the angels are capable in the participation of the divine essence. Therefore, through these intelligible effects of God, man knew God then more clearly than we know Him.[16]

Rationality in the fallen state is thus diminished, so that the knowledge of God of which the human being is now capable is an indirect knowledge, gleaned through the observation of effects and moving, by means of inductive logic, to the recognition of their primary causation. Thus for Thomas, in the spirit of Aristotle, rationality must focus first on the empirical (*principium cognoscendi est a sensu*), whereas in the Augustinian tradition, which had been dominant until that point in Christian history, reasoning was conceived of as a more internal, meditative process, and the line between reason and revelation was thus much less distinct than it is with Thomas.

Freedom. The second most common "endowment" named by the broad traditions of Christianity as locus of the *imago Dei* is the human will. That this creature — again, unlike the others — is capable of volition is a characteristic that could hardly be overlooked by any who begin with the presupposition that the *imago* must refer to an inherent and unique human capacity. It is also quite natural that this particular quality is often cited along with rationality, for thought and decision are, of course, inextricably interwoven. In fact, I have not discovered instances in which willing was regarded as an alternative to reasoning in this connection. For it would be difficult to move toward an act of the will apart from cognition; and all thought, though it does not always issue in discernible acts, seems to involve decision making. Thus Irenaeus, the first major theologian to exegete the *imago* concept, names both rationality and freedom of the will as constituting the image of God in human beings.

This combination continues throughout Christian history — though, quite predictably, one can detect a shift toward the accentuation of freedom in the post-Reformation period and especially in the Modern period. As we approach the nineteenth century, this emphasis on human freedom easily combines with terms like "spiritual being," "personality," and especially "moral capacity." Thus the Lord Bishop of Durham at the beginning of the twentieth century writes:

What is the Image? Is it reason, in its highest sense? Or power to know God? Or actual holiness, positive sanctifying knowledge of God? Or immortality? Or sovereignty over the creatures? We reject the last as inadequate. And as to the theory of positive holiness, it is a fact against it that fallen men are viewed in Scripture as "made in the image of God" (Gen. ix,6; Jas. iii,9); the original making of man in that image is a fact permanent for all men.

The solution which to us seems most comprehensive is that the Image lies in the mysterious gift of Personality, bringing not only mental but, much more, moral capacity, and true free-will and free-agency, such that man within his sphere becomes a true self-guiding Cause, as God in His sphere.

And there follows the contrast that by this time has become mandatory:

The beasts are not so. They are not moral, not responsible, not disengaged from material circumstance; not true causes. Man is all this; and so can know God as like knows like. God, the Archetype of all Personality, supremely self-conscious, self-acting, moral, has made man to be, in the remarkable words of the Apocrypha, "the image of His own peculiar nature" (Wisd. ii, 23, *eikona tēs idias idiotētos*).[17]

James Orr of Glasgow, in a volume written during this same period, casts his definition of the *imago* in similar language:

Positively . . . this image, or resemblance to God, must be supposed to lie primarily in man's nature. . . . The resemblance cannot be looked for . . . in his body, nor in the animal functions of his soul. It must be looked for, therefore, in that higher constitution of his being which makes him spiritual. It is in the powers and activities of man as personal spirit that we are to seek his affinity to God and resemblance to Him. The image of God intended in Scripture, in other words, is a mental and moral image. It is to be sought for in the fact that man is a person—a spiritual, self-conscious being; and in the attributes of that personality—his rationality and capacity for moral life, including in the latter knowledge of moral law, self-determining freedom, and social affections. . . . [18]

While "in the first human beings," writes Orr, the image "was, must have been, largely potential," still, "a dewdrop may reflect the sun;

and man, in one sense in his childhood, may yet have reflected in a clear intellect, harmonious affections, and an uncorrupted will, the undimmed image of his Maker."[19]

This introduction of the concept of the image as "potentiality" is no doubt a consequence of the challenge to conventional theology on the part of evolutionary theory. It is no longer quite authentic in sophisticated theological circles to assess all this on the basis of a retrospective contemplation of the "original pair." I. A. Dorner of Berlin, accordingly, made much of the distinction between the *imago* as an "endowment" already granted the newly created beings in the Garden of Eden, and as "man's destination." The "idea of man, as it is conceived in God's world-plan," he writes in his much-used *System of Christian Doctrine,* " . . . is not exhausted in the fact of his being a teleologically co-ordinated unity of nature and soul. The soul," he continues,

> has not merely Nature for its contents, but is susceptible also to the infinite, the divine. . . . Mere natural beings have no such ideal, no proper historical development, because no freedom. But man is a being summoned to freedom and historical development. . . . The freedom of man, even of empirical man, is in essential connection with the morally necessary, the divine; and by this fact, not by mere *liberum arbitrium*, is he potentially, i.e. by his very destination, the image of the ethical God.[20]

Another influential voice of the same era, Charles Hodge of Princeton, combines rationality and freedom again, linking the two with the key conception of "spirit." Under the subheading of humanity's "intellectual and moral nature," Hodge writes:

> God is a Spirit, the human soul is a spirit. The essential attributes of a spirit are reason, conscience and will. A spirit is a rational, moral, and therefore also, a free agent. In making man after his own image, therefore, God endowed him with those attributes which belong to his own nature as a spirit. Man is thereby distinguished from all other inhabitants of this world, and raised immeasurably above them. He belongs to the same order of being as God himself.

And again: "He is the image of God, and bears and reflects the divine likeness among the inhabitants of the earth, because he is a spirit, an intelligent, voluntary agent; and as such he is rightfully invested with universal dominion."[21]

While nineteenth- and early twentieth-century writers tend to devote particular attention to the attribute of freedom, combining it, as we have seen in these references, with a strong sense of moral vocation that was characteristic of that age and implying (what Hodge in the last citation makes quite explicit) that these attributes make the human being capable of mastery in the world, the antecedents of this practice can be traced to the classical period. We already noted in passing that Irenaeus found the *imago* lodged in both human rationality and human freedom. Augustine is even more exemplary of this combination. In fact, his anthropology in many ways focuses on the will—its original freedom, its bondage on account of the Fall, its renewal through grace. The original integrity of the creature (*status integritatis*) is certainly bound up with its rational capacities; but these are brought to a point of convergence in the will. What is distinctive in the human creature is its freedom to choose: to affirm created being in spite of its limitations; to actualize its potential righteousness; to refrain from sin (*posse non peccare*), and so forth. Of course, for Augustine, as for Luther, the Fall signals the loss of precisely this freedom: the "free will" becomes the will "in bondage." And in his anti-Pelagian phase particularly, Augustine stressed the total incapacity of the fallen creature to extricate itself from sin (*non posse non peccare*). Yet since the work of grace in Christ is restorative of the original state, it is signficant that it is the will of the human being that the Spirit liberates and causes to be transformed.[22]

This location of the *imago Dei* in human willing—not in isolation from rationality but transcending mere intellection and expressing itself in decision—seems to me to come much nearer to the picture of the human given in the tradition of Jerusalem, as distinct from that of Athens. For it is not merely in understanding, but in the kind of understanding that leads to act—to obedience—that biblical faith locates its sense of human "grandeur": "And if I . . . understand all mysteries and have all knowledge . . . but have not love, I am nothing" (I Cor. 13:2). If we are looking for human qualities as the locus of the divine image, we could probably not improve on the identification of the *imago* with the human capacity for free decision and action.

But should we, in the first place, be looking for such qualities? There can be no doubt that such a search has been undertaken in all branches of the church—and with remarkable inventiveness! If one sets out, in the name of concretizing the language of the *imago*, to discover the highest excellencies with which our species has been gifted, one can expect, over 2000 years, to reap a bountiful harvest. Not only rationality and volition, but moral sense, spiritual being, speech, upright stature and bearing, the capacity for self-transcendence — even the fact that human beings cook their food — can be named in such a quest. But what if all such "endowments" are only secondary, that is, means, not ends? The *imago Dei*, says Karl Barth bluntly, "is not a quality of man."[23]

What is it then? Barth's response (which we already noted in passing) emerges out of quite a different mindset from those whose testimonies we have so far examined. He insists that the image of God "does not consist in anything that man is or does" but simply in being human: "He would not be man if he were not the image of God. He is the image of God in the fact that he is man." God desires to have vis-à-vis himself a being "which in all of its non-deity and therefore its differentiation can be a real partner; which is capable of action and responsibility in relation to Him; to which His own divine form of life is not alien. . . . "[24]

With this statement we have moved out of the sphere in which the human being is being assessed for its attributes and into one where what matters most is its *relatedness*.

III. THE RELATIONAL CONCEPTION OF THE IMAGE OF GOD

Whereas the substantialistic conception of the *imago Dei* locates the image in us, that is, as a quality of our human nature (*physis*), the relational conception conceives of the *imago* as an inclination or proclivity occurring within the relationship. What is presupposed by this interpretation of the *eikōn Theou* is quite simply the relationship between Creator and creature. The image of God is something that "happens" as a consequence of this relationship. The human creature images (used as verb) its Creator because and insofar as it is "turned toward" God. To be *imago Dei* does not mean to have something but to be and do something: to image God.

While intimations of this way of regarding the *imago* symbol can be found in classical (and especially, as we have seen, Augustinian) theology, it is clearly with the Reformers of the sixteenth century that the break with substantialism occurs — in this as well as in many other respects. David Cairns believes, with some reason, that Luther's rejection of theologies of the *imago* that locate it in indelible human capacities is linked with his fear of compromising his own central teaching of justification by grace alone, through faith alone (*sola gratia, sola fide*).[25] If the human creature is understood to possess qualities already—as an inherent dimension of its *physis*—that can seem to have a positive religious significance such as rationality and freedom, this (Cairns believes) vitiates the exclusiveness of grace and faith. Certainly Luther did not want to undercut his gospel of "sheer grace" by accepting the tradition (strong in St. Thomas) that grace can relate itself to (i.e., cooperate with) nature without difficulty. But I do not agree with Cairns that this is Luther's primary reason for rejecting the medieval conventions of the *imago*, including even important dimensions of the interpretation of his beloved Augustine.[26] The more plausible explanation is that Luther had been moved in a fundamental way by the relational character of the whole biblical testimony. Intuitively—because he was so thoroughly governed by the biblical material—he grasped the fact that the primary categories of Hebraic-Christian belief are *all* relational. His abhorrence of the Schoolmen's "speculations"[27] is the negative side of his fresh discovery of the biblical "ontology of community."[28] Under the impact of this discovery, Luther gradually battled his way through the heavy layers of Hellenistic and Scholastic categorization, most of it substantialistic, toward a redefinition of each of the Faith's first principles: *grace* was not a substance but a deed, a continuing gift-deed of the living God to living creatures;[29] *faith* was not the assent to objectifiable dogmas or propositions about God, but assent to God's person and presence, an ongoing response of trust (*Vertrauen*) that is the creature's right response to the gift of grace; *sin* was not a quantitative thing, measurable in misdeeds and wicked thoughts that could be reckoned up, confessed, and balanced off through equally quantifiable acts of penance, but rather the abrogation of relationship, turning away from God; *righteousness*—a word Luther learned to abhor while it was interpreted as a quality that he knew he did not and could not possess—became for him the designation of a new and right relationship with God.[30] And so on.

It was inevitable, given this monumental reconstruction of the primary categories of belief (for which, certainly, there were precedents,[31] but which until the Reformation did not become sufficiently robust to challenge the established conventions), that Luther would also have to part company with the patterns of interpretation that hovered around the *imago* symbol. He is, of course—as is so often said—no "systematic" theologian; but there are seldom genuine contradictions in his thought. It would have been grossly inconsistent

for him to have embraced conceptions of grace, faith, sin, righteousness, and other key terms in which the chief assumption is what is
occurring between Creator and creature, and then to retain a theological convention that traces the meaning of the *imago Dei* to some
quality the creature possesses in its detachment, within itself.

While disagreeing with Professor Cairns about Luther's motivation in this connection, I am in full agreement with his conclusion,
namely, that Luther regarded the image of God as being "entirely
determined by man's response to God."[32] So basic is the relational
assumption in Luther's theology of the *imago* that he finds he must
deny the presence of any "remnant" of the image of God in fallen humanity, that is, in humanity which has abrogated its relationship
with God. Because, of course, if the image is dependent on a positive
relationship between Creator and creature; if it is, as we have put it
in the foregoing, not a possession or endowment but something that
is consequent on this relationship — then when the relationship is an-
nulled the imaging of God that was its consequence is indeed
"lost."[33]

Whenever this "lost" of Luther and other Reformers was (and
is) heard within the camp of the substantialists, it sounds like an ab-
surdity.[34] For, given the identification of the *imago* in that long-
standing tradition with rationality and freedom of will, the insistence that the image of God has been wholly forfeited through the
Fall can only seem to many tantamount to insisting that human beings are no longer in any sense rational or free. Luther's false reputation as a Christian "irrationalist" or a pure fideist is partly based on
this misunderstanding. While he did not trust the rationality of fallen
humanity (for he knew before Freud how the wily will is able to "ra-
tionalize"), he certainly did not think the human creature in the sinful
state incapable of thought. The point is, however, that for Luther the
image of God is not to be located in this way. Of the "speculations"
of Augustine and "the fathers" along substantialist lines, he writes:

> Although these not unattractive speculations point conclusively
> to keen and leisurely minds, they contribute very little toward the
> correct explanation of the image of God.
>
> Therefore although I do not condemn or find fault with
> those thoughts by which everything is brought into relationship
> with the Trinity [he is referring to Augustine's teaching concern-
> ing the "vestiges of the Trinity" in humanity as memory, intellect,
> and will] I am not at all sure that they are very useful. . . . [35]

"If these powers are the image of God," he quips, "it will also follow that Satan was created according to the image of God, since he surely has these natural endowments, such as memory and a very superior intellect and a most determined will, to a far higher degree than we have them."[36]

In his commentary on Genesis, Luther is obviously still struggling with the formulae that identify the *imago* with such "powers." One waits in vain for him to make a quite clear and unambiguous statement of the relational concept of the *imago* (he did not have the benefit of hindsight). Nevertheless, the presupposition of the whole discussion is the nature of the relationship of pre-Fall Adam/Eve with their Creator. This becomes transparent in Luther's repeated contrast between the awful anxiety of the fallen species and the entire lack of such anxiety in pre-fallen humanity. The latter

> not only knew God and believed that He was good, but also . . . lived in a life that was wholly godly; that is, he was without the fear of death or of any other danger, and was content with God's favor. In this form it reveals itself in the instance of Eve, who speaks with the serpent without any fear, as we do with a lamb or a dog. For this reason, too, if they should transgress His command, God announces the punishment: "On whatever day you eat from this tree, you will die by death," as though He said, "Adam and Eve, now you are living without fear; death you have not experienced, nor have you seen it. This is My image, by which you are living, just as God lives. But if you sin, you will lose this image, and you will die."[37]

In other words, in the state of original trust, as we may phrase it, the human creature images God's own freedom for life. (Jesus anticipates Luther's sentiment here with his famous, "Be not anxious for your life. . . . ") But with the alienation of the human from its creative source, such openness to existence is replaced by existential anxiety and an orientation toward death — a profound insight, for which Freud, Marx, and Heidegger might well be grateful.

While Luther implies the relational concept of the *imago Dei* throughout his scriptural commentaries and elsewhere, John Calvin expresses it directly. Cairns has noted that Calvin has more to say about the image of God than does any other theologian since Augustine, and that he regards the concept "dynamically."[38] It is obvious from his treatment of the theme in both his *Commentary on Genesis* and the *Institutes* that, like Luther, the Geneva Reformer finds it necessary to wrestle with the entrenched conventions that identify the *imago Dei* with innate human capacities. Commenting on the long-established distinction between "image" and "likeness," Calvin feels at liberty to take on even such giants as Augustine, who, he says, "beyond all others speculates with excessive refinement, for the purpose of fabricating a Trinity in man." For, Calvin continues,

> in laying hold of the three faculties of the soul enumerated by Aristotle, the intellect, the memory, and the will, he afterwards out of one Trinity derives many. If any reader, having leisure, wishes to enjoy such speculations, let him read the tenth and four-teenth books on the Trinity, also the eleven books of the "City of God." I acknowledge, indeed, that there is something in man which refers to the Father, and the Son, and the Spirit; and I have no difficulty in admitting the above distinction of the faculties of the soul . . . ; but a definition of the image of God ought to rest on a firmer basis than such subtleties.[39]

Thus Calvin rejects interpretations of the *imago* that locate it in this or that aspect of the human *physis*. First he dismisses out of hand "the Anthropomorphites," who "were too gross in seeking this resemblance in the human body."[40] Even those who do not presuppose a physical form in the deity but consider the human being to reflect the divine being "in the body," because God's "admirable workmanship there shines brightly," are "by no means consonant with Scripture."[41] To those who, with Chrysostom, find "the similitude of God" located in "the dominion committed to man; as though he resembled God only in this character, that he was constituted heir and possessor of all things,"[42] Calvin responds that this is by no means a satisfactory answer to the meaning of the *imago* either. While it may have "some portion, though very small, of the image of God,"[43] it does not do justice to the "internal" character of the biblical expression.[44]

Clearly, Calvin thinks, the "seat" (i.e., the place in human being where imaging occurs) of the *imago* is "the soul." Yet Calvin is adamant in rejecting any suggestion of an ontic connectedness (*analogia entis*) between God and the human creature at the point of the latter's psyche:

> It is necessary to combat the Manichaean error, which Servetus has attempted to revive and propagate in the present age. Because God is said to have breathed into man the breath of life,

they supposed that the soul was an emanation from the substance of God; as though some portion of the infinite Deity had been conveyed into man. But it may be easily and briefly shown how many shameful and gross absurdities are the necessary consequences of this diabolical error. For if the soul of man be an emanation from the essence of God, it will follow that the Divine nature is not only mutable and subject to passions, but also to ignorance, desires, and vices of every kind. . . . It is a certain truth, quoted by Paul from Aratus, that "we are the offspring of God," but in quality, *not in substance*. . . . Creation is not a transfusion, but an origination of existence from nothing.[45]

Calvin admits, with the great tradition we have traced above, that the two outstanding capacities of the human spirit are rationality and will: " . . . the human soul has two faculties which relate to our present design, the understanding and the will."[46] But he is not ready to identify these capacities as if they constituted the image of God. Rather, the *imago* refers to

the integrity which Adam possessed, when he was endued with a right understanding . . . when he had affections regulated by reason, and all his senses governed in proper order, and when, in the excellency of his nature, he truly resembled the excellence of his Creator. And though the principal seat of the Divine image was in the mind and heart or in the soul and its faculties, yet there was no part of man, not even the body, which was not adorned with some rays of its glory.[47]

This last phrase — "rays of its glory" — brings us close to Calvin's central informing concept in his formulation of the theology of the image. All creation, as God's handiwork, reflects the *gloria Dei*: "It is certain that the lineaments of the Divine glory are conspicuous in every part of the world."[48] If, however, "the image of God is said to be in man," this is because the human creature, as God's covenant partner, reflects the divine glory in a peculiar sense. This thought tempts Calvin, as it did so many other Christian thinkers before and after him, to indulge in the gratuitous habit of denigrating the nonhuman creatures in order to exalt the human: the *imago* "separates [the human being] from the vulgar herd." But it is not representative of the thought of this Reformer to leave the matter there. For the primary idea that is obviously emerging as he struggles with this doctrinal symbol is not the distinction between human and nonhuman in terms of superior qualities in the former; rather, it has to do with the specific vocation of the human being. This vocation is: representatively and articulately to mirror the *doxa theou* from a position within the creation. Such a vocation is possible not because of any quality or talent or power belonging to the human creature as such, but because, so long as it is turned toward its Creator, this creature reflects (images) the Creator within creation as a mirror reflects the sun.

Thus we arrive at Calvin's most important metaphor for the *imago* teaching: the mirror. The human creature "ought to be accounted a mirror of the Divine glory."[49] "There is no doubt," writes T. F. Torrance in his *Calvin's Doctrine of Man*, "that Calvin always thinks of the *imago* in terms of a mirror." But precisely this metaphor precludes any interpretation of the image of God as an endowment, for "only while the mirror actually reflects an object does it have the image of that object. There is no such thing in Calvin's thought as an *imago* dissociated from the act of reflecting. He does use such expressions as *engrave* and *sculptured*, but only in a metaphorical sense and never dissociated from the idea of the mirror."[50] Therefore, when Calvin associates the image of God with the "original integrity" of "Adam" — "when he was endued with a right understanding" — he is not singling out the human understanding and will as if they were the image, but he is presupposing something about the fundamental orientation of the creature vis-à-vis the Creator: that it is positioned before God, responding positively to God's sovereign presence; in a word — Calvin's perennial word! — *obedient*. "That is man's true rectitude: to be created in the image of God is to be opposite to or to respond to Him in such a way that God may be able to behold Himself in man as in a mirror."[51]

But naturally, the mirror will reflect whatever it is turned toward. The reflecting — the imaging — depends on the position of the mirror in relation to an object. In the words of Paul Ramsey,

> The image of God is . . . to be understood as a relationship within which man sometimes stands, whenever like a mirror he obediently reflects God's will in his life and actions. Man is a theological animal to the root of his essential being. However significant from other points of view may be man's capacity as a culture-producing, history-bearing animal, or however important the fact that man is "a living nature which possesses reason," nothing about man not presently involved in response to God can

be called God's image. The mirror itself is not the image; the mirror images; God's image is in the mirror. The image of God, according to this view, consists of man's position before God, or, rather, the image of God is reflected in man because of his position before him.[52]

Corresponding to this concept of the image of God as human orientation toward God—as its negative side or antithesis—is the whole Reformation conception of sin as estrangement from God. For the Reformers and their followers, the informing "picture" in both of these key concepts of the faith is the notion of relationship. Therefore, while the mirror may serve as a metaphor in the theology of the *imago*, only human relationships provide an adequate analogy. Mirrors do not turn toward or away from anything, but persons do; mirrors are not affected by their turning toward or away from any object whatever, but persons are. Every human being knows the absolutely determinative character of our posture vis-à-vis the others who matter most in our existence from day to day. Turned toward these others, we manifest certain responses to life in general: we reflect the well-being that belongs to our primary relationships. Certain qualities are elicited from us in the context of these relationships. The qualities may be there already as potentiality, but until they are evoked by the other they are dormant. (As Simone de Beauvoir said of her womanhood, "I was born female, I became a woman"—that is, in response to the other.) Contrariwise, when such relationships are broken, these same qualities are frequently replaced by other qualities, usually their antitheses. Trust turns to distrust and a general wariness in relation to the world. Comfort turns to neurotic loneliness. Feelings of disorientation and alienation are exchanged for a sense of belonging. And so forth.

Just here we may observe something of considerable historical importance in this whole discussion of the *imago Dei*, namely, that while there are obvious points of overlap between the two conceptions of the *imago*, they are so fundamentally different that communication between theological schools influenced by them becomes virtually impossible. As we have already noticed in passing, when, for instance, the sixteenth-century Reformers insisted that the *imago* had been "lost"—or if not "utterly annihilated and effaced . . . yet . . . so corrupted that whatever remains is but a horrible deformity"[53]—they were presupposing what we are calling here the relational conception of the image of God. When the "mirror" turns away from God and toward, say, pleasure, or the quest for security in things, or satisfaction in the self, it exchanges the divine image for something else. That is, when the human creature falls away from God, it loses the qualities that pertain to the relationship with God—just as the son in Jesus' famous parable, turning away from his father's house, forfeits certain conditions that pertained because of the relationship with his father. Neither Luther nor Calvin intended to claim anything so patently ridiculous as that the Fall implied the loss of any human capacity either to reason or to will. On the contrary, what they meant was that the human being, having violated the primary relationship of its existence, was no longer capable of manifesting the integrating factors that were present to it because of that relationship. Our anxiety, our estrangement, our inordinate fear of what might happen tomorrow, our consequent wrong use of reason and the bondage of our will—these follow upon the rudimentary disorientation of human life in relation to its source and ground, God. In our state of estrangement from this source and ground we no longer image God, not because we have lost some inherent quality of our creaturehood but because we are literally *disoriented*. Thus in all of our thoughts, words, and deeds, even the best and bravest of them, we manifest the peculiarities of a broken relationship rather than the qualities accompanying a positive communion with the source of our being. This is the basic preunderstanding of the Reformers (and it is picked up by their successors, such as Kierkegaard, Brunner,[54] Barth, and others), who took as their point of departure for the whole discussion of the *imago* a thoroughly and consistently relational understanding of reality.

What we must attempt to achieve over and above this Reformation line of thought is to extricate it from the residue of substantialist thinking in which it is still, perhaps inevitably, entangled. The relational understanding of the *imago* does not have to be derived or explicated by examining *anthropos* with a view toward discovering inherent qualities of being unique to our species as compared and contrasted with the other creatures of God. In fact, there is no need whatsoever, when examining this position, to resort to the questionable enterprise of comparing and contrasting humankind with "otherkind." Quite the contrary, as I shall hope to demonstrate in the succeeding chapters of this study: the whole intention of the relational conception of the image of God is to position the human creature responsibly in relation to the other creatures; not to demonstrate that this creature is higher, or more complex, or worthier, but to designate a specific function of this creature—a very positive function—in relation to the others. Relationship is of the essence of this creature's nature and vocation. The relationship to which it is heir is a multiple one, having to do not only with God, whom it is called to image within the creation, but also and simultaneously with the other creatures of God, who are served by its peculiar imaging of God. If it is "endowed" with any qualities that are different from the qualities with which other creatures of God are endowed, these human qualities should not be considered ends in themselves but only means for the fulfilling of its relational ends. This points to the direction in which we must move. It means that we shall move with—but now also beyond—the Reformers.

The further development of this direction requires a major transition in thought, and therefore it will be convenient to treat it in another chapter. For the moment we notice only this: that there is already in our own heritage a strong mandate to think all of this through relationally. The image of God is not our possession simply by virtue of the fact that we are human beings and not cats or trees. We do not possess any thing that could be called *imago Dei*. We are obligated—by our own tradition—to think verbally about all this. We image God, that is to say, if and when and as we stand in a positive (responsive) relationship with God. Ultimately, therefore, as Ramsey has succinctly said, the term *imago Dei* "can be defined only derivatively by decisive reference to the basic 'primitive idea' in Christian ethics, i.e. the idea of Christian love which itself in turn can be adequately defined only by indicating Christ Jesus." He continues:

> Jesus' pure humility and prompt obedience to God and his actions expressing pure and instant love for neighbor: these were in fact the same thing, the same image, the very image of God. Standing wholly within the relationship of imaging God's will, "with unveiled face, reflecting as a mirror the glory of God" [Goodspeed's translation of II Cor. 3:18]: these are in reality the same. There is no obedience, no response to God, there are no religious duties beyond this: Thou shalt love. . . . [55]

It is no accident that when Jesus sums up the law—and we should hear the word "law" (Torah) not in the legalistic way that we Christians are accustomed to hearing it, but as a summation, in the imperative mood, of our whole essential nature and vocation—it is no accident that he sums it up in terms of loving. For Jesus, as for the

Reformers and others throughout Christian history, this loving encompassed two spheres: God and the neighbor (i.e., others of our kind). What we now have to discover (and I think it will be a discovery and not an invention, because it is at least implicit in this Torah) is that there is yet another sphere, totally inseparable from these two, that also claims our love: nature, the extrahuman world, the inarticulate creation that is nonetheless "unsilent" (Sittler).

Kierkegaard rightly summarized the whole discussion of the *imago Dei* when he wrote: " . . . we can resemble God only in loving."[56] How does this imaging of God extend itself to our poor, vulnerable Sister Earth, so bereft of love by centuries of lust on the part of the "rational animal" that is one of its inhabitants?

IV. IMPLICATIONS FOR OUR THEME

The relational conception of the *imago Dei* implies that the human creature does have a special calling within the created order. The title of this study is intended to suggest the nature of that calling: it is a matter of "imaging God." Those who today are, justifiably, keen on ridding the human ego of its superiority complex with respect to the other creatures may be disappointed to hear from yet another Christian source that *anthropos* has a "special calling." But before they dismiss this hypothesis, let them consider certain implications of the relational understanding of the *imago Dei* as we have examined it here, remembering also the scriptural background explored in the previous chapter.

While, according to this understanding of human being, *anthropos* does have a particular vocation within the creaturely sphere; and while this vocation is bound up with its being a creature capable of multiple and mediatorial relations, there is not in this theology of the *imago Dei* the same propensity that one finds within substantialist interpretations to present essential humanity in a way that makes it necessary to denigrate other creatures. If we look for the essence of the human in rationality, for instance, we automatically assume a hierarchical structuring of the world and must relegate all creatures that do not possess the subtlety and skill of human reasoning to lower strata on the ladder of being. Moreover, as our Western history so flagrantly demonstrates, this valuational process is prejudicial not only to nonhuman beings but also to all human beings who on account of their condition or their innate abilities are not capable of "measuring up" to the highest conceptions of what it means to reason. One could speculate endlessly on how much damage has been done to children, to the mentally handicapped, and to the uneducated and illiterate in Western civilization on account of this avowedly "Christian" practice of identifying the highest and best — the truly human! — with rationality.

Or to women! It is by no means incidental to the history of this doctrinal symbol that it has gone hand in hand with a typology of the sexes in which the female of the species could be consigned to a level of being and worth significantly lower than the male because of her alleged inferiority as a thinking being.[57] Serious students of Christianity, regardless of their sex, are obligated to ask critical questions about the function of the *imago* symbol in this connection. Societies do not simply and instinctively arrive at such stereotypes — that the male thinks and the female feels. A good deal of ideational preparation must exist for such typologies to emerge and to condition the thought of centuries. Given the central significance of the *imago Dei* symbol in the evolving thought of Christendom, fixated as it has been upon the endowment of rationality, we cannot doubt that this symbol has played a major role in the oppression of women.

In the same vein, we could speak of the split between educated and uneducated, clerical and lay, theological professional and ordinary believer within the Christian community itself. Particularly in Protestantism (which, despite the emphases we have noted in the two major Reformers, came to place an enormous weight of glory on the comprehension of doctrine in the seventeenth century) Christians have been classified according to their rational-theological state of awareness. Faith itself, which in Protestant orthodoxies subsequent to the Reformation was characteristically reduced to the assent to propositions about religious truth,[58] has been and frequently still is conceived of as a function of enlightened reason. The consequence of this is that more faith, or a more admirable faith, could be attributed to those whose intellectual capacities and/or opportunities for scholarship enabled them to acquire greater knowledge. To this day, for most churchgoers the minister is regarded as the Christian of superior faith — and largely because he/she has a professional degree.

In short, whenever ratiocination is lauded as the chief good and end in life, every being — nonhuman and human — not manifesting this capacity, or manifesting it insufficiently, must be relegated to a lower category of existence and value. This not only unduly elevates the human being's capacity for reasoning and willing; it obscures two other factors that cannot legitimately be ignored in this connection. I refer to the fact that we are physical beings and the fact that our rationality is by no means unambiguously good!

As we have had occasion to notice more than once in the foregoing and might realize even more fully through a more detailed study of this history, the association of the *imago* with thought and will is inseparable from the dissociation of "essential humanness" from the body. Almost from the outset, the body seems an embarrassment to Christian theology and spirituality. Contemplating the long history of this embarrassment; reflecting, for instance, on the enormous influence on the Christian tradition of intellectuals like Paul, Origen, Augustine, and countless others who obviously had difficulty with their own sexuality; and considering as well the monastic, the celibate, and asexual state of so many of those who are responsible for having bequeathed us this tradition—one cannot avoid asking whether the inordinate attention this tradition paid to ratiocination is not in part explicable as a flight from the body. It is a delight—because it is so exceptional—to read in Calvin that "there was no part of man, not even the body, which was not adorned with some rays of its [the divine image's] glory."[59] But almost as soon as he has dared to say it, Calvin, himself an ascetic in the Protestant mode, feels constrained to take it all back. For him, as for so many others in this religious tradition, the Fall spoiled human glory especially at its allegedly weakest, most vulnerable point—naturally the body! In short, the almost exclusive concentration of the theology of the *imago* on the so-called spiritual endowments of the human creature has robbed the faith of its potential for developing positive relational links between humanity and other physical beings. Whatever one may say of the reputed anthropocentrism of the Hebraic scriptures, there is certainly not the same temptation in that source as in evolving Christian authorities to depreciate human physicality. By the same token, any contemporary attempt to recover the significance of the human body and the inseparability of human spirituality from human physicality must go back behind Christian traditions to the older traditions of Judaism.

Secondly, there is the ambiguity of human rationality—something Luther understood rather well but which was hardly applied with any consistency to the church's reflection on the meaning of the *imago Dei*. It is not necessary, of course, to castigate reason as such, and no sane person in our chaotic and dangerous city-culture today would purposely court a Dionysian frenzy of antirationality. But while most of the architects of the Christian tradition have been able to speak willingly about the limits of rationality, relatively few of them have developed or cultivated the suspicion that it may be precisely our vaunted human rationality that has consistently bedeviled the world. What, if not reason, plotted the downfall of just persons, wars against weaker nations, instruments of torture, betrayal of good causes, and so forth? A really painstaking study of Hitler's extermination camps produces one impression that is more devastating than the mass murders as such: the diabolical rationality of the whole enterprise, the "Final Solution."

Did Anselm of Canterbury, that calm monk of Bec, trained in the ordered life of the Schoolmen, have any existential awareness of the evil dimension of human rationality when he insisted that "faith seeks understanding"? For Thomas Aquinas, *ratio* behaves in a most civilized and cooperative manner. What would he have made of the Manhattan Project? With our rationality in full cry, we have now created a technological society in which it is almost impossible to live like the truly human beings exemplified by the One who walked with his disciples in the wheat fields and slept in a storm-tossed boat and ate fish from unpolluted waters. Under the aegis of a finally untrammelled reason—answerable to no gods, no holy writ, no moral law—we have built a *civitas terrena* poised on the edge of oblivion. There is no longer any place in the postmodern world for an unqualified celebration of human rationality and volition.

Christianity, through its conceptualization of the *imago Dei* symbol and in other ways, has contributed very significantly to the apotheosis of these endowments; and if Christianity is to acquire or retain any credibility among the sensitive in our time, it must not only confess its culpability in that connection, but it must show that there are alternatives to the uncritical celebration of rationality and the unwarranted elevation of *Homo sapiens* within its own deepest wells of wisdom.

What the historical survey and generalization undertaken in this chapter has attempted is a glimpse of the foundational ontic basis of such alternatives. There is another way of thinking about what it means that the human being is *imago Dei*—quite other than the interpretation that has dominated in Western Christendom. This other way does not deny rationality, freedom, spirituality, moral sensibility, and many of the other qualities that substantialist thought has brought forward in its elaboration of the Priestly writer's evocative turn of phrase. Such "speculations" and "subtleties," as Calvin says, have their own fascination. But the other, minority tradition of the *imago* points to an image of the human that presupposes and conjures up an entirely different arrangement of things. It introduces us to a view of the universe and the human place in it that contains, in fact, a radical critique of every hierarchical ordering of earthly life, every elevation of one species at the expense of others, and every attempt either to divinize or demonize the human creature. It introduces us to nothing less than a new conception of being itself, a new ontology — which is new only insofar as our civilization, though "Christian," has never yet appropriated the radical vision of what it means "to be" in the tradition of Jerusalem.

CHAPTER FOUR

The Ontology of Communion

I. INTRODUCTION: BEING MEANS BEING-WITH

From both the biblical analysis and our perusal of the historical development of the *imago* symbol we derive a single, simple, and even obvious point (which is, however, always being lost in the maze of ecclesiastical conceptualization): namely, that according to the tradition of Jerusalem, we are created for relationship. Relatedness — and specifically the modality of relatedness designated by the biblical word "love" (*agape, ḥesed*) — is the essence of our humanity as the Creator-Redeemer of this tradition intends it.

The relational understanding of the *imago Dei*, in other words, is not a tour de force, or an interpretation imposed on the biblical term by a later (perhaps "personalist," or "existentialist") world view. On the contrary, it is a reflection of this far more inclusive ontological assumption of biblical faith — that being as such is relational. Far from superimposing on the biblical term their own post-Scholastic or prehumanistic assumptions, the Reformers who exegeted the *eikōn Theou* more or less relationally were struggling toward an ontology more commensurate with Scripture than was the metaphysics they inherited from the established theological-doctrinal tradition in which they stood.

They were, after all, primarily students of the Bible. As such, it is unlikely that they could have been satisfied with substantialist cate-

gories, when most of what they encountered in Holy Writ was relational through and through: this record of a people's history; these
complex narratives of the often dramatic relationships between
fathers and sons, mothers and children, brothers and brothers, lovers,
rivals; these anguished prayers and inspired praises; these dialogues
with God and with one another; these stories, steeped in particularity; this tale of wandering, of fiercely remembered promises, of
prophetic rage, of apocalyptic spontaneity, of despair and vision. In
short, the whole presentation of truth in the one source they took to
be absolutely and finally binding (*sola Scriptura*) was relational.

With hindsight we may judge, reading their expositions of the
meaning of the *imago Dei*, among other things, that these sixteenth-
century expositors of Scripture and faith were caught between two
quite different, if not mutually exclusive, theories of the nature of being: one was largely a product of the tradition of Athens, the other of
Jerusalem. But the Athenian ontology had had centuries to establish
itself by the time of the Reformation and to incorporate into itself
(for instance, by way of the allegorical interpretation of Scripture)
the externalities of biblical thought. The Reformers, therefore, were
wrestling with forces greater than they themselves (and many of
their chroniclers since then) realized. One doubts whether they were
aware of the fact that when they called for a return to the sources, they
were not just seeking an alternative authority but were questioning a
centuries-long tradition concerning the nature of reality. What must
have seemed to their contemporaries as it still seems to many of ours
a crude sort of fixation on the biblical text was in reality the fascination of a faith that senses, without fully comprehending it, that there
is indeed "a strange new world in the Bible" (Barth). The speculations
of the Schoolmen had taught them how to universalize particulari-
ties, how to translate into static categories and eternally true dogmas
the lively and dialogical mysteries of ever-changing relationships between God and the people of God portrayed on the pages of Scripture. But they took the words of Scripture so seriously that they
could not as readily transcend the particularity of the stories, the
events, and the persons of which those words spoke.

Besides, one must say at least of Luther that, for all his erudi-
tion, he was and remained a child who, as Harnack says of him,
"romped in the church like a child at home."[1] He had a child's
sense — or an artist's sense, which may be the same thing — that reality
must not be so thoroughly transhistorical and supranatural that it is
no longer conceived to be present, if hidden, in the very things that

happen between persons and things and God. Nominalism of a sort may have been a vehicle for this sense of the significance of the particular, but I should locate it rather in Luther's peasant sensibility, his Germanic rootedness in the world — that other, positive side of Nordic melancholy. He could not, I think, break through the biblical narrative itself into pure (i.e., abstract) doctrine. If there is to be doctrine, it must be there in the story, for "the Gospel is nothing but the story of God's little son, and of his humbling."[2]

The question of the Reformers' sources and influences apart, what concerns us here is that the relational conception of the image of God, which the Reformers intuited, is a consequence of and a window into an entire — and entirely different — way of conceiving the "first science," the science of being itself. Joseph Sittler describes this biblical ontology succinctly when he says,

> Reality is known only in relations. . . . There is no ontology of isolated entities, of instances, of forms, of processes, whether we are reflecting about God or man or society or the cosmos. The only adequate ontological structure we may utilize for thinking things Christianly is an ontology of community, communion, ecology — and all three words point conceptually to thought of a common kind. "Being itself" may be a relation, not an entitative thing.

And precisely on the grounds of such a supposition, Sittler concludes: "The fundamental term *imago Dei* is not a term that points to a substance, an attribute, or a specifiable quality, but one which specifies a relation."[3]

What is implied anthropologically in the ontology of the tradition of Jerusalem is that the human being in God's intention, as created and in the process of redemption, is a being-in-relationship. So if we are looking for the meaning of essential humanity, then we must look for it, not by examining humanity-in-the-abstract and not by studying a human person in his or her solitude, with his or her rational, volitional, and other capacities intact, but by considering human beings in the context of their many-dimensioned relationships. The I.Q. test does not disclose the essence of the human any more than does the accumulation of deeds and achievements ("good works") that are products of an active and perhaps aggressive will. Under the impact of substantialist interpretations of the *imago*, combined with other influences of a similar character, we have been conditioned to locate the essence of *Homo sapiens* (as the nomenclature itself testifies) in rationality, freedom, spirituality, consciousness, moral sensibility, memory, and many other qualities of being. The relational conception of the *imago*, resting on the ontological presupposition that being itself is relational, insists rather that all of these endowments are only secondary considerations — means, not ends. They are means, namely, to the end that we may be able to enter into the rather complex constellation of relationships for which we are intended.

If this is taken seriously, it implies a thoroughgoing critique of much that has been done in the name of Western, "Christian" civilization. As Sittler says, it conflicts in particular with "the very structure of a good deal of post-Enlightenment thought. . . . "[4] For we have been taught to value most the qualities of mind and will that are exemplified by the most self-possessed members of our species, rather than the relationships for which such qualities may equip a human being. To possess a superior intellect, to exercise unusual daring, insight, and decisiveness in our choices, to be exceptionally dexterous manually and technically — such are the aptitudes we covet for ourselves and our progeny. If, along the way, we can also manage to be popular, genial, and civil in our associations with others, and generally well-rounded personalities, this is naturally a bonus. But the whole tradition of Jerusalem turns this thinking on its head and insists: You were given these endowments, these capacities for understanding and willing, making and doing, in order to enter into and sustain at some depth the relationships with the counterparts of your being, apart from whom you are "hollow" beings. What do such talents profit anyone if they are buried in what is supposed to be self-realization? "If I speak in the tongues of men and angels. . . . And if I have prophetic powers, and understand all mysteries and all knowledge . . . and have not love, I am nothing" (I Cor. 13:1). (What if that were carved in stone over the doors of our theological seminaries and graduate schools!)

To state the matter in the form of a kind of theorem or axiom: the basic ontological category of the tradition of Jerusalem is not, as with Athens, that of "being" as such, but *being with*. Or, as an equation: Being = Being-With.

It is awkward to express this in English without its sounding contrived or, even worse, sentimental! In German, however, a language both sufficiently free of foreign (especially Latin) influence and sufficiently flexible to permit the creation of new words that retain the "primitive" picture within themselves, one can speak of *Mit-*

sein (literally "with-being"). Heidegger, who invented this word (as was his wont), was in his own way conducting a polemic against the metaphysical traditions of Athens, but not in the name of the tradition of Jerusalem, even though his influence on both Protestant and Catholic theology has been great. Aligning himself with the pre-Socratic thinkers who, he believed, enjoyed a "privileged immediacy of ontological vision,"[5] Heidegger sought to overcome the abstraction of being, a process stemming from "the two crucial vantage points of metaphysics after Plato, and of science and technology after Aristotle and Descartes" and informing the whole direction of Western civilization.[6] His object was, as it were, to relocate being in time, in the world: "To be human is to be immersed, implanted, rooted in the earth, in the quotidian matter and matter-of-factness of the world. . . . A philosophy which abstracts, which seeks to elevate itself above the everydayness of the everyday, is empty."[7] And "Being-in-the-world," says Heidegger, "is a *being-with.*" For "the 'world's worldhood' is such that the existence of others is absolutely essential to its facticity, to its 'being-there' at all."[8]

Although Heidegger's language is highly specialized and difficult, a term like *Mitsein* does not fall on the ears of German-speaking persons as something entirely unheard-of (as "being-with" seems to English-speakers). In fact, it interacts positively with many other words that are part of everyday speech in German: neighbors are *Mitmenschen* (literally, "with-people"); colleagues or fellow workers are *Mitarbeiter* ("with-workers"), with whom one can engage in *Mitwirkung* ("cooperation"). When one's friend is ill or dies, one feels *Mitleid* ("with-suffering" = compassion) and expresses one's *Mitleidenschaft* ("sympathy"). Literally dozens of words in the German tongue assume the prefix *mit* ("with"): *mitbringen* ("bring along with"), *Mitbewohner* ("coinhabitant"), *miteinander* ("together"), *mitfahren* ("accompany"), *Mithelfer* ("with-helper," i.e., assistant), *mitreden* ("with-speak" = converse), and so forth. Such words, coming from a language that did not undergo as thorough a transformation through its contact with Latin as did English, sustain an immediacy of connection between the act/state/experience and its expression in language that is rarely achieved in English. The "picture" is present in the word itself. And the basic picture that these *mit*-words conjure up is one that is also rare, and becoming more so, in the technicized society whose "forgetfulness of being" was Heidegger's fundamental concern. It is the picture of a world in which all things interact, a world where mystery means the encounter of being-with-being (*Untereinandersein*), a world in which reality is discovered in reciprocity.

It is, in fact, not very far away from the world-picture of ancient Israel. *Shalom*, a word used by the Hebrews to express what they believed to be "God's intention for the creation," is perhaps the most poignant of all human words aiming to articulate the mutuality of all being.

> Its basic meaning is wholeness—a state of harmony among God, humanity and all creation. . . . All elements of creation are interrelated. Each element participates in the whole creation, and if any element is denied wholeness and well-being (shalom), all are thereby diminished. This relational character of creation is rooted in all creatures' common origin in a God who not only created all that is but who continues to be active in the world, seeking our shalom.[9]

Given not only the abstraction of being in Western philosophical and theological traditions, and not only the consequent technicization and "thingification" of nature, plus a background of nineteenth-century bourgeois individualism, it is extremely difficult for persons in our society—Christian or not—to achieve the kind of *metanoia* that is necessary if one is to imagine oneself part of a world like this. Simply as a matter of course, our society conditions us to think of being—if we think of it at all—as an impersonal, abstract idea, or a kind of undifferentiated substance ("existence") in which we participate in some vague sense. Or else—and this is more likely the case for the majority of people—the concept of being is entirely too abstract for us, and we can only deal with it by translating it at once into the plural—"beings." This, as Heidegger would say, only reflects the "flight from being" in which we as a people are involved; Marx would say that it reflects our "alienation." It is difficult, not only conceptually but at a deeper level of thought and feeling, for us to conceive of the world as a creation in which "all elements are interrelated"—in which "to be" is "to be with."

At the same time, the very extremity of our isolation from one another, our sense of abandonment and void, has made significant numbers of us long for such a world; and this means a new openness to "the ontology of communion." Thus, theologically and religiously speaking, we find ourselves in an apologetic situation that

makes it possible to recover some of the alternative categories belonging to the oldest strata of the Judaeo-Christian tradition. There
is a certain readiness for these alternatives on the part of many people, who recognize at varying levels of comprehension the failure of
the dominant concepts, goals, and values of our civilization.

It is thus not surprising, for example, when a denomination as
steeped in neo-Protestant individualism as my own, the United
Church of Canada, adopts as its own a new credal statement that begins with the words, "We are not alone. . . . " The statement is
confessional in a genuine sense of the word, because it engages precisely that over against which faith in our epoch has to pit its frail
courage: the experience of solitariness, of disaffection, of abandonment, of being alone. Such a confession confronts without equiv-
ocation the very anxiety that as a people North Americans find it
hard to acknowledge: the despair of those who have sensed but cannot admit the death-of-God/death-of-meaning. All appearances to
the contrary, it affirms, "We are not alone, we live in God's world.
. . . " Simply in our being there we are being-in-relationship; our
sheer existing points beyond itself. We are creatures whose being
implies relatedness. The solitary, isolated, self-sufficient human
being—the "self-made man" that still exists for us as a rhetorical
ideal—is, in fact, a contradiction in terms. To be, to be-in-the-
world, is to be with.

The "ontology of communion" is a natural, and necessary, outcome of the biblical conception of God. For even God in this tradition is "not alone." There is no interest in the Judaeo-Christian scriptures in God-alone, such as one finds in some religious and
philosophical traditions. The biblical God is busy from the first sentence of Genesis making beings who can participate in his own over-
flowing *Mitsein*. Not only the creation theology of these writings,
but even more pointedly their covenant theology (which Barth
rightly finds to be the internal motivation of creation[10]); not only the
steadfast love (*ḥesed*) but also the anger, wrath, jealousy of this
God—all betray God's apparently innate drive toward an ever more
actualized relatedness: "I will be your God, and you will be my people!" God may be transcendent—yes, even more holy, awesome, and
"other" than the most remote deities of the philosophers. Yet all of
God's otherness is directed to the service of a single biblical theme:
the absolute purity and intensity of the divine *agape*. " 'God is' means
'God loves.' "

Whatever else we may have to understand and acknowledge in relation to the divine being, it will always have to be a definition of this being of His as the One who loves. All our further insights about who and what God is must revolve round this mystery — the mystery of His loving. In a certain sense they can only be repetitions and amplification of the one statement that "God loves."[11]

This applies not only to the so-called perfections or attributes of God, which, as they are often treated, present a very different picture of God, one made fearsome by power rather than awesome in love; it applies also to the much-misunderstood doctrine of the Trinity. Freed from the strictures of technical jargon, the Trinity is nothing more or less than an extension of the fundamental ontic insistence that God too is being-with, that is, "God is love" (I Jn. 4:16). Therefore, the primary declaration of the New Testament, namely, that this God whose very being is a yearning for ever more actualized expressions of mutuality has now in the fullest possible way become God-with-us (Emmanuel), should not come as a surprise to anyone who has carefully followed the course of Israel's history.[12]

To claim that the rudimentary ontology of the biblical tradition is being-with is to say that all being, from the Being who is the source and ground of being to the smallest of created things, is being-in-relationship. This does not mean that the reality, goodness, and beauty of individual life is denied. We are not speaking about a merger of being, as in Neoplatonism or pantheism. We are referring here to an alongsideness, a vis-à-vis, a dialogue, a give and take, a back and forth. "With" does not and should not translate immediately into that other familiar biblical preposition, "in." "In" certainly belongs to the terminology of Scripture, especially to Pauline mysticism: we are *en Christo* ("in Christ"). Perhaps in some ultimate sense this *in* points to the most fully realized state of communion, in relation to which our being "with" Christ ("I have called you friends") is only an eschatological foretaste. But the mystical relationship implicit in the preposition *in* must not be allowed to cross over the fine line between communion (*com + unus*) and ontic union. Ontic union belongs to the tradition of Athens — to the mystery religions, for example, with their goal of incorporation into the deity and the consequent loss of self. The primary relational category of biblical faith, love, precludes such a blurring of distinctions.

"With" is indispensable to this ontology; it implies identification with differentiation. I am not you, you are not me; yet, *mirabile dictu*, with all our insularity, our aloneness, our persistent egoism, we are nonetheless graciously enabled to meet and engage each other. We are not alone.

The New Testament's concept of the church is apropos here, and not only because of its admirable exemplification of the principle of being-with, but because (as we have seen in the discussion of the biblical background of the *imago Dei*) at the epistemological level the being into which we are called in the Christian *koinonia* is the primary source of our understanding of God's intention for *human* being as a whole. In the New Testament's imagery of the vine and the branches, or of the bride and bridegroom, the first Christians preserved the Hebraic ontology of relatedness—identification-with-differentiation. But it is Paul's symbol of the *soma Christou* that most ably represents this conception of the "new being" that is the gift of divine grace.

As members of Christ's *corpus*, Christians are brought into a relationship with the Christ that on the one hand draws on the idea of mystical union, yet at the same time sustains the polar concept of distinction. However close may be the communion of the church with Christ, Christ remains "the head" of the body; and on this basis Protestant theology, where it has been true to its own reforming principles, has always resisted the idea of the church as a straightforward "extension of the Incarnation."[13] Within the *koinonia* believers are also "members of one another"; yet "all the members do not have the same function" (Rom. 12), and far from having their own individual identity and worth threatened by the solidarity of their communion with and in Christ, the interrelatedness of the body upholds the personal uniqueness of each:

> For the body does not consist of one member but of many. If the foot should say, "Because I am not a hand, I do not belong to the body," that would not make it any less a part of the body. And if the ear should say, "Because I am not an eye, I do not belong to the body," that would not make it any less a part of the body. If the whole body were an eye, where would be the hearing? If the whole body were an ear, where would be the sense of smell? But as it is, God arranged the organs in the body, each one of them, as he chose. If all were a single organ, where would the body be? As it is, there are many parts, yet one body. The eye cannot say to the hand, "I have no need of you," nor again the head

to the feet, "I have no need of you." On the contrary, the parts of the body which seem to be weaker are indispensable, and those parts of the body which we think less honorable we invest with greater honor, and our unpresentable parts are treated with greater modesty, which our more presentable parts do not require. But God has so adjusted the body, giving the greater honor to the inferior part, that there may be no discord in the body, but that the members may have the same care for one another. If one member suffers, all suffer together; if one member is honored, all rejoice together.

Now you are the body of Christ and individually members of it.

(I Cor. 12:14–27)

It is not accidental that the apostle goes on directly to speak about the nature of love (I Cor. 13); for the most immediate manner of articulating this basic ontology of the tradition of Jerusalem is precisely that. This being-with is finally nothing more and nothing less than love. And love, as Paul proceeds so unforgettably to characterize it, consists precisely in a delicate and always grace-enabled balance between two equally dangerous threats to itself: on the one hand, the danger of succumbing to the differentiation principle contained in love and thus, for example, "insisting on having one's own way" (v. 5); on the other hand, giving in to the dimension of identity in love, and so engulfing or being engulfed by the other — a temptation in regard to which the lover must be "patient and kind" (v. 4), allowing the beloved a certain space, a certain freedom.

When we attempt to comprehend the ontology of communion, and therefore (according to this tradition) our own nature and calling as human creatures, it should not be necessary to say anything beyond this one word — love. God's being, we have said, means God's loving; therefore, Kierkegaard was absolutely right when he concluded that we image God only in loving.

Unfortunately, the ease with which this word "love" is used in our culture — its various reductions in secular society, and perhaps even more devastatingly, its gross sentimentalization by the religious — has rendered it almost incapable of bearing the weight of the ontic and noetic assumptions for which it (and finally it alone) is an adequate expression. Serious theology must take unusual pains to ensure that this rudimentary idea of both theology and ethics, love, will not be misconstrued. Far from being an easy affirmation of the mawkish truisms verbalized in thousands of ways throughout our media-conscious culture, love in this ancient tradition refers to the foundational reality of the world: *God* is love, and for love all that is has its being.

The ethic that follows this ontology is thus an immediate and inescapable dimension of the metaphysic itself. There is no separation here of theology and ethics, indicative and imperative, no need to reason one's way inductively from one to the other. The ontology of love (namely, that God is love, and that we are *imago Dei*) already contains the love-ethic. If our being is as such a being-with, then the good that we are obliged to pursue is not something externally imposed but the making good of our own essence, *being* who we *are*. Such a vocation may indeed call for our perfecting of such personal endowments as intellection, the capacity to determine and to will, spiritual sensitivity, and many other talents that we as persons have undoubtedly been graced with. But we do not achieve the good we are to seek by perfecting these talents as such, but only when through them we have been enabled to approximate the fullness of relatedness for which these qualities equip us. We move toward real humanity, not when we have achieved all manner of personal successes of brain, will, or body, but when through the media of brain, will, and body we have entered as unreservedly as possible into communion with "the other."[14]

II. THE THREE DIMENSIONS OF HUMAN BEING-WITH

But now we must openly confront the question that the foregoing discussion has begged: Who is this "other" whom we have been brought into being to commune with?

The answer that springs to the religiously catechized mind, almost as a conditioned response, is of course God. St. Augustine set the tone for all subsequent reflection on this subject when, in the most famous sentence of his *Confessions*, he stated: *Tu fecisti nos ad te, Domine, et inquietum est cor nostrum donec requiescat in te* ("You created us for yourself, Lord, and our heart is unquiet until it reposes in you.") This response is correct in its way: our being is, according to the Jerusalem tradition, oriented toward its ground and source, God. What is wrong with the answer in this form is its incompleteness; biblical ontology requires a more inclusive answer. It was for this reason that Jesus, when he summarized the law, included at once a second focus of our human being-with: the neighbor (*Mitmensch*). Paul, as we observed earlier, could later have the love of neighbor express the whole law (Rom. 13:8); for he knew that authentic neighbor-love implies the love of God. The Torah, which is not merely derived from the biblical understanding of the nature of being but is itself an expression of the ontology of communion rendered in the imperative mood, points us toward God when it points us toward our *Mitmenschen*, and vice versa. The two dimensions of our relatedness are inseparable in every respect except linguistically.

What I intend and hope to affirm now — for reasons I trust have already been well established — is that already implicit within this biblical logic of being is yet a third dimension: the inarticulate but "unsilent" creation, the physical universe that is our home, the creatures whose "otherness" is more conspicuous still than the otherness of those of our own kind — in short, what we call nature. I do not think that it is necessary to strain the tradition of Jerusalem to locate this third dimension. It is true that it is not explicitly named in the love commandment. It is also true that there are fewer, and less impressive, references to the natural world in Scripture than we should be happy to find there (in the light of the present crisis of the environment). Nevertheless, I shall contend, it belongs to the basic ontology of this tradition that the extrahuman creation constitutes a third focus of the love commandment, and one that shares with the first and second dimensions their inseparability. It is not unimportant that we may find in the Bible explicit pointers in the direction of this love for the natural order: in its creation sagas, in many of the psalms and much of the wisdom literature (for example, the famous address to Job out of the whirlwind), in various laws of the older covenant protecting the rights of animals, in the teachings and remembered acts of Jesus, and so forth. But this explicit — and always somewhat tenuous — evidence of Scripture needs to be undergirded by something more foundational.

This, I propose, is where it is mandatory for theology today to become more articulate concerning the biblical ontology, the "ontology of communion, community, ecology" (as Professor Sittler has appropriately labeled it). What is important, after all, is not that we should be able to read somewhere in Scripture, "And thou shalt love the natural order as thyself too!" Rather, what matters is the Bible's basic attitude toward creation, toward salvation, toward the material universe (including the human body), toward other forms of life—toward life itself. If what we encounter in the Bible's jux-taposition of the divine and human is indeed an ontology of related-ness, we can hardly be content with an articulation of this theory of being that stops with the divine and the human. To be sure, that is precisely where most Christian theology heretofore has stopped! The drama in which it has taken interest is the drama of human his-tory, the "divine-human encounter" (Brunner). Nature has been regarded as a neutral thing, a backdrop against which the historical drama is enacted. But this nonchalance concerning the third dimen-sion of human relatedness was the consequence of luxury assump-tions that thoughtful Christians can no longer afford. Heretofore, the natural order has remained inarticulate, has not asserted itself; or rather, humanity could remain unconscious of "nature's warning voice." But the silent partner of our covenantal being is no longer willing to remain dumb before its shearers. Joseph Sittler writes:

> We are embarrassed today because purely historical categories are no longer capable of operating sociologically or in the life sciences or in any other kind of descriptive science. And why? They have come to this incapacity because our generation has witnessed the drawing of the life and vitality and the potentialities of nature into the realm of history. The life of nature is now pathetically open to the decisional life that man lives as a historical being. For the first time man has added to his natural curiosity and creativity a perverse aggressiveness whereby nature is absolutely suppliant before him in such a way that she lives by his sufferance and can die by his decision.
>
> This possibility has actually never existed until our genera-tion. That means that theological categories may no longer be only historical categories. They have got to deal with man as his-tory and as nature; and therefore, categories of creation, redemp-tion, and sanctification have got to operate with the same scope as the fundamental categories of man and God. And this requires not only that Christian and Jewish morality shall be offended by pollution but that theology must do more: it must be reconceived, under the shock of filth, into fresh scope and profundity.[15]

The "reconceiving" of theology involves the imaginative and spirited rethinking of what in the Athens tradition was considered the "first science," the science of being.[16] To come to terms with the new and life-threatening phenomena that have presented themselves today to the consciousness of all thinking persons, constituting a "shock of nonbeing" on a cosmic scale, we are compelled to reconsider what we mean by being. It is, as Sittler insists, not enough for Christian ethicists to devise new analyses and strategies for the meeting of the various crises by which our consciousness is shocked. Theology, which is foundational for ethics, must return to basic questions, beginning with the question of being itself. It is true, as Paul Tillich himself observed, that "there is no ontological thought in biblical religion. . . . " But it is equally true (as he goes on at once to remark) that "there is no symbol or no theological concept in [the Bible] which does not have ontological implications."[17] The law of God (Torah), like the gospel itself, arises out of prophetic contemplation of life, of being, as the nature of being is disclosed to the prophetic imagination. Faith discerns "what must be done" as it returns, in supplication and awe, to the foundational reality that is "revealed" in the core events of salvific history, under the impact of the contemporary problematic. What evokes explicit commandments — commands that are more than mere exhortations because they are grounded in perceived reality (*ontos*) — is the combination of a renewed reflection on the broad traditions concerning the being, meaning, and direction of the creation under God, and the emergence in history of particular circumstances that call for "a word from the Lord."

The process to which we are invited and compelled is, therefore, by no means novel. What the rabbi Jesus was about when, in the Sermon on the Mount, he explicated certain implications of the law against bearing false witness, committing adultery, murder, and so forth, was precisely this (and it was not a novelty with him either): in the light of contextual realities of which he was especially conscious, he gave expression to commands that he believed were already implicit in the tradition. There had come a time when the community of belief had to be told that lust was already adultery and hate already murderous. There had come a time when this community, surrounded by enemies, had to be told that the commandment to love the neighbor and the "stranger within the gate" already contained the imperative "Love your enemies" (Mt. 5:43f.).

Similarly, there has come a time — our own — when it is necessary for the rabbinic and prophetic ministry of the people of God to announce that the love of the natural order is already implicit in the biblical ontology. It is not a new commandment, though it must be newly announced. It was present already from the outset — indeed from the foundations of the world. It was present already in the being of the creation. Even before the Creator articulated it, "saw" it (Gen. 1:10, 25, 31), the "goodness" of the whole work of creation, mirroring God's own glory (Calvin), was "there." So was the interrelatedness of all its aspects (surely the point of the ordered sequence of the creation in six days). There was already a bond of being between humanity and all else, second only to the bond between the human pair themselves, which in turn was second only to the bond of being between creature and Creator. *Shalom* is not merely an ideal to be striven for but a reality to be acknowledged and lived. The same love commandment already implicit in that bond of ontic relatedness and mutuality binding male and female, Creator and creature, extends itself naturally and without constraint or contrivance to the relationship between humankind and otherkind.

It requires only the occasion. And with the introduction, millenia later, of an inestimable threat to otherkind, the occasion has arrived. "Under the shock of filth," what is implicit has now to become explicit: the inarticulate but no-longer-silent creation must be loved. Perhaps this dimension of the love commandment implicit in the tradition of Jerusalem must for us become the most immediate of the three. Paul, in the midst of an imperium where human beings (especially non-Romans) counted for less than systems and principles, found himself expressing the whole Torah in the command to love the neighbor (Rom. 13:8). It may be that we shall have to learn to express the whole law of God in the command to love the earth. For it is precisely for the lack of such earthward orientation of human love that the planet's life is today threatened. As bearers of this ancient, relational ontology of the people of Israel, our context evokes from us a commandment that the classical expressions of our faith did not yet have to explicate, though it was tacitly present from the outset: that we love this world.

We name, then, three dimensions of human relatedness.[18] The human being is being-with-God, who is source and ground of all being; it is being-with-the-human-counterpart (*Mitmenschen*); and it is being-with-nature. Humanity in God's intention means existing in dynamic, harmonious relationships with these three counterparts of our being. To be *imago Dei* implies that, standing within the relationship with God, the human creature reflects God's vicarious and gracious *Mitsein* in its life vis-à-vis these others. To state the matter in other terms — terms that largely through Karl Barth have become part of the theological vocabulary: essential humanity involves a coexistence that is at the same time proexistence. Being with the other, in the perspective of this faith tradition, implies being for the other. By contrast, sin in this same tradition is a condition not only of being–alone (attempting autonomy) but also being–against. At bottom, sin is quite simply the negation (or the attempt at negating) of the relational structuring of the being for which we were created. We may express the distinctions in a formula as follows:

Essential (intended or authentic) humanity means:

being-with (coexistence)
= being-for (proexistence)
= being-together (communion, community, covenant)

Existential (distorted, inauthentic, "fallen") humanity means:

being-alone (autonomy)
= being-against (estrangement, alienation)
= being-above (pride = the attempt at mastery) *or*
being-below (sloth = escape from responsibility)

This relational mode of formulating the rudimentary biblical concept of being or ontology applies to all three dimensions of our orientation as human beings. With respect to all "the others," whether they be our own kind, other species, or the creative Source, the being to which we are called as distinct from the distorted being that we know all too well is an unequivocal mutuality and reciprocity. If we can grasp this basic presupposition of the Bible's version of "first science," then the question What should the role of the human being be in the natural order? will in effect answer itself. If we do not grasp this fundamental assumption about the nature of being itself, then no amount of exhortation concerning the improvement of human attitudes toward the natural world will make much difference. The change that is called for by the manifold crisis of our environment is one that must take place, as I maintained in the Introduction, internally — in our manner of imagining ourselves. If we believe ourselves to be beings whose very existing implies a coexisting that is simultaneously a proexisting, then this form of the human self may at last begin to express itself with respect to the natural order. Biblical creational theology maintains that we were made for being-with. Biblical redemption theology says that it is possible, through grace, for us to begin to realize this creational intention even in the midst of our distortion of it. The biblical imperative is that this possibility, "under the shock of filth," be a necessity.

III. NOT THREE DISTINCT RELATIONSHIPS

In the foregoing discussion I have said that the human being manifests a "threefold relatedness," or that his/her life is oriented toward "three dimensions or foci." Admittedly, this is inelegant language. Would it not be simpler, as well as more conventional, to say that humanity in God's intention is created for three relationships: one with God, one with other human beings, and one with the natural order?

It would indeed be simpler. But it would also be misleading. For one of the most significant things that must be said about the "relationships" in question is that according to biblical faith they are inextricably bound up with one another. It is impossible to separate them into three different categories, even though it is certainly necessary to distinguish among them.

The reader will recognize that we have here something like an anthropological parallel with trinitarian doctrine. (Given the Augustinian convention that associates the Trinity with the *imago Dei*, there may be a legitimate precedent for this, though we employ it differently.)[19] Like the Trinity, the three foci of human relatedness are "three yet one": three distinct, hypostatic points of reference, but all of a piece.

From the side of their distinctness, we may and must speak of the Godward orientation of our being-with, of the humanward orientation, and of the orientation toward nature. But it must be understood that these three dimensions of our total relatedness as human creatures are inseparable in reality, even if for purposes of understanding and discussion we must separate them (a necessity imposed on theology, as on all analysis, by the dynamic character of its subject matter). So inseparable are these three dimensions of our relatedness in life as distinct from theory, that John's First Epistle can remind us that anyone claiming to love God while hating his neighbor is nothing short of "a liar" (4:20). Jesus' connecting phrase between the two prongs of the love commandment (that the second is "like unto" the first), as well as Paul's summation of the whole Torah in neighbor-love, make the same point but more positively: rightly to love the neighbor is to love God, and vice versa.

To this, following the logic of the ontology we are put in touch with by the *imago Dei*, relationally conceived, we must now make explicit the third focus: love toward the inarticulate creation. Rightly to love God and our *Mitmenschen* is also to love our home the earth and its myriad creatures and parts. These three are indivisible dimensions of the same love. Their indivisibility becomes evident today if one asks, for instance, what kind of love for the neighbor would manifest itself in greedy and rapacious attitudes toward the earth, its resources, and its species. Can one possibly be said to love God and one's own kind if one treats God's creation and one's neighbor's habitat with disrespect? The question becomes all the more pointed if we ask it knowing (as we certainly must!) that the "neighbor" in question refers now to a global community, and to generations yet to come who will inherit the kind of biosphere that we leave them.

It is necessary to emphasize the interconnectedness of the threefold relatedness in which the human creature stands according to the ontology of Jerusalem because the unfortunate effect of much Christian doctrine and practice is to have divorced the relationship with God from the humanward and earthward dimensions of our being-with. All too consistently, empirical Christianity has fostered a virtual segregation of the "vertical" and "horizontal," the "heavenward" and "earthward," the "sacred" and "secular," the kingdom of God and the kingdoms of this world. Consequently, it has been possible in the modern period for those who manifested the greatest concern for humanity and the natural world to become thoroughly disengaged from the church. The early humanist movement, which (as we know from the biographies of Zwingli, Calvin, Erasmus, Melanchthon, and others) is inseparable from the Reformation, very soon channeled its energies into nonecclesial forms and causes. The same could be said of the Romantic movement of the nineteenth century (one of whose prime movers was the father of liberal theology, Friedrich Schleiermacher), with its recovery of a special sensibility (*Gefühl*) toward nature. The church seemed incapable of retaining either the humanitarian or the nature-loving spirit within itself. Its field of interest was—too exclusively—divinity.[20]

Also, tragically enough, because the church of the post-Reformation period permitted itself to become the custodian of the human relation to God, neglecting both of the other foci of our ontic relatedness, Western society's attitude toward nature in particular became, in a short time, thoroughly devoid of any of those qualities that could appropriately be described within the categories of relationship—or even spirituality. Having placed the relationship with God in a class by itself, with an accompanying high spirituality,

Western Christians developed a relationship with both nonhuman nature and the human species that was increasingly secular, flat, and one-dimensional.[21] These dimensions of our relatedness were thus robbed of the qualities of transcendence and mystery, since those qualities were ascribed so exclusively to divinity.

Thus part of the corrective that is necessary in building new human attitudes toward nature is to reconnect, as it were, the divine/vertical/sacred dimension of human relatedness to the earthly/horizontal/secular dimension. Without detracting from the spirituality that correctly pertains to our relationship with God (would it not, in fact, enhance it?), we must learn to attribute to our relationships with other human beings and with the nonhuman universe such spiritual attitudes as the sense of their awesome otherness, wonder, mystery, hiddenness, fascination, inner depth, and meaning—in short, their transcendence. And the only profound way we can achieve this within the parameters of our Judaeo-Christian tradition is by recovering something of the interconnectedness of its basic ontology: that is, the recognition that while God remains God and is not simply to be confused in a pantheistic way with the creation, all the creatures, being God's, bear about them some portion of the glory that is their Creator's.[22] The same awe and reverence that informs our relationship with God should therefore inform our relationship with other human beings and with the extrahuman creation. For these are not distinct and separate relationships, but three aspects of a thrust outward, out beyond ourselves—a common quest for "the other" that finds this other in God, humanity, and nature, and is not truly fulfilled until it has discovered all three of its intended counterparts. Following the logic of St. John, may we not say, then, from the negative perspective, that one who claims to love God or neighbor while hating the earth is "a liar"? Or, positively phrasing it by using Augustine's famous formula, may we not say, "Thou has created us for thyself, for one another, and for thy creation, and our hearts are restless until they repose in all three"?

It is, of course, impossible to calculate such hypothetical possibilities. Nevertheless, one may wonder in such times as ours whether it would not greatly alter the situation of the earth if even only a minority of its citizens—especially its First World citizens!—began to think and act as if the reverence that they have been taught to feel for the divine should also be reflected, quite concretely, in their attitudes toward the creation, human and extrahuman.

IV. WE RECEIVE OUR BEING

A final point must be made before we leave this discussion of the character of biblical ontology. It concerns the dynamic, as distinct from fixed or static, character of this ontology — or, one might say, the process character of being in the perspective of this tradition. We encountered it particularly in our discussion of the ecclesiological application of the *imago Dei* in the New Testament, where it is assumed that the conformity of the Christian community to the *imago Christi* is an eschatological process. In order to prepare for this aspect of the discussion, let us quickly recapitulate the argument up to this point:

(a) When we ask who *anthropos* is, that is, what is the essential or intended character and vocation of the human being according to the Judaeo-Christian tradition, Christian theological conventions turn us toward the doctrinal symbol of the *imago Dei*.

(b) If we trace the history of the theology of the *imago*, we find two distinctive conceptions, one that thinks of the image of God as a substance or endowment of human being, the other regarding it as a consequence of the divine-human relationship.

(c) The biblical usage of this term, as well as the best traditions of Reformation theology in particular, suggest that the relational understanding of the *imago* symbol is the appropriate one so far as the tradition of Jerusalem is concerned; for it corroborates rather precisely the other primary categories of biblical faith (grace, hope, and especially love), which are all relational in nature.

(d) The quintessence of the relational understanding of the *imago Dei* is its underlying presupposition that the human creature is created for relationship, that is, that relatedness-in-love is of our very essence and vocation as creatures of the God who *is* love. We image God in loving.

(e) The relatedness or being-with that is of the essence of our humanity is not one-dimensional — not merely Godward, or exclusively "religious" in character — but has three distinctive foci: God, other human beings, and extrahuman creation (the latter being an aspect of the Torah that is implicit in biblical ontology, which is evoked and made explicit in our historical moment because of the crises of nature).

(f) These three dimensions or foci of our human relatedness are integrally and inseparably linked with one another, to the extent that there is no appropriate relationship with God that is not at the same time a new being-with our own kind and otherkind, and vice versa.

What we must now go on to observe is something about the internal character of this being. One way of stating what I should like to affirm about the character of this being is that it is not so much a matter of "being" as of "becoming": that is, it is not something that has simply been given but something that is being given. It is not accomplished once for all, but it is in process; it is dynamic and not static. Combining this with the insight that this being is a relational reality (being-*with*), we may derive the conclusion that, according to the ontological perspective of this tradition, we receive our being in our being-with.

There are two claims implicit here. First, we receive our being: we are continuously given being. It is like the manna of the wilderness; it is the "daily bread" for which Jesus taught his disciples to pray. In other words, to notice the obverse side of this insight, we do not *have* being. As we have noted earlier, the language of possession is inappropriate to the ontology of this tradition. In reality, we possess nothing. As Luther said, "Wir sind Bettler" ("we are beggars"). We do not even have our being. We are contingent, "absolutely dependent" (Schleiermacher). In fact, if we *are*, it is because two other human beings had a relationship with each other; and both of them *are* (or were) for the same reason. If, in fact, we continue to *be*, it is because we are daily sustained by thousands of other beings, seen and unseen, that make our continuance possible. If we wake up each morning for a certain number of years to find that, yes, we still exist, it is not because we have within ourselves the wherewithal for our own perpetuation. We are not self-generating or self-sufficient. We are recipients at every level of our being—physical, psychic, spiritual, emotional, and so forth.

But there is a second claim in the statement that "we receive our being in our being-with," and it has to do with the "whence" of our being. From what or whom do we receive our being?

Again, almost as a conditioned response, the religious mentality answers that we receive our being from God, the source and ground of all that is. God, who creates *ex nihilo*; God, who continually re-creates (*creatio continua*); God, without whose grace we and the whole creation, as Calvin insisted,[23] would slip away into oblivion (a sentiment that late twentieth-century humanity, perched on the edge of nuclear holocaust, can perhaps once again appreciate): God and God alone is the "whence" of our being. Faith can never afford to stop confessing our total dependence on the creating and sustaining, redeeming and sanctifying love of God. To none other are we ultimately accountable for our being and continuing-in-being.

Yet it is necessary once again to be wary, lest we fall into what may be called the religious heresy, that is, the heresy of segregating sacred and secular, the heresy of robbing God's creation of its rightful transcendence in an inept endeavor to honor God's personal transcendence. If we take the three-dimensionality of our being-with seriously, then we must recognize in each dimension—and in all of them in concert—the source of our being. Thus when we affirm, as we must, that God is the whence of our being, we do not mean that each of us receives his being directly in some unusual, supranatural manner, straight from the Creator and without reference to or mediation from the other counterparts of our being. The confession that God is the source and ground of our being is, rather, simultaneously a confession of our dependence on these created "others": the parents who conceived and nurtured us; the siblings whose companionship (and rivalry) shaped our formative years; the friends, co-workers, neighbors, teachers, students, and colleagues with whom we are linked in voluntary or involuntary communality; the dogs and cats whose presence in our childhood and at other times may have been even more significant than that of people; the animals and plants that sustain our bodies and the wine that makes our souls glad; the trees, the particular landscapes, the mountains, the sea, the rivers and prairies; the sun and skies; the ground with which, despite false pride, we have an aboriginal affinity: through each and all of these, creatures though they be, our being has been shaped and is being sustained. I know perfectly well that I would not be who I have become or am becoming without the quite specific faces that have beamed upon me or scolded and questioned me from my youth up; or the quite particular climate in which I was reared and have lived most of my life (the snow); or the animals I have loved—and who loved me more than I them; or the trees, the splendid trees.

We know, if we are honest, that we *receive* our being, that it comes, prodigiously, from beyond our own inherent capacity for living—for "going on," whether physically or psychically.[24] Faith names this "beyond" God, and Christian confession rightly acknowledges the being that comes from this transcendent source as "grace," for it is a sheer and undeserved gift! But the recognition that life is gift should not, surely, lead to the kind of total separation of grace and nature that has too often characterized the religious (especially the Protestant) mentality. Grace is dialectically related to nature: "Grace is not nature and nature is not grace. But grace and nature are related."[25] Grace is not simply to be equated with natural occurrence, because such an equation would deprive the human spirit of the sense of wonder at the unusual, the unexpected, the undeserved. But neither is grace to be perceived as a supernatural alternative to nature. "Nothing natural is the cause of grace; anything natural (or historical) may be an occasion of it."[26] The awe that produces in us the sense of "sheer gift" (*sola gratia*) is not born of the experience that nature is simply bypassed: that conception of the miraculous, so important to the "religious" mentality, is regularly chastised in Scripture.[27] Rather, grace refers to the experience of seeing in and through the regular, ordinary, and even predictable occurrences of life a depth and a mystery that infinitely transcends the phenomena that are its vehicles.

This may and must be said especially about that occurrence that is the primary locus of Christians' wonder at the grace of the eternal: "Jesus Christ and him crucified." Of this, Joseph Sittler in a moving passage has written:

> The disclosure of grace in the enormous paradox of the cross is the "focal point" for man's encounter with grace. The grace of God is humanly, historically, and episodically incandescent in Calvary. That occasion, indeed, was and is so crucial an occasion that the mind and devotion of the devout is tempted to forget, in its grateful Christocentrism, that Jesus was not centered in Jesus at all. He is called the Christ precisely because of that. Our theology can be Christocentric as regards the reality and crucial occasion of grace precisely because that Christology lives within the grace of the Holy Trinity. The holy occasion of the discovery of the grace of God may indeed be the mountaintop experience, but the place and content of the experience is not identical with the experienced in its origin and fullness and destiny. That is why the occasion must be both absolutely valued and absolutely qualified. For the decisive context of life is time as continuity and not time as moment; continuity, not break; steadiness, not staccato; what goes on and not only what shakes up.[28]

By all means, then, God and God alone is the ultimate source of the being that we receive. But the "mysterious ways" in which "God moves" to bequeath to us this ongoing gift are ultimately inseparable from the very ordinary ways that are at work in history and nature, in our daily existence in its continuity with time past and time future, in our interaction with one another and with "the things that are made" (Rom. 1).

It is, I think, because Christians have been so fearful of making this connection between grace and nature — as if in that way we could preserve a little space for God amidst the growing modern preoccupation with matter — that the religion of the West has been so reluctant to admit of any great mystery in the world itself, and has consequently treated the world as if it were a thing — a very large collection of things — put here for human use. The corrective to this situation, however, does not have to be introduced from the East. The "journey to the East" undertaken by numerous sensitive souls in our period might well pause longer than it has been wont to do in Jerusalem. For in the tradition of Jerusalem, and particularly in its relational understanding of being, there is a remedy for the theo- and Christo-monism, that is, the sort of theism that honors God and Christ by desacralizing humanity and the earth. And it is a remedy more immediately applicable to the West than are Eastern potions, since the disease itself is eminently Western. To be sure, we shall not hear from the tradition of Jerusalem that the world as such is God. But we shall hear that it is God's.[29] And that is precisely what we need to hear, not only we whose essential secularity has given us the illusion of ownership, of possession, and of mastery, but also we whose religiosity has robbed us of the rudimentary human experience of being "awed by the world."[30] The world is God's: therefore, the language of possession is inappropriate to faith. The world is God's: therefore, everything in it has for faith the quality of sheer gift.

We receive our being, then, from God, that is, from God's world, that is, from one another, that is, from the earth and the myriad elements and creatures. Receiving and giving, giving and receiving: who could miss this recurrent emphasis in the teaching of Jesus, for example?[31] Our tradition presents us with a picture of the universe as an ecologically harmonious system of interrelated, interdependent beings. The picture is already beautifully expressed in the creational symbol of "the Garden," that place of mutuality from which the human being was expelled just because of its bid for autonomy. The picture also stands however at the omega-point, the *telos*, of the process, in both the Old and the New Testament versions of the peaceable kingdom. Most important of all, so far as our experience and knowledge of this ecological grace is concerned, this same picture is the foundational concept of the community into which the people of God are called: the church, the "body"—a movement that clearly lives from its Head but is also sustained by the variety of its members, with their particular gifts and offices and callings. Thus, in both its theology of creation and its theology of redemption, Christian faith assumes not only the interconnectedness of all the counterparts of our being but also the flow of the life source that permeates and employs them all. And, far from being mere theoretical knowledge (*gnosis*), this ecological grace is a matter of experience. We have already tasted of this banquet in the eucharistic "foretaste" of the kingdom that is called *koinonia*.

V. CONCLUSION AND TRANSITION: AWED BY THE WORLD

The conclusion these reflections on the nature of being in the tradition of Jerusalem move toward is an intensely practical one. We are led by such meditation to understand that we shall not have made good this conception of what it means "to be" until we have translated into earthward forms of spirituality the sense of mystery and reverence that we have too exclusively attributed to divinity alone. Our present earthly crises have, to be sure, provided the incentive for us to rethink the tradition of Jerusalem along such lines as these. But it is not the first time that contextual realities have evoked from theology and from its primary sources emphases that had been overlooked, neglected, or unexplored by the past. If it had been taken seriously from the outset of the Christian movement that a world that could be described as God's own good creation must, for all its materiality, manifest something of the holiness of its Maker; if the Hellenistic tendency to denigrate matter had not led Christians into a too consistently ambiguous posture with respect to the earth; if the movement of the Redeemer toward creation (the Incarnation) had not been vitiated by a "religious" interest in redemption *from* creation—then it would not have been necessary at this point for representatives of this tradition to call for a more reverential attitude toward this world in the name of the triune God.

The point of the present exercise in biblical ontology—the ontology of communion, as I have called it, following Sittler—has been to show that the potential of our tradition for such reverence has nonetheless been there all along. Where it has not surfaced often in official doctrine and praxis (indeed, there have been few Francises of Assisi), it has nevertheless continued in oblique and hidden ways to inform countercultural or unofficial aspects of our "Christian" society.

Indeed, the natural sciences, which official religion has consistently feared (because, one suspects, they threatened to transfer to the world some of the wonder religion wanted to reserve for its own special preserve) — even the natural sciences learned from this same Judaeo-Christian ontology that human spirituality is cheapened when it fastens on the divine in such a way as to exclude nature and even history from the realm of transcendent wonder. Thus it happens again in our time, when the silly battle of Religion and Science has more or less spent itself, that scientists may everywhere be heard exemplifying, according to their kind, the dictum of Aquinas, that great pupil of "the father of modern Science," Albertus Magnus: *Gratia non tollet naturam, sed perficit* ("Grace does not destroy nature, but perfects it").[32] Those who fix their gaze most intently on the natural world are frequently those least able to account for nature through nature alone. With an unforgettable account of one of them, I close this chapter:

> . . . I saw a judgment upon life, and . . . it was not passed by men. Those who stare at birds in cages may not care for it. It comes from far away out of my past, in a place of pouring waters and green leaves. I shall never see an episode like it if I live to be a hundred, nor do I think that one man in a million has ever seen it, because man is an intruder into such stillness. The light must be right, and the observer must remain unseen. No man sets up such an experiment. What he sees, he sees by chance.
>
> You may put it that I had come over a mountain, that I had slogged through fern and pine needles for half a long day, and that on the edge of a little glade with one long, crooked branch extending across it, I had sat down to rest with my back against a stump. Through accident I was concealed from the glade, although I could see into it perfectly.
>
> The sun was warm there, and the murmurs of forest life blurred softly away into my sleep. When I awoke, dimly aware of some commotion and outcry in the clearing, the light was slanting down through the pines in such a way that the glade was lit like some vast cathedral. I could see the dust motes of wood pollen in the long shaft of light, and there on the extended branch

sat an enormous raven with a red and squirming nestling in his beak.

The sound that awoke me was the outraged cries of the nestling's parents, who flew helplessly in circles about the clearing. The sleek black monster was indifferent to them. He gulped, whetted his beak on the dead branch a moment, and sat still. Up to that point the little tragedy had followed the usual pattern. But suddenly, out of all that area of woodland, a soft sound of complaint began to rise. Into the glade fluttered small birds of half a dozen varieties drawn by the anguished outcries of the tiny parents.

No one dared to attack the raven. But they cried there in some instinctive common misery, the bereaved and the unbereaved. The glade filled with their soft rustling and their cries. They fluttered as though to point their wings at the murderer. There was a dim intangible ethic he had violated, that they knew. He was a bird of death.

And he, the murderer, the black bird at the heart of life, sat on there, glistening in the common light, formidable, unmoving, unperturbed, untouchable.

The sighing died. It was then I saw the judgment. It was the judgment of life against death. I will never see it again so forcefully presented. I will never hear it again in notes so tragically prolonged. For in the midst of protest, they forgot the violence. There, in that clearing, the crystal note of a song sparrow lifted hesitantly in the hush. And finally, after painful fluttering, another took the song, and then another, the song passing from one bird to another, doubtfully at first, as though some evil thing were being slowly forgotten. Till suddenly they took heart and sang from many throats joyously together as birds are known to sing. They sang because life is sweet and sunlight beautiful. They sang under the brooding shadow of the raven. In simple truth they had forgotten the raven, for they were singers of life, and not of death.[33]

CHAPTER FIVE

Dimensions of Human Relatedness

I. INTRODUCTION: THE TRIUNITY OF BEING-WITH

We began this study with the confession that what needs changing if we are to avert some of the crises that have appeared on our near horizon is not nature but human nature. Our own civilization has appropriated an image of the human that has finally, perhaps inevitably, resulted in a manifold threat to the biosphere. If we are to expect any sort of alternative to the bleak future of a desecrated or uninhabitable planet that promises to be the outcome of human pursuits perfected in this First World, we must seek to comprehend and to change some of the very traits that have made us "first" — such as the calculating rationality and the determined willing that we have brought to our life in and with the natural order.

For Christians, this mandate contains a double directive: On the one hand, our *cultus* has been so closely and formatively aligned with First World civilization that now, facing such crises, we are obliged to examine our past very critically, with a view to repenting of some of the counsels we have allowed to go out into our world and to shape it. On the other hand, the situation propels us into a positive search for meaning and direction: are there insights, wisdom, and ways, perhaps hidden and unexplored within our greater tradition, that can help us rebuild the world and, more specifically, reimagine ourselves as human beings within it?

Determining to confront the problematic of our "Christianized" culture at its doctrinal source, we have addressed this inquiry to the symbol that more than any other has borne the awesome weight of Western humanity's high self-estimate: *imago Dei*. What we have seen is that this same symbol, which has served as the theological ideological rallying point for the human need to distinguish our species from "the common herd," sustains—through an alternative tradition that passes straight through the Reformation—a very different way of regarding the essence of the human.[1] Under the impact of our contextual necessity to reimagine ourselves, the *imago Dei* symbol as conceived within this alternative tradition could become newly significant. For in that interpretation it appears as a terse semiotic expression for a whole ontology that radically questions every hierarchical conception of being and, more particularly, all anthropological doctrines that, on the basis of a more complex mechanism of cognition and volition, place the human creature in a position of sheer domination with respect to all other creatures.

The biblical ontology that conceives of human being—and all being—in relational terms does not deny the uniqueness of the human creature. There is no need to reject outright Aristotle's definition of *anthropos* as "a rational animal," or to repudiate those who marvel at human capacities for deciding, determining, planning, judging, changing, and so forth. However, what the equation "being = being-with" does require of us is that we view all such capacities and endowments according to their function as attributes enabling us to become what we are intended to be: serving and representative creatures, stewards whose complexity of mental, spiritual, and volitional powers makes it possible for us, within the creation, to image the holy and suffering love of the Creator. If we bring that perspective to bear on the question of our being and meaning, it challenges almost everything that can be identified as the primary "values" and pursuits of First World peoples. At the same time, it presents a lively alternative for those of us among the peoples of the First World who cannot yet brush aside a critique of our civilization that emanates from this particular (biblical) source.

In the preceding chapter I attempted to characterize what I believe is the first principle of the ontology of the tradition of Jerusalem, namely, that it is an ontology of communion: that being as such, within the parameters of this tradition, must always be understood to mean "being-with." Our human being implies within itself a movement toward "the other." The correlate and counterpart of our human being, the "other" to whom the essential self is open, is not in any simple sense God only; for God, whom we image, is also in this tradition being-with (Emmanuel). It is, therefore, impossible for us to be in a relationship with God without in that same movement toward the Other called God being turned toward the others called neighbors (*Mitmenschen*) and toward the inarticulate creation.

Tangentially relating this to Augustine's "vestiges of the Trinity," I suggested that there is an indissoluble unity in the three-dimensionality of this human relatedness, so that to separate one focus of our being from the other two is to distort the whole picture. Like the theology that the early church found to be implicit in the biblical witness to God, biblical ontology as a whole is not polymorphous but uniform. The doctrine of the Trinity evolved during the first four centuries of the Common Era, partly, in order to avoid the simplistic, polytheistic conclusion that had suggested itself to many both inside and outside the church, namely, that Christians were believers in three gods (tritheism) or three manifestations or modes of the same god (Monarchianism). A similar process, I believe, must now take place in our basic ontological understanding as it applies to Christian anthropology. Human being, like God's, is not multiple or fragmented; rather, our being is internally oriented toward three distinctive counterparts. These three are so inseparable both in their externality with respect to us and in our internal apprehension of them that a right orientation toward any one of them implies a right orientation toward the other two as well.

While trinitarian theology guarded against tritheism on the one side, it was also intended to ward off an undialectical monotheism. The error of the Monarchians, the church declared, was that they did not comprehend the need for maintaining the distinctions (Father/Son/Spirit) within the godhead, and so ended in an absurd theology that had so thoroughly apotheosized Jesus that it no longer made any sense of the primitive church's confession of his full humanity. There is, I should say, a corresponding need within the ontology of human relatedness to maintain the hypostatic distinctiveness of each of the three dimensions or counterparts of human being, while at the same time emphasizing their indissoluble unity. After all, while the love of God and of neighbor are inseparable, it is not simply the same thing to love one's neighbor and to love God. The neighbor is not God, though he/she may indeed be God's *Stellvertreter(in)* — may indeed be Christ "incognito" (Luther).[2] Yet I am not ultimately answerable to my neighbor; my neighbor is not permitted to "play God" in relation to me, nor I to her or him. Moreover, God's "needs" are not identical with those of my neighbor. The latter's are always greater than those of the former, and in fact, what God requires of me is normally communicated to me through the concrete requirements of my neighbor. Thus, no matter how much my behavior toward my neighbor entails and reflects my relationship with God, and vice versa, there are distinctions between the ways in which I work out my being-with each of them.

This is also true with respect to the third counterpart of my being, the extrahuman world. It is not the same thing—though it is never an entirely different thing either—to love my own kind and to love the otherkind. This distinction is brought home to us today at every turn, as we try, on the one hand, to behave toward the natural order with stewardly care and, on the other hand, to be responsible neighbors to our fellow humans. It is by no means easy, in other words, to simultaneously devise a responsible ethic of the environment and a responsible ethic of social justice. Who wants to be perceived as a conserver of natural resources at the expense of starvation and deprivation on the part of the oppressed among one's own kind?[3]

Thus God, neighbor, and nature confront me with different responsibilities just as they each offer me different gifts. This difference, as well as the essential interconnectedness of the three counterparts of my relatedness, must be honored.

The intention of this chapter and the next is to explore in particular the distinctiveness of each dimension of the threefold orientation of human being, whose essential unity we have already established. What is involved in each of the three foci of our being, and how do they act upon and condition one another?

Because the primary concentration of our study is the relationship between humanity and extrahuman nature, we shall reserve that dimension of human relatedness for a separate chapter (six). Here we shall inquire briefly about human being in relation to God and to our own kind, both for the intrinsic importance of these aspects of our total *Mitsein* and as necessary presuppositional reflection preparatory to the relationship with the natural order.

II. BEING-WITH-GOD

Christian faith affirms that essential humanity means humanity "with" God: "We are not alone. . . . " Obviously the little preposition *with* in such a sentence carries a wealth of meaning. In a

real sense, the whole aim of the four thousand years of religious tradition in which we stand could be expressed through an extended
meditation on this one preposition. God, who is as such Being-in-
relationship, will have alongside himself beings with whom there is
communion. And to achieve this aim, God will not only create such
beings but, when they have renounced their essential relatedness in
favor of an assumed and baseless autonomy, will go to impossible
lengths to secure their companionship.

The tradition explores the meaning of this first aspect of human
relatedness under the rubric of our human creaturehood. Being-
with-God means being creature vis-à-vis Creator. It means ac-
knowledging the limits and the possibilities of our particular form of
creaturehood, and of seeing the limits not as confining limitations but
as gracious boundaries within which we are invited to freely work
out our particular possibilities. To be "with" God in our being implies
that we are neither "in" God, as if indistinct from deity (pantheism),
nor utterly "apart from" God, as wholly isolated beings (deism).
Rather, our creational glory is to have our being alongside the being
of the Creator: "I have called you friends."

As we know, the Bible, with its insistent concretization of
truth, will spell this out in myriad ways — especially, of course, in the
concept of the covenant. The covenant concept is the most recurrent
concretization in Scripture of the ontology that we have called the
ontology of communion. But the Bible also employs other concrete
expressions of this ontology, including analogies of relationship that
carry great emotional depth for us: We are God's "children" — sons
and daughters, offspring, progeny; God is our father, mother, friend,
lover. The metaphors of the family, of marriage, of human friendship and fellowship, even of animal instinct ("as a hen gathers her
chicks") are invoked to depict the intimacy of human being-
with-God.

The character of this relationship is such, however, that it is not
at all automatic or simply "necessary" (in the medieval sense of the
term). We cannot cease to be beings whose lives are intended for relationship with God ("thou has created us for thyself . . . "); yet neither is this relationship simply given, fully actualized, to our existence as such. For God does not will to have beings who could *only*
be with God as his covenant partners, children, and friends — beings
who have no other choice in the matter! The *with* of this relatedness
has to be continuously affirmed by us, as we saw in connection with
the biblical exposition of the *imago Dei*. The *with* of this relatedness

depends on our being turned, mirror-like, toward God. Otherwise it is an empty concept, a mere formula.

For this *with* implies reciprocity and it contains dimensions of both determination and volition. We are such beings that only in our being-with-God, willingly and affirmatively, do we make good our own potential for being. In other words, the determinational (or "given") element in the tradition is that human being, created for coexistence with the Creator, is less than fully human apart from its being-with-God. But this "given" element is held in tension with the volitional element: We are not compelled, simply by our being as such, to exist in spiritual proximity with the divine Being. In fact, we are free to deny altogether our coexistence with the Creator and to seek to "have" our being apart from our being-with-God. We are quite at liberty to leave "the father's house" and to make our own way in the world. When we do so (as in fact we do!) we become distortions of our essential being, because we have really been made for this relationship, and outside of it we are "restless" (Augustine). Yet we are given every opportunity to pursue an independent course; for God wills to have alongside himself beings who are "with" God freely, and not as if they were "programmed" for it.

Again, the whole drama of the human pilgrimage with God, as it is unfolded in the biblical account, could be told from the perspective of this juxtaposition of determination and volition. The aim of the God who is portrayed in these writings is nothing more or less than to elicit from the human creature an amen to its existence as one whose life is being-with-God. But God will not resort to coercion or manipulation—though God frequently threatens to do so in the biblical story. For it must be an amen willed by the creature itself (as Peter Abelard knew in a way that Anselm of Canterbury did not[4]). Thus God goes to what must seem to many extreme and even absurd ("foolish," says Paul) lengths to demonstrate the depths of God's own being-with the creature in God's effort to secure from the creature a corresponding affirmation of its being-with its Creator. And if we ask what the "people of God" is—what Israel is and what the church is—then we should answer very simply that the people of God is only this: that sphere where human beings begin to make such an affirmation, where they begin—hesitantly, to be sure, but not insignificantly—to say amen to their human creaturehood, that is, their being-with-God.

Karl Barth, in what is surely one of the most poignantly beautiful passages in all the literature of Christian dogmatics, depicts the

Christian life as the beginning of the genuine humanity into which
anthropos, from the outset of its historic pilgrimage and as conceived
within the parameters of this biblical tradition, has been beckoned:

> Of all creatures the Christian is one who not merely is a crea-
> ture, but actually says "Yes" to being a creature. Innumerable crea-
> tures do not seem even to be asked to make this affirmation. Man
> is asked. But man as such is neither able nor willing to make it.
> From the very first man as such has continual illusions about him-
> self. He wants always to be more than a creature. He does not want
> merely to be under the universal Lordship of God. But the Chris-
> tian makes the affirmation that is demanded of man. . . .
>
> The fact that he does confess [his creaturehood] is not a kind
> of triumph for his individual honesty. Other people are just as
> honest, perhaps more so. But he is simply made real by what he
> sees. And as such he is simply availing himself of a permission and
> invitation. He is going through an open door, but one which he
> himself has not opened, into a banqueting hall. And there he will-
> ingly takes his place at the table, in the company of publicans, in the
> company of beasts and plants and stones, accepting solidarity with
> them, being present simply as they are present, as creatures of God.
>
> In practice, of course, he is faced every day afresh with the
> riddles of the world-process, with the precipices and plains, the
> blinding lights and obscurities, of the general creaturely occur-
> rence to which his own life's history also belongs. Of course he can
> only keep on asking: Whence? and Whither? and Why? and Where-
> fore? Of course he has no master-key to all the mysteries of the
> great process of existence as they crowd in upon him every mo-
> ment in a new form, to all the mysteries in the historical process of
> all created reality. On the contrary, he will be the one person who
> knows that there is no value in any of the master-keys which man
> has thought to discover and possess. He is the one who will always
> be the most surprised, the most affected, the most apprehensive
> and the most joyful in the face of events. He will not be like an ant
> which has foreseen everything in advance, but like a child in the
> forest, or on Christmas Eve: one who is always rightly astonished
> by events, by the encounters and experiences which overtake him,
> by the cares and duties laid upon him. He is the one who is con-
> stantly forced to begin afresh, wrestling with the possibilities
> which open out to him and the impossibilities which oppose him.
> If we may put it in this way, life in the world, with all its joys and

sorrows and contemplation and activities will always be for him a really interesting matter, or, to use a bolder expression, it will be an adventure for which he for his part has ultimately and basically no qualifications of his own.[5]

Two facets of this wonderfully poetic description of authentic humanity deserve special notice with regard to our present discussion. The first has to do with its christological presupposition. This, of course, is not surprising given Barth's overall program as a theologian. We draw attention to it, however, because of its connection with a point made much earlier in our discussion, namely, the fact that in the New Testament's theology of the *imago Dei*, Jesus as Christ is depicted as the truly human being who is as such *eikōn Theou*, and Christians are those who through incorporation into the life of Christ are "being conformed" to the image of God that Christ incarnates. It is entirely consistent with this Pauline view of the *imago* when Barth discusses human authenticity by describing the life *en Christo*—the life into which we are beckoned through hearing, through baptism, through the *testimonium internum Spiritus sancti*.

What is even more significant about the passage in this respect is that it illustrates in the most graphic way the eschatological nature of this process of identification and incorporation. It is, as we have put it in the present discussion, a matter of being "beckoned into" a new identity. It is a beginning—every day a new beginning. The creature who says yes to its creaturehood does not in that moment have the satisfaction of receiving the answers to all its questions. In the first place, it is not an achievement on its part that it does say yes; it is simply "made real by what it sees," a door is opened to it that it did not open, and so forth. There is no question of a permanent alteration, no thing is given this creature. For the "adventure" on which it has embarked by grace through faith it has "ultimately and basically no qualifications." In other words, here Barth not only links the anthropological with the christological exposition of the *imago* but also (and therefore!) upholds the relational ontology of the tradition.

The second aspect of the Barth quotation to which special attention should be drawn in the present context is the way in which Barth, in a passage dealing primarily with the relationship between the human creature and the Creator, inevitably touches on the relationship between humankind and otherkind in the process. Entering a banquet he had not anticipated through a door he had not opened, the one who is "being made real" (*vere homo*) sits down at table not only with publicans (i.e., sinners like himself) but also "in the company of beasts and plants and stones, accepting solidarity with them, being present simply as they are present, as creatures of God"—and doing this "gladly"! I say that Barth moves inevitably from the human-divine relationship to the human-nature relationship because, as I have insisted in the foregoing chapter, there can be no profound discussion of human creaturehood that does not make ontic connection with all the other creatures. To discover our own creaturehood is in that moment to discover our solidarity with all the other creatures. Barth has here shown his typical (i.e., intuitive but also highly skilled and professional) grasp of the inseparability of the three-dimensionality of our human relatedness.

The primary methodological observation that must be made about this first focus of our human being-with, that is, our relatedness to God, is of course that it is first. When Christian faith affirms that essential—as opposed to distorted ("existential")—humanity is being-with-God, it is insisting that this particular orientation of our being has an ontic priority. Of the three counterparts of our being, only this one counterpart can be named without qualification as both generative and authoritative. We owe our being to God; only to God, therefore, are we finally accountable for our being and what flows from it. That we are bound up with one another and with all creaturely life; and that the gift of being is continuously given us by means of all the other creatures and elements of creation—this we have affirmed. But only One is the generative source of life, and only to that One are we obliged to answer for our lives (this being, of course, the primary significance of the Last Judgment motif in Scripture).

There are some very important practical consequences of this insistence on the priority of the human relationship with God. Among them is the recognition, which has been indispensable to all prophetic faith, that while we exist in solidarity with other human and nonhuman creatures, each of us is also granted a measure of independence vis-à-vis all the others. We are certainly responsible to and for one another, but we are not ultimately accountable to any besides our Creator and Lord. None of us is owned by others of our kind or by the various processes of nature—nor do we own them. Therefore, we are free to be *for* them what we believe God—to whom we and they are accountable—wills us to be. The dialectic of individuality and communality, as well as that of freedom and responsibility, is dependent on this ontic priority of the human relatedness to God.

Nevertheless, a certain warning has to be issued whenever this kind of observation is made. It is that while this first dimension of our human *Mitsein* is first—that is to say, has an onto-theological priority—this must never be turned into an ethical priority. For instance, this is the warning of Jesus' parable of the Last Judgment in Matthew 25:31ff. Those who are especially conscious of the fact that they have been with the Lord (by their own definition) are sent away into hell because their inordinate "God"-consciousness has blinded them to the hungry, naked, and imprisoned among their own kind. On the other hand, those who have been with the needy ones of the earth, despite their obvious surprise at being regarded as companions of the Lord, are invited to participate in the joys of the divine kingdom. The theological priority that rightly acknowledges that our primary ontic orientation as human beings is toward our Creator must never be transmuted into an ethical priority. Ethically speaking—that is to say, in terms of the daily actualization of our faith in God—being-with-God must always mean being-with-the-neighbor, particularly the needy neighbor, as this and other teachings of Jesus make clear.

Being-with-God can only become an excuse for not being-with-the-earthly (human and nonhuman) counterparts of ourselves if faith is subjected to a "religious" distortion. It is permissible to say that our being-with-God has priority because divine grace (i.e., God's reality and presence) is the *conditio sine qua non* of our creaturely *Mitsein*. Even this must not be claimed, however, in such a way as to suggest certain definitive patterns or formulae for our relatedness to the divine being. There are countless ways in which God's presence is real in human life, some of them recognized, practiced, and articulate, others (possibly most) not so much known and expressed as simply lived. God should not be equated with speech about God, or with explicitly theological, liturgical, or moral patterns of behavior regularly associated with divinity. We court the Gnostic heresy when we make the reality of God synonymous with knowledge (*gnosis*) of God and of God's ways with us. Suffice it to say that our relationship with God, whether acknowledged or simply lived, is the source of our courage to go outside ourselves and to seek the other. It is the source of our wisdom, whatever wisdom we have, in working out our responsibility for and solidarity with other created beings. But it is never a sufficient end in itself. The Bible is critical of nothing so much as of an interest in God that stops there. The fruits by which genuine faith in God is known are very tangible, worldly fruits. Authentic being-with-God does not express itself in a greater interest in the extraterrestrial and the supramundane but in a more intensive engagement of God's beloved world.

III. BEING-WITH-HUMANKIND

The second dimension of human relatedness (which in the biblical tradition must certainly be named second, however "like unto the first" it is) is our orientation toward our own kind. Since my intention is to move fairly quickly through these first two dimensions of human relatedness to the third, which is the primary focus of this study, I shall concentrate here chiefly on aspects of the subject that deal almost as much with the human relationship with nonhuman nature as with other human beings.

From the outset, it is necessary to note an important insight of critical theology in the articulation of this aspect of our relatedness. To be with other human beings means to be alongside them, on an equal footing, as it were — not above but with, not below but with. That is, it is neither a position of superiority nor one of servitude; neither oppressed nor oppressor. This recognition is what informs all expression of liberation theology today. In other words, the source of this insistence is not the Marxist concept of the classless society, as many critics of liberation theology seem to think, but the biblical ontology of communion, upon which, in fact, Marx himself was dependent.

For within this relational ontology of the tradition of Jerusalem is an implicit criticism of hierarchical arrangements of human community, and in spite of the agelong effort of powers within the community of faith to submerge this criticism, it has never been quite possible to do so. Again and again, prophetic ("Abrahamic" — H. Camara) minorities have been formed around the remembrance of this biblical sense of human classlessness *coram Deo*. And this will continue as long as the memory of this tradition lasts, for it is no incidental aspect of the tradition. The *with* in our subheading (being-with-humankind) carries that connotation. It registers an implicit polemic against every form of society in which some people are permitted to assume positions of higher worth in relation to other human beings: men in relation to women, adults in relation to children, the healthy and whole in relation to the handicapped, the more intelligent in relation to the less, the property-holding few in relation to the many without "substance," those of one skin pigmentation in relation to those of another, and so forth. Under the conditions of historical existence, this tradition realizes well that there will always be a tendency for persons and groups to climb to prominence on the backs of others, and conversely, from the perspective of the sin of sloth, a propensity for some to offer their backs to the climbers. But while maintaining a consistent realism about this, prophetic faith cannot regard such a struggle for preeminence and station as in accordance with the will of God. Theological liberalism, and especially the Social Gospel, was quite faithful to this prophetic tradition when it insisted that the immediate implication of human being-with-God ("the fatherhood of God") is solidarity with other human beings ("the brotherhood of Man"). God's parenthood, so to speak, radically conditions the relationship between human creatures — siblings! Given the priority of our being-with-God (God's sovereignty, in traditional Reformed dogma), no human creature can be legitimately regarded as subordinate or superior to another. "Call no man your father on earth, for you have one Father, who is in heaven. Neither be called masters, for you have one master, the Christ" (Mt. 23:9–10, par.).

At the same time, given the fact that God's own sovereignty is expressed supremely in suffering servanthood (see the New Testament exposition of the *imago*), the imaging of God in our relations with one another must mean that every human being is called to take upon him/herself the service of the other. No one is a servant, but everyone should serve. Thus Jesus' statement in Matthew cited above is followed immediately — and logically — by the command: "He who is greatest among you shall be your servant . . . " (23:11).

This service may be the direct and obvious kind of *leitourgia* (liturgy = public service) such as that undertaken by the Samaritan of our Lord's parable. But it may also be the kind of service rendered by those who bear authority, as with the centurian who came to Jesus begging him to heal his mortally ill daughter (Mt. 8:9ff.). For the biblical conception of the equality of human beings under God does not preclude the necessity of order, office, or authority (*exousia*). Authority is requisite to the well-being of the human community.[6] The New Testament does not hesitate, therefore, to speak about obedience to legitimate authorities — parents, husbands and wives, governing authorities, ecclesiastical authorities. What has not always been understood, however (only think of the fearful history of the exegesis of Romans 13!), is that Scripture contains an implicit and explicit distinction between legitimate and illegitimate authority. Considering, for example, the sagas of the kings of ancient Israel, with the prophetic witness against most of them, one cannot turn to Paul's admonition in Romans 13, "Be subject to the governing authorities . . . ," as though that prophetic witness against authority did not exist. The only authentic authority in this tradition is authority that serves. Only stewardly authority is consistent with the primary informing concept of this faith, that is, love. God's own authority is nothing more or less than God's love articulating itself in the imperative mood. In our earthly offices of authority, therefore, we image God only when our authority reflects God's, that is, only in our love for those in relation to whom we bear authority. Self-love and personal aggrandizement, so frequently the marks of earthly authority, have no place in this ontology of communion:

> And he said to them, "The kings of the Gentiles exercise lordship over them; and those in authority over them are called benefactors. But not so with you; rather, let the greatest among you become as the youngest, and the leader as one who serves. For which is greater, one who sits at table, or one who serves? Is it not the one who sits at table? But I am among you as one who serves."
> (Lk. 22:25–27)

A second and more complex connotation of the fact that our being is "with" those of our own species is its positing of a dialectical tension between participation and transcendence. "The self," wrote Reinhold Niebuhr, "is engaged in a perpetual dialogue with other selves in which its dependence upon others becomes apparent but which also proves its independence over all relationships."[7] As our little preposition faithfully signifies, to be "with" another human being means, on the one hand, to participate intimately in the life of the other; on the other hand, it implies a certain distance. Human beings are drawn to one another, for the human self "can not be truly fulfilled if it is not drawn out of itself into the life of the other."[8] Drawing again on Heidegger:

> The key factor of Heidegger's analysis of man with regard to religion is his constant emphasis on the openness of man beyond himself. Man is not sufficient unto himself and wholly in-

dependent of any transcendent reality, but is first of all Being-in-the-world, and thereby a Being-with-others. Although the rigorous description of human existence which is given in *Sein und Zeit* concentrates on the individual rather than the communitarian aspects of man, Heidegger's understanding of language as determinative of human nature and his constant references to mankind (*Mensch*) and the mortals (*die Sterblichen*) prove that he considers the individual man to be essentially related to other men as well as to the world in general.[9]

While the self is "essentially related to" others, "drawn out of itself into the life of the other," it remains distinct. The human-to-human relation, even at its most intimate, contains the paradox of participation and transcendence: persons "recognize in each other the mystery of similarity and uniqueness."[10] The other, who is like, remains irreducibly other. I can in a genuine way be with this other only as I permit him the right to his otherness. The other transcends me and rightly evades my attempts to make her "mine":

> The self recognizes the other as the limit of its expansiveness. It is the "other"; and the otherness includes a final mystery which even the most imaginative love cannot penetrate. It is an independent and unique life which, ultimately considered, can not be fitted into any, even common, purpose or project. There must therefore be an element of reservation and reverence for the other in even the most mutual relations.[11]

Or, as Eberhard Jüngel puts it,

> . . . in love one I and another I encounter each other in such a way that they become for each other beloved Thous. I must always become a Thou to the other person if I am not to be had by the other I in such a way that I become an It. In love there is no having which does not arise out of surrender.[12]

In other words, the Hebraic and Christian ontology of communion maintains a significant dialogical tension between involvement and detachment in human relations — aspects of which, as we shall see presently, must also be applied to the relationship between humankind and otherkind. To speak quite concretely, if John and Mary and Peter were living in accordance with God's intention, they would certainly be living in close communion with one another; but they would not be merged together in such a way that they could no longer individually speak of "I" but only of "we."[13] Their individual identities as John, Mary, and Peter would be maintained; indeed, as we should deduce from everything the New Testament claims about the Christian *koinonia*,[14] the communion (as distinct from undialectical "union") that seems to be God's intention for human beings in community would imply that the individual identities of persons are enhanced by their communality if it is rightly ordered. The element of participation not only does not threaten to overcome individuality, it positively encourages the process of self-realization. From this perspective, communities that are ordered by the sacrifice of the self to the collectivity (as in Zamiatin's *We* and indeed most of the other great antiutopian novels of our era[15]) are destructive communities. A constructive community is one that elicits from each of its members their fullest potential as individuals, for without personal self-realization the community itself is immeasurably impoverished.

This dialectic of participation and transcendence is of intense significance for our understanding of the nature of the church, and it is in fact implied in all the major metaphors and analogies of the church in the gospels and epistles—vine and branches, bride and bridegroom, and especially the one body with its many members. But if we remember that the church in this literature is not merely a special ("sacred") community within the larger human society but an eschatological paradigm for human community at large—the sphere where Christ's true imaging of God is becoming a gracious possibility for many—then we can see that the dialectic we are discussing can be applied to every form of human community.

To marriage, for example.[16] Despite gross misunderstanding of Mark 10:8 and parallels, biblical teaching resists every suggestion that the marriage "union" annuls the individuality of the two persons involved. Jesus' statement that "the two shall become one" is, indeed, a strong endorsement of the participation principle; and when it is lifted out of the total context of the biblical ontology of human relatedness, and is at the same time influenced by "romantic" conceptions of this particular human relation that tend sentimentally to vitiate the transcendence principle, it can produce a very questionable ethic of connubiality. Feminist theology is justified in protesting against this tendency in historical theology; for not only has this text been used to overaccentuate the participation principle, but—since in the resulting merger of being the male partner could be thought the dominant one—it has been tantamount to claiming that marriage, in fact, effects the incorporation of the woman into the man. Combined with such scriptural notions as the creation of the woman from the body of Adam,[17] and the Pauline sentiment that the woman is the man's *imago* as the man is God's, this particular gospel pronouncement concerning the "one flesh" has all too consistently confirmed sexist moral codes that have assumed the husband's virtual ownership of the wife and thus imposed on women forms of conjugal morality far more stringent and inflexible than those binding men in the marriage covenant.

A thoroughly relational understanding of human being rules out such a conception of marriage; for this ontology assumes the kind of mutuality in the encounter between human beings that can never be reduced to the language of possession: neither partner can be "owned." Each remains thou in respect to the other. The truth is, the whole notion of marriage as a union is misleading and dangerous from the perspective of this ontological tradition. It would be more accurate to speak of the communion of marriage, as has been done in the better conventions of Catholic sacramentalism. Marriage is certainly an intensive and intimate form of human co- and pro-existence; but it is not one from which the principle of transcendence can be eliminated. Regarding marriage as a merger of being not only replaces the "with" of this ontological tradition with an "in" that is drawn from extrabiblical sources such as the mystery cults of the ancient world; what is more important is that it displaces the basic conception of being that stands behind this whole tradition, a conception for which the language we have been using in this discussion ("being-with") is nothing more than a rather ungainly, though perhaps useful, linguistic device.

As I have maintained earlier, this device—or something comparable—is necessary because of the cultural reduction of the language that does belong to the biblical tradition, namely, the language of love. If theology could assume that the language of love would be received in the biblical sense, it would not have to resort to such clumsy linguistic figures of speech. But precisely love—above all that language—is so consistently corrupted in our culture, both in its secular and religious manifestations, that theology must prepare very carefully for its deployment. This is especially true where intimate human relationships are concerned, particularly the male-female relationship. For in these relationships, sexual stereotyping on the one hand and romantic sentimentalism on the other have especially bedeviled the meaning of love as it comes to us out of the tradition of Jerusalem. Love (*ḥesed, agape*) in that tradition, being defined first of all by the described behavior of Yahweh/God vis-à-vis "the chosen," does steadfastly resist both temptations intrinsic to intimate human relations, the temptation to dominate and the temptation to dissolve the self. Against the temptation to dominate, biblical love maintains a strong sense of mutuality, solidarity, participation in the life of the other; against the temptation to lose the self through absorption in the other, this love insists on the inviolability, mystery, transcendence of the other. Love in this sense is the relational category par excellence. Obviously, it is meaningless to speak of love apart from proximity, mutuality, participation; but it is equally obvious — however obscured by practice — that there can be no talk of relationship unless the principle of transcendence is sustained. Love presupposes that the other is truly other, is not simply an extension of my being, and thus never "mine." Love seeks neither to use the other nor to be engulfed in the other. It upholds and evokes the singularity, uniqueness, and ineffability of the other. In love the other becomes truly "Thou," enabling me to become "I."

This same dialectic of participation and transcendence should be applied, *mutatis mutandis*, to every other kind of human relationship. Today, for instance, a grave question confronting the whole human race is how to sustain the two desirable goals of, on the one hand, realizing a more peaceful and just global form of civilization and, on the other, preserving national and regional cultures, languages, and customs that are precious to their bearers. Clearly, a planetary society that faces extinction if it cannot discover ways through the impasse of national conflicts must call into question the ancient assumption and practice of the absolute sovereignty of individual states.[18] But how can a global civilization be achieved without reducing the quality of human life? Is it to be achieved through the application of a "melting-pot" theory, in which the uniqueness of each state or tribe is sacrificed to the greater unity of them all? Such counsel can readily be offered by superstates, because they can assume that their own dominance is highly probable in the resulting mix of cultures.[19] But a technological mass culture in which all the color and variety of divergent traditions has been replaced by the plastic monotony of a universal consumer society hardly appeals to the imagination and intelligence of the race. Clearly, in the necessary move toward global civilization the peoples of the earth are obliged to improvise forms of mutuality that combine the principles of participation and transcendence.[20]

In sum, the ontology of the tradition of Jerusalem suggests very distinct ethical guidelines for human relatedness at every level. It insists on equality of worth while recognizing diversity of gifts and offices. It denies every form of servitude while commanding each freely to serve the other. It provides the ontic basis for reciprocity of being between persons by holding in tension communal solidarity with respect for individuality.

The skeptic in each of us is quick to point out that such a delicate equilibrium between conflicting traits of the human spirit betrays a grand idealism. Who but a dreamer could expect to find on this earth actual human communities, great or small, where such wondrous balances were actually sustained? Does not the obvious and often glaring diversity (or inequality!) of gifts bequeathed to persons, and the differing vocations that they make possible, inevitably lead to hierarchies of human worth? Is not habitual service of the other always on the verge of servitude? And who could maintain the celestial poise of involvement-with-detachment implied in such a majestic imperative as "Love thy neighbor as thyself"?

Two responses should be given to this perennial skepticism of a disillusioned humanity. First, biblical faith is well aware of the enormity of the antithetical state over against which it sets this ontology and ethic of relatedness, that is, the state of an enduring egoism and isolationism, and of the subtle fear of rejection that masquerades as self-sufficiency (being-alone); the state of personal and social enmity, estrangement, mutual suspicion, and the spirit of revenge (being-against). In short, biblical faith understands sin at least as well as the existentialists do. It does not hesitate even to point up the continuation of such behavior among those who have been graced with the visitation of that insistent Spirit who breaks down "the dividing walls of hostility" and would create *koinonia* where there is "neither Jew nor Greek, bond nor free, male nor female." There would certainly have been no need for Paul to write three-quarters of what he did write to those young congregations of the Mediterranean world had he assumed that their new status as persons *en Christo* and so "with" one another was entirely discontinuous with the "old being" of sin and death. With him—and with all those ever since who have retained this kind of biblical realism—there is little danger of starry-eyed utopianism. Their message assumes that the new *Mitsein* given through Christ is given as possibility, process, and vision; that is, it is a new reality breaking in on the old. They are fully aware of the "not yet" of the eschatological conception of human community that their gospel implies.

However, they are also conscious of an "already"; for they believe that a grace is at work that, despite human recalcitrance, enables approximations of the new being-with to be realized. We may begin to image God in our human relationships, and not just continue to reflect the old patterns we have been conditioned by. Therefore, the tradition of Jerusalem resists cynicism more steadfastly than it resists idealism. And this implies the second response that theology must make to enduring doubt, including the doubt of the faithful: that the point of departure for faith's vision of human community is not an ideal that must be striven for or a social program dependent on human enthusiasm, work, loyalty, and determination. In short, it is not a matter first of law but of gospel, that is, of possibility and permission. We may be "with" one another in a new way; we may image God's *Mitsein* in our relationships with one another, because God is newly and effectively with and for us in Christ. Having been befriended by the Other who is the transcendent counterpart of our existence, our characteristic resistance to the others (our human counterparts) is being broken down.

Our pathetic quest for autonomy has been and is being challenged by a "theonomous" love that allows us to be ourselves while enabling us to discover something within ourselves that longs for real proximity to others. Our fear of serving, lest we become servants, has been and is being conquered by a Spirit who leads us into the truth that the greatest humanity is a humanity that serves. Our covetousness of the gifts of others has been and is being replaced by gratitude for the diversity of gifts among humankind and for the richness of community that this diversity makes possible. It is beginning to be possible for us to accept authority without resentment, to bear it without vanity. The worldly patterns of relationships between persons, with their subtle sanctioning of hierarchical structures and fixed typologies, are under strict judgment in our midst. And though their forms are not easily vanquished, the substance has gone out of them: men can begin, in this community of faith, to recognize the full humanity of women; the dominant races can begin to treat members of subjected peoples as equals; the economically secure can begin to acknowledge the claim on them of the poor and wretched of earth; adults can begin to appreciate children and youth, and vice versa.

And this new prospect of human mutuality, made possible and made mandatory every day, can begin to express itself in radical new forms of community. In such community, justice, mercy, truth, and peace — as well as contrition for their absence — begin to be possible, and not just as ideals but as reflections of the justice, mercy, truth, and peace we have received and continue to receive daily from the God who is "with us." While we undoubtedly continue to exhibit the old alienation that pertains between fallen creatures, there is also now a new reality that breaks through our relationships with one another. The Spirit of reconciliation invades our lives with the apparent intention of fully replacing habitual patterns of mistrust and bourgeois restraint. So behind the worn and predictable visages with which we daily confront one another there is now a new image of the self: like an impulsive child, it insists on presenting itself. A new face, luminous with a vivacity not our own (yet somehow also ours) is being fashioned for us as we are turned toward the God whose image is manifested in the Christ:

> And we all, with unveiled face, beholding the glory of the Lord, are being changed into his likeness from one degree of glory to another; for this comes from the Lord who is the Spirit.
>
> (II Cor. 3:18)

We are again speaking, of course, of the church. The church is the sphere where the quest for new images is occurring in an open way. Not that it is the only such sphere, for God's Spirit is not bound by the churches; and not that it is anything more than a place of quest and beginnings. Yet in this community of suffering and prayer we experience, in a way that is at once more intense and more candid, the yearning of those who know that new possibilities have been given, and that different patterns of human relatedness are at least available. It would be a falsification of the reality of the churches to claim for them more than this — for instance, to insist that the new with-being that is offered is already realized within the Christian *koinonia*. The aura of unreality that does cling to much middle-class Christianity today stems precisely from this exaggeration, this bourgeois appropriation of realized eschatology. We are speaking of beginnings only.

Yet we may and should speak of beginnings. For whatever the

actual state of the empirical church, we know that in that sphere human beings are beckoned into new relationships with one another, and that this beckoning is more than a command; it is gospel. We can begin there, and thus also in the larger community beyond this sphere of explicit faith, to turn toward one another. The face of forgiveness, acceptance, and love that has been shown us in the compassionate countenance of the God of Golgotha can be reflected in the faces that we show to one another. We can also begin there—and thus beyond the bounds of this fellowship as well—to live out of a trust that overcomes the ancient addiction to suspicion that infects our race. We can begin there—and thus also in the larger community of humankind—to seek and find intimations of the communality that is our de facto status as creatures, though we resist it strenuously and take refuge in the illusion of self-sufficiency. We can begin there—and thus find the necessary support for the same praxis within the life of the world—to defy the barriers to peace and justice that arise when human beings are conditioned to regard other human beings as "the enemy," or to think them less than fully human.

In short, within the community of the Cross we can begin to *image God* in our relationships with others of our kind. It is undoubtedly unimpressive, this beginning, with respect to what might be and finally must be. It is only a beginning, and each day a new beginning. Yet compared with the being-alone and being-against that is the actual, visible, and increasingly menacing condition of our civilization, the *Mitsein* of the ecumenical Christian church may be appreciated today as a reality for which most Christians are insufficiently grateful. It may well be that the church of the near future, no doubt numerically reduced but also less beholden to worldly powers and superpowers, will prove the one inter- and transnational movement capable of upholding and communicating a vision of world community that is not just another cloaked ideology of empire.[21]

CHAPTER SIX

Being-With-Nature

I. "MAN AGAINST NATURE"—
AGAINST HUMANITY!

The editor of a book of short stories entitled *Man Against Nature*[1] introduces his collection by relating his experience in a submarine:

> The crew about me were men against nature, wresting from the ocean a privilege she accorded only to fish and the sounding whale. It was made possible by machines, of course; and sometimes as I moved about the sub and saw the incredible array of dials and knobs and felt the great power of the boat I wondered if it weren't also a matter of men against machine. It seemed fabulous that mere men could be trained to subdue such a complex monster. Then I thought of Hillary and Tenzing reaching the top of Mt. Everest in their oxygen masks and their clothes which a highly industrialized nation had made possible; and I thought of the men at White Sands, New Mexico, experimenting with rockets, and those in the same state releasing atomic power; and I realized afresh how much of the conquest of nature is preceded by the conquest of the machine, and how sometimes it seems that the machine is threatening to become the master.

This was written thirty years ago, and the submarine was not a Trident.

"There are, in the large," writes Joseph Sittler, "two ways by which man has sought to do justice to the realm of meaning in the natural world; two forms of relationship by which he has sought to come to terms with what he cannot silence. First, nature can be subsumed under man. . . . [Second] Man is subsumed under nature. . . . "

But neither, concludes Sittler, is appropriate:

> Neither of these ways is adequate, and man knows it. For neither one does justice either to the amplitude and glory of man's spirit or to the felt meaningfulness of the world of nature. Christian theology, obedient to the biblical account of nature, has asserted a third possibility: that man ought properly stand alongside nature as her cherishing brother, for she too is God's creation and bears God's image.[2]

While it may be true that in some profound sense "man knows" this, however, there is unfortunately too little evidence of that knowledge in the annals of human behavior. It is clear even to the casual student of Western history that the attitude toward the natural world that has prevailed in our civilization is not one that could be described accurately with the word "alongside" (Heidegger's *Sein bei*), or in the phrase that heads this chapter. It would be coming closer to reality if we were to use the preposition "above" instead of the preposition "with" in that phrase: nature subsumed under man. We have already encountered ample evidence of that designation in our survey of the historic fate of the *imago Dei* symbol, where time and again the singularity of *Homo sapiens* has been secured at the expense of all other creatures above which this "rational animal" is alleged to exist and reign.

But would not true objectivity concerning Western attitudes toward nature require that we employ still stronger language? While the human transcendence of nature is certainly a consistent motif in the evolution of Western humanity's self-image, there has been, besides, a dimension in our relationship with the natural order that is more aggressive than the preposition "above" normally suggests. It would not be possible to grasp the ethos of the postindustrial West without some sense of the real enmity shown toward the natural world by its most dominant societies. Until the very recent consciousness of nature's fragility and the limits of its resilience (a consciousness that has somewhat mitigated the bravado of our rhetoric, though not of our deeds), the most common expression of our public attitude toward the natural world was our declared determination to "conquer nature." Thus it is not mere ecological emotionalism when a current appeal of Greenpeace in connection with its effort to save the whales begins, "Let us not delude ourselves. What the human race has done to the great whales is WAR!"[3]

Some will point out that the language of the "conquest of nature" is metaphor, and there is truth in that claim. Giving to the recent past the most charitable interpretation, we may say that from the Enlightenment onward the objective of the collective human spirit at its most "advanced" has been not to destroy but to domesticate nature, thus bringing it more fully into the service of the human community. Yet language is more telling than is sometimes intended. Why this particular metaphor? Why, indeed, has the entire project of the modern West so often found encapsulation in the motto "man against nature"? It is an expression that, in its pre-1960 setting, could be used and heard in a highly positive manner, as a laudable project necessary to the progress of civilization.

It is true that the human impulses being enacted under the aegis of such rhetoric are not easy to comprehend. But if one studies eighteenth-century gardens with their symmetrical patterns, their cubical and spherical and most untreelike trees, their controlled horticulture; or if one follows this same inclination as it expresses itself today in the tailored lawns of suburbia, sometimes actually made of plastic—one senses beneath the surface of a domesticated and often patently contrived beauty a darker motif that may not be different in kind from what is present in our grand projects of the industrial-technical exploitation of natural resources. I mean the determination to *control*. Not the somehow noble attempt to compete against the elements so poignantly depicted in imaginative literature, such as Hemingway's *The Old Man and the Sea*,[4] an attempt whose nobility is inseparable from its pathos. The determination of modern technicized rationalism to bring nature to heel does not arise out of sheer human need, nor is it fully explicated by the desire to tap nature's potential or to enjoy its beauty. In fact, if the Western spirit had been motivated by either truly pragmatic or truly aesthetic concerns in its dealings with nonhuman nature, it would hardly have been as extravagant in its subjugation of the natural order or as wasteful in its conquest of nature's limited resources. One cannot contemplate the chemical pollution of the Great Lakes,[5] the devastated state of Canadian forests, or the unnatural concrete ugliness of our North American cities without developing a deep suspicion that some propensity has been at work among us that far exceeds our aesthetic or even our material necessities.

This propensity is sometimes excused as a mentality that evolved out of the pioneer's obvious need to "clear away" a rampant and overabundant nature in order to make room for human habitation. One is permitted to doubt, however, that that is a sufficient explanation for the phenomena—some four or five centuries after the beginnings of European settlement on this continent—of "dead" lakes,[6] the permanent extinction of animal and plant species, cities and highway communities bereft of natural beauty, and the industrial spoilation of marshlands, maple forests, waterways, and so forth. One suspects that full justice could be done to the explanation of such phenomena only through recourse to concepts normally reserved for distorted human relations—such as alienation, estrangement, revenge, and "war."

For underneath the modern decision to master nature is a long history of human anxiety in the face of nature's otherness, its seeming indifference to human pursuits, its resistance to human ambition. This history cannot be traced with accuracy, for it almost certainly predates recorded history, and its genesis is not to be located in external events but in internal, psychic states that can only be described through symbols, myths, and stories. It is the heath in Shakespeare's *King Lear* and *Macbeth*—"both a real place and a place in the mind."[7] It is the primeval dark and the cold. The mythology of Genesis 3, which links the alienation of humanity from nature with the alienation of human from human and the abrogation of the creation bond between humanity and God, is certainly an attempt to express this state.[8] So is Genesis 11, where the race of Adam takes to the building of cities to escape the naked encounter with the earth.

Perhaps, after all, it is not possible to improve on the word "sin" in this connection. Certainly, it is not sufficient to draw attention to the historical events and movements that have given form and direction to our hostility toward nature: the Manichaean sense of nature's innate evil; the Neoplatonic feeling for the inferior yet nefarious and cloying power of matter; the "Christian" spiritualization of reality, with its identification of the essential with mind and will and its denigration of the body. Behind all such historical phenomena is a mystery of aboriginal fear and estrangement that has something to do with the sundering of basic human relatedness at every level of our being, not only our being-with-nature.

One thing is evident: the mastering of nature that has driven and still drives the spiritual engine of Western civilization is not to be accounted for solely on the basis of a positive, perhaps promethean desire to measure, predict, and use nature's bounties, as is frequently alleged. There is an unavoidable negative, not to say nihilistic, element in this relationship. We think ourselves above nature, to be sure, but our behavior betrays more than the pride of superior intellect and the will to power; it betrays an enmity that defies rational explanation. Perhaps despite our avowed transcendence of the natural order, we know ourselves to be part of it, to be at the mercy of the same processes that carry off strong beasts and bring decay to giant trees; and therefore we struggle the more desperately to rise above it.

> For the fate of the sons of men and the fate of beasts is the same; as one dies, so dies the other. They all have the same breath, and man has no advantage over the beasts; for all is vanity. All go to one place; all are from the dust, and all turn to dust again.
>
> (Eccles. 3:19–20)

But as the words of Koheleth make transparent, enmity toward nature must in that case be traced to self-loathing. "Man against nature" translates into "man against humanity."

II. THE NEW SOLIDARITY OF THE VULNERABLE

The inseparability of our attitude toward the natural world and our attitude toward ourselves as a species has become newly conspicuous in our time. Former generations could imagine themselves masters of nature while remaining oblivious to the implications of such an *imago hominis* for the human species itself. Now, however, it cannot be avoided: there can be no mastery of nature that does not finally disclose itself as the necessity of mastering human nature. The increasingly controlled forms of human society that have come to be in the twentieth century are extensions of the bid for control over nature already expressed in the seventeenth century by Descartes, Hobbes, and many others. If one starts out to dominate the natural world, one cannot stop short at that reputedly "rational animal" who, however rational, is also animal — and by all accounts creation's most problematical animal. "Man against nature" becomes "man against humanity" in this sense too, that it contains the obvious directive that what is "natural" within the human species must be brought under control.

To be sure, that lesson was already taken very seriously by our eighteenth- and nineteenth-century forebears who, in their educational systems and moral codes, strove to eliminate or at least manage the "unruly" passions of children and adults alike. What they did not admit, however—what has become more conspicuous in our time—is that what is "natural" to our species and must be brought under control is not limited to the human lusts and passions but includes the very traits our forebears had identified as "higher." The logic of mastery, as artists and novelists have grasped more imaginatively than either scientists or social scientists have, goes far beyond the control of the emotions to embrace every product of human ingenuity that may introduce elements of unpredictability or radical nonconformity into the social fabric. And in a society threatened on every side by passionate minorities (dramatized by hostage-taking and hijacking), the social will to apply this logic becomes increasingly irresistible. Hence when B. F. Skinner and the behaviorists propose that the human race can no longer afford "freedom and dignity," they are not speaking out of some merely idiosyncratic psychological whim; they are giving voice to the same sentiment expressed by ordinary citizens who call for the reinstatement of the death penalty and the return of a more authoritarian form of public education. It is just that the behaviorists are more humane than most of the citizens in question, because they want to achieve control through conditioning rather than through punishment and threat.

But the process of mastering human nature does not stop with the elimination of spontaneity and nonconformity. With human as with nonhuman nature, the endeavor to control contains a radically destructive component. This component, which could be sensed already in the nineteenth century by such astute observers as William Blake, expresses itself powerfully in the technology of nuclearism. Nothing in the world of technique, says Jacques Ellul, is so impressive as the machinery of war;[9] and on no aspect of our corporate existence do we spend so much money, talent, and emotional energy. Thus, by a strange but perhaps all too logical twist of destiny, it has come to pass that the very "endowments" that we imagined set our species apart from all the others—reason, will, technique—have contrived to bring us into an inescapable solidarity with all the others. No more than they—and perhaps less than they—can we escape the wrath that may come of our own ingenuity. In Neville Shute's *On the Beach*, that first literary shocker of what has become a genre, the human beings awaiting death from nuclear fallout curse the rabbits who may well outlast them.[10] "I said in my heart, with regard to the sons of men, that God is testing them to show them that they are but beasts" (Eccles. 3:17).

This newly recognized solidarity with all living things — dying things! — has had the effect, where it has penetrated the human imagination, of defying the whole hierarchical view of creation that has dominated our civilization. More than Darwin, nuclearism and its attendant crises have forced us to rethink attitudes toward the natural world and our place in it. Clarence Glacken writes:

> When, in the fifth century, St. Augustine wrote in the *City of God* of man's place in nature, he referred to man's position in the divine hierarchy, created by God, in which those having life are ranked above those which do not have it; those who have the power of generation or desire for it are above those lacking it. Among living things, those that are sentient are above those that are not, as animals are above trees. And among the sentient, the intelligent are above those lacking it, and among the intelligent immortal angels are above mortal man. When T. H. Huxley, in the nineteenth century, wrote of man and nature, he was concerned with man's place in an evolutionary scale, with man as a product of evolution from simpler forms of life. When we use the phrase, man's place in nature, we mean neither of these, for we are living neither in the age of St. Augustine nor of T. H. Huxley. Today it means the place of human cultures in the natural world; it has to do with attitudes towards all of life and its environment, attitudes which are germinating in new seed beds in which the value of life and of nature must be seen against the now almost limitless obliterative capacities of man, at least on this earth. It is this last consideration that is forcing us into new formulations and that most decisively sets us apart from the past.[11]

III. POSSIBILITIES AND LIMITATIONS: THE BIBLICAL BACKGROUND

Since we have acknowledged Christian culpability in the unfolding drama of "man against nature" from the outset of this study, there is nothing to be gained at this juncture from a reiteration of that confession. What we are obliged to ask ourselves as Christians today is not only whether we have sinned in this as in other matters, but whether among our sins of omission there are aspects of our own better traditions through whose neglect or rejection we have overlooked correctives and alternatives to the questionable counsels we have offered. In the light of the new solidarity with the rest of nature into which technique has led a bewildered promethean humanity, can we recover some of these buried treasures of the tradition of Jerusalem that may help our kind acquire a more appropriate conception of its place in the natural order?

It has been the presupposition of this whole work that we both may and must answer that question in the affirmative. Not to attempt to do so is tacitly to admit the defeat of the tradition. But on what basis shall we make the attempt? My answer has been: through a rethinking of the rudimentary understanding of being that informs the tradition of Jerusalem but was too soon absorbed into more powerful ontologies and became, for the most part, ineffectual. Through the recovery of this "more primordial interpretation" of being (Heidegger),[12] namely, being understood relationally, we may derive not only a better understanding of the human relationship with God and neighbor but also of the human relationship with nonhuman nature.

In proposing this route, I do not wish to overlook or to underestimate the direct evidence of Scripture concerning the tradition's theology of nature and the human relationship with nature. There has been a good deal of imaginative probing of Scripture — particularly of the Old Testament — by scholars of the Bible who have been sensitized to the same concerns that have been the motivation for this book.[13]

As an instance of this scholarship — and one that closely parallels some of the major concerns of this book — we may consider a work by Bruce C. Birch. In *The Predicament of the Prosperous*, cowritten with ethicist Larry L. Rassmussen,[14] Professor Birch has drawn attention to much of the biblical material suggestive of an approach to this subject that is implicitly or explicitly critical of the "Christian" world's past approach. He notes, for one thing, that in the much-neglected Wisdom Literature it is nature rather than history that most characteristically provides the paradigm for divine truth. Citing Proverbs 3:19–20 ("The Lord by wisdom founded the earth; by understanding he established the heavens; by his knowledge the deeps broke forth, and the clouds drop down the dew"), Birch comments:

God as deliverer is not mentioned in the wisdom texts, nor is there any mention of any of the great saving events of Israel's history such as the Exodus. Creation and not history is the arena where God's presence is sought. Creation provides for the orderly parameters within which human existence is lived. Creation is affirmed as benevolent, embodying the possibilities of goodness. To be wise, then, is to recognize and actualize the potential for full life already inherent in the created order. To know God is to discern the harmonious order for which we were created: *persons to God; persons to each other; and persons to the rest of nature.*[15]

But it is not only in the Wisdom Literature—including Jesus' appropriation of it[16]—that we may discover direct biblical evidence of an alternative view of the relationship between God, humanity, and nature. The creational myths are also fruitful here. The saga of Genesis 1:1–2:4a contains a number of motifs pertinent to this question. One is its theocentrism: "God is the only actor in this story. . . . One can hardly take Genesis 1 seriously and continue to act as though humanity is self-sufficient." A second is the writer's insistence on the essential goodness of creation: "*All* creation participates in the goodness that God as creator intended for the world." The third motif, Birch notes, is "the important commission to stewardship given to humanity in this account":

> Humanity is created in the image of God, both male and female (Gen. 1:27). Here we wish only to note that the image of God stressed in this account is that of God the sovereign. In the ancient Near East kings would often erect their own image in far-off reaches of their empire to represent their sovereignty. Hence, we might suggest that whatever else is implied by creation in the image of God, it at least suggests that humanity is to represent God's own concern to maintain the goodness of all creation. The commission that follows is to a kind of trusteeship, not a granting to humanity of inherent power to use as humans themselves see fit. "Be fruitful and multiply, and fill the earth and subdue it; and have dominion over the fish of the sea and over the birds of the air and over every living thing that moves upon the earth" (v. 28). Except for Genesis 1 this theme of human dominion is found in the Old Testament only in Psalm 8. In both instances exercise of dominion is accountable to God; it is not license for human indulgence.[17]

Both of the creation sagas, Professor Birch affirms, "are rich with tradition important to our faith" today, even if both also have their attendant "dangers"; but "they do not exhaust the subject of creation theology," as too many present-day thinkers seem to assume. Proverbs 16:4 and Psalm 24:1 ("The earth is the Lord's and the fulness thereof . . . ") assume that "nature is itself God's creation and has intrinsic worth before God apart from relationship to the human."[18] Psalm 19:1 ("The heavens are telling the glory of God; and the firmament proclaims his handiwork") and many similar passages from the Psalms and prophets "are filled with such creation hymns witnessing to the evidence of God's glory not in history but in the natural order." In Job 38–41, the astonishing variety of the creation is celebrated by a God who addresses presumptuous *anthropos*; and "Jesus' stilling of the sea (Mk. 4:39) has been seen by some as nature's witness to and acknowledgment of Jesus' messiahship even before the disciples have fully recognized who he was."

Numerous other Scripture references pertinent to our subject indicate this tradition's sense of God's own *Naturgefühl*, and his cautioning of human beings who may not reflect this same sensitivity. Thus one of the reasons for keeping the Sabbath is so that "your ox and your ass may have rest" (Ex. 23:12); again, the Sabbath year and jubilee require that the land should be left fallow (Lev. 25:5); and again—apropos our earlier references to the human "conquest" of nature—wars against other human communities must never devolve into war against nature itself: "When you besiege a city for a long time, making war against it in order to take it, you shall not destroy the trees by wielding an axe against them; for you may eat of them, but you shall not cut them down. Are the trees in the field men that they should be besieged by you?" (Deut. 20:19).

From yet another perspective (one to which we have already alluded, and shall develop further presently), Professor Birch notes that many times over the Bible depicts the human condition in terms of participation in nature. While Psalm 8 tempts the hierarchically minded to elevate the human above the natural with its "thou hast made him a little lower than God," Psalm 144 answers the question "what is man?" with the sobering reminder that "man is like a breath, his days are like a passing shadow." Psalm 49:12 presses the point still farther: "Man cannot abide in his pomp, he is like the beasts that perish." Birch believes that "the best of many passages that show humanity within nature is Psalm 104":[19]

> God is praised as creator and all sorts of things in creation are
> enumerated as witnesses to God's glory as creator: the heavens,

the seas, the valleys, the mountains, wild asses, cattle, trees, birds, goats, badger, moon, sun, and lions. Then in v. 23 almost casually it states, "Man goes forth to his work and to his labor until the evening." Verses 27–30 then conclude of all God's creatures: These all look to thee, to give them their food in due season. . . . [20]

All such biblical material—and it is not minor—demonstrates the tradition's recognition of human "shared finitude with all God's creation," reminds us of our "rootedness in creation," and—especially, of course, with Genesis 3—depicts our distortion of our own selves in terms of precisely that attempt to rise above the creaturely status.[21]

Concomitantly, redemption in the continuity of the two Testaments involves the restoration of the human to its rightful place within nature; more than that, it assumes the redemption (shalom) of the whole creation:

> Is the redemptive activity of God and the redemptive work of Christ directed and limited to the human? Many would say so, but it hardly seems possible biblically. Unless we see human life lived in a vacuum, redemption must involve the rest of nature as well because redemption is precisely God's effort to restore the whole network of relationships that have been broken by sin. This is why new creation is such a helpful image of God's redemptive work. . . .

Birch and Rassmussen provide references from both Testaments: Isaiah 55:12–13; Romans 8:21; Colossians 1:15; Isaiah 11:6–9.[22]

A similar approach to Professor Birch's is taken by H. Paul Santmire in the final chapter of his historical survey of Christian attitudes to nature entitled *The Travail of Nature: The Ambiguous Ecological Promise of Christian Theology.*[23] Santmire believes that while the history of Christian thought is certainly "ambiguous" in relation to nature, the Bible itself contains for us—confronting, as we must, new problems in this area—a "new option." He calls this option "an ecological reading of biblical theology."[24] Contrary to those who insist that " 'man stands at the center of the whole picture,' " Santmire claims that "it is possible to construe [the historical categories in which biblical theology is of course steeped] more generously and more universally than the proponents of the anthropocentric approach have generally done: not in terms of God and humanity over against nature, but in terms of God and humanity *with* nature. This could be called an ecological hermeneutic of history. It is predicated on the assumption of a divine and human concomitance with nature, rather than a divine and human disjunction from nature."[25]

Santmire finds this approach upheld by numerous themes in the Old Testament. The importance of the land in Yahweh's promise to the people of Israel, a theme on which Walter Brueggemann has concentrated,[26] is one of them: "it will no longer do to talk about Yahweh and his people . . . but we must speak about Yahweh and his people and his land," Brueggemann writes. Another is the "flowering of creation theology in Israel's monarchical and postmonarchical periods," which, with Brueggemann and Westermann, Santmire insists does not represent the influence on Israel's election-centered faith of "alien elements" emanating from Canaanite nature religions (the position taken by von Rad, Wright, and Lampe),[27] but is an extension of Israel's own theocentric faith: God who is Lord of history is praised also "for the majestic power that he exercises throughout the world of nature."[28] Santmire traces this theme in the work of the Priestly writer of Genesis 1 and in many of the Psalms, especially the so-called Royal Psalms. With Birch and Sittler, he finds "the richest expression of the fecundity theme" in Psalm 104.[29]

Turning to the New Testament, Santmire believes it possible to find the "ecological motif" in much of what we read there. Jesus' message was focused on the coming of the kingdom, an eschatological theme; nevertheless, while this certainly contains an anthropocentric concentration, it also assumes the renewal and "final transformation" of earth, "in keeping with the prophetic-apocalyptic expectations [Jesus] had inherited."[30] In fact, he writes, "the historical Jesus, insofar as we have access to him through the faith-colored lenses of the New Testament writings, can be thought of as an ecological figure as well as an eschatological figure."[31]

Paul's "apocalyptic theology" is also rich in ecologically significant ideas: the groaning of the whole creation, the universal lordship of the Christ, redemption as healing and the renovation of the world, and so forth. Of course, it is true that Paul, with much of the New Testament's witness, is primarily concerned with the mission of the church and therefore cannot give priority to "these universalizing cosmic concerns." Yet Santmire observes, quoting J. C. Beker, that the " 'somatic worldly component of [Paul's] anthropology cannot be spiritualized away. . . . Paul's church is not an aggregate of justified sinners or a sacramental institute or a means for private self-salvation but the avant-garde of the new creation in a hostile world. . . . ' " Therefore, while "no biblically legitimate creation theology of cosmic Christology will prompt its adherents to forsake the life and mission of the people of God under the cross," Paul's *theologia crucis* may in fact be the best for an ecological theology:

> Paul was no less passionately concerned with the mission of the church and the theology of the cross than any other Christian writer. But it may just be the case that his apocalyptic theology, predicated on his vision of the eschatological triumph of God, might be best suited, of all the other New Testament theological "trajectories" or traditions which we know, to offer us the framework to preserve the integrity of the church's life and mission, in all its aspects, in a world dominated by a spirit of alienation from nature and the threat of universal death.[32]

But all the same, says Santmire, the "ambiguity of Christian thought about nature" is already encountered in the New Testament:

> . . . this ecological reading of the New Testament theology of nature, however, has its limits. The portrayal of the mind of early Christianity, wherein we see the influence of the metaphor of migration to a good land and the metaphor of fecundity — the ecological motif — coming to expression in one grand vision of the ultimate realization of the divine purpose for all things, in the coming new heavens and the new earth, or in the integration and unification of the whole creation under the cosmic rule of Christ, does not represent the dominant thinking of all those New Testament writings which portray Christ in a cosmic context.

The earthward, ecological motif is offset by what Santmire throughout his survey of Christian thought concerning nature has called "the spiritual motif." It is particularly strong in John's Gospel and also (in a different way) in Hebrews (see 12:22–23). The metaphor here is one of ascent, and the vision is that of a spiritual world. "The Pauline vision of the Christian standing in solidarity with the whole creation at the very end is thereby eclipsed."

We are left, Santmire concludes, with a question: "Is the final aim of God, in his governance of all things, to bring into being at the very end a glorified kingdom of spirits alone . . . ? Or is the final aim of God, in his governance of all things, to communicate his life to another in a way which calls forth at the very end new heavens

and a new earth . . . , a transfigured cosmos where peace is universally established between all creatures at last?" A "large majority of
modern biblical scholars," Santmire thinks, would opt for the
former interpretation—the spiritual motif. He himself believes that
a case can be made for "an ecological reading of biblical faith":

> If contemporary Christian theologians took that kind of approach
> to biblical theology seriously . . . that could lead to a new birth
> of Christian thought about nature. The travail of nature in Chris-
> tian theology could come to a blessed ending.[33]

IV. THE NEED FOR FOUNDATIONS

Biblical exegesis, we may conclude, provides much impressive material that is relevant to thinking Christians' search today
for a better theology of nature. At the same time it should be forth-
rightly acknowledged (as Santmire does) that the biblical evidence
already participates in the "ambiguity" about this subject that has
typified the history of Christendom. Direct evidence from Scripture
is indispensable to Christian faith and theology. But if Christian
thought and praxis are to achieve, in a given historical context, sufficient transcendence of the multiple witness (not to mention "ambiguity") of the Bible to enable them to integrate its message and act,
they must always attempt to discern the deeper substrata of biblical
faith. On the basis of these it can engage its historical context with
a gospel that is fundamentally biblical even if it is not directly so, and
even if "things" can be found in the Bible that may seem to contradict it or convey another message. This search for the substrata
of the biblical and historical traditions of church, impelled by the
church's need to address a prophetic word and deed to its context,
is the primary task of critical and constructive ("systematic")
theology.

Such a general methodological observation is illustrated by the
present discussion. We can hardly expect the Bible authors to have
spoken directly to the crises we confront. They did not have to deal
with a beaten natural world, or with human beings whose technical
genius had brought them to the point where they can destroy trees
not only with axes, one at a time, but with acid rain, from afar, and
by the millions! The remarkable thing is that there is as much as there
is in this ancient literature by way of compassion for nature and the
recognition of human solidarity with it.

But if we ask for the foundations of this compassion and

recognition, we are brought back to the ontological basis that has been the subject of this investigation. Direct biblical evidence such as we have briefly noted from Professors Birch and Santmire and others must be taken very seriously; but it should also be understood as superstructure, much of it, presupposing substructural foundations, or — to mix the metaphor — as the tip of the iceberg. Beneath this direct evidence, concealed or at least usually more implicit than explicit, lies a conception of reality itself that quite naturally produces the specific ideas about the world, nature, and the human relationship with nature that scriptural exegetes, under the impact of environmental deterioration, have begun to notice. Professor Birch confirms this himself when he chooses the title "These All Look to Thee — A Relational Theology of Nature" for his heading over most of the material I have cited in the previous section. He writes:

> In the dominant Biblical understanding of humanity and nature the key is not distinct orders of creation nor is it an almost mystical view of cosmic oneness. The key is relationship. God, humanity, and nature are to be in harmonious relationship. Humanity and nature are both valued before God and the full life of each depends on the full life of the other. In fact, Hebrew has no separate word for nature (in our meaning of the natural order outside humanity). We are already implying a dichotomy in our use of the word nature that the Hebrews did not recognize. Each order has its name but all (human and nonhuman, animate and inanimate) were part of the single creation of God. Thus, we might well explore the Biblical witness to a relational theology of nature.[34]

What I have proposed in the foregoing is that this "relational theology of nature" is, in fact, only a necessary extension of the tradition's relational conception of being itself — all being, including God's. Therefore, we are not importing something or overtaxing the biblical heritage when, in the face of conventional theology's silence on the subject, we conclude that nevertheless the human relationship with nature within the tradition of Jerusalem is more intimate than Christians have habitually supposed. If the whole ontology of this tradition is explicable only on the grounds of a reciprocity of being (being-with), then to avoid applying this fundamental ontological perspective to what we call "nature" would be tantamount to demonstrating our insensibility to this "first science" as it articulates itself in the Hebraic ethos.

Could it not be, in fact, that precisely this insensibility is what lies behind the silence on the subject of nature, or the ambiguity on the part of historical Christianity? A review of Christian thought, including the *imago Dei* symbol, strongly suggests that the potential of biblical material for engendering a distinctive ontology was seldom explored, let alone exploited. Not only the obvious prominence of Stoic, Platonic, Neoplatonic, and other categories, but even more tellingly the persistence of an allegorical approach to the scriptures of Israel, implies that from the earliest times Christian thinkers missed the point that the biblical writings presuppose an incipient "metaphysics" of their own. Instead òf exploring that alternative theory of reality, most of the theologians of the developing traditions of both Eastern and Western Christianity approached the scriptures of the Old Testament as stories, fables, allegories, or simply "history" containing hidden truths that were to be unearthed with the aid of metaphysical assumptions drawn from the traditions of Athens or Rome. Besides, given the unworldly and antiworldly bias of so many of those theologians, even the events recorded in the Synoptic Gospels had to be subjected to this dehistoricizing process, so that the transcendent truth — *theologia eterna!* — could be extracted. It seems not to have occurred to Origen, for example, that Jerusalem might have a distinctive "first science" of its own; that the scriptures of Israel are not presented in the language of history, encounter, and dialogue for nothing, but that all of this bespeaks a way of conceiving "being."

But the habit of neglecting the relational ontology of Jerusalem is not limited to Christian beginnings. So entrenched is it, in fact, that Christian scholars are still reluctant to apply the term "ontology" to theological and biblical matters. Since the impression was created that ontological reflection belongs to the tradition of Athens, theologians desirous of an apologetic rapprochement between "Athens" and "Jerusalem" attempt to demonstrate that the philosophical quest for the meaning of being parallels or is continuous with "Biblical Religion";[35] while others, correctly more conscious of the distinction between the two traditions, confine ontology to the classical and medieval thought worlds and contrast it with the historical-dramatic approach of Scripture.[36] In both instances a specific content is assumed for the term "ontology" — namely a content derived from the philosophical quest of ancient Mediterranean civilizations and those who, in the medieval and modern worlds, took that tradition for their foundation. But when this is done, and done consistently for centuries, it has the result of implicitly denying that Jerusalem has any understanding or preunderstanding of the nature of being! Of course, Jerusalem does not speak of "metaphysics," and the term "ontology" is as foreign to it as to the native peoples of North America. But the psalmist who asked, "What is man that thou art mindful of him?" and the Yahwist who called God "I am," and the Wisdom writer who compared the fate of human beings with that of the beasts, and the prophets who felt the presence of the "wholly other," and the Gospel writers who recorded the words and deeds of One who dared to say, "Before Abraham was, I am"—all these most certainly were searchers after "ultimate reality."

And finders too! What distinguishes them from Athens is not that they did not search for the meaning of being, but that the mode of their search was different, and what they found was different. Very different in most cases, I think. If, instead of delving into the depths of the psyche in the manner of the Platonists, or observing the interactions of nature and the *polis* as did Aristotle and later empiricists, the seers of the tradition of Jerusalem busy themselves with descriptions of historical events, God's "mighty acts," human interchange, dialogue, prayer, lament, and the like, it is because what they have grasped in their "search for ultimate reality" is particularistic and dialogical through and through. It cannot be reduced to universals, and it cannot be resolved in theories that transcend the dialogical state. Even the eschatological resolution of the historical drama, when, as Paul puts it, there will be only yes and not also no, still assumes relationship as its fundamental ontic presupposition.

If, then, ontology connotes the resolution of dialogue and the end of particularity and preoccupation with the purely spiritual and abstract, ontology is indeed incompatible with the tradition of Jerusalem. But if ontology means the struggle of the human mind to comprehend the rudimentary character of reality; and if reality itself is conceivably dialogical, steeped in particularity, concrete relationships; in short, if reality could be thought of in the language of grace, faith, hope, and love—then, of course, Jerusalem has an ontology. It is an ontology of communion, reciprocity, and mutuality of being. It is an ontology that finds ultimacy not in undifferentiated substance (*nous, logos, ousia*) but in the bodying forth of being that exists, and in what happens between the existent realities.

If such an ontology of communion had been seriously and consistently pursued by Christian theology, would it have been necessary for us today, late in time, to scurry about for some better conception of the relationship between human beings and the natural order? One does not know. Perhaps "the occasion" (the *crisis* of this relationship) would still have had to come about to invoke that conception. But this much seems obvious: it would have been there — much more obviously there — to invoke. For if the being of all that is, including God, is being-in-relationship; if " 'being itself' is a relation, not an entitative thing" (Sittler); if relatedness applies to everything of which being is posited — then it would be difficult, to say the least, to reduce anything that is to the status of "thing." And perhaps a civilization under the impact of such an ontology would have had quite a different fate from that of our own. •

V. WITH: IDENTIFICATION AND DIFFERENTIATION

To affirm that human being is not only being-with God the Source and being-with neighbor the coequal but also being-with all creation is to situate "nature" within the same spiritual and conceptual framework that applies to the other two foci of our relatedness. Stating the same thing in another way: The peculiar form of receptivity that we bring to our contemplation of nature is not of a different kind from the attitudes of mind and spirit with which we consider our proximity to God and to our own kind. It is not as if there were three types of mentality or spirituality — one appropriate to divinity, another to humanity, and a third to nature. Rather, whether we reflect on God, on our own species, or on trees, rocks, and whales, we are engaged in the same mode of contemplation, investigation, or reverie. For all three, however distinct from each other, however unique in their demands on us, however different in their manner of imparting themselves to us, are present to us in such a way that the being of each mirrors the being of the others. Christ is our needy neighbor at our door at midnight (Lk. 11:5), and all things that are made reflect the glory of God (Rom. 1:20).

Thus, with respect to the rest of nature as with the other two dimensions of our being-with, we experience a paradoxical sense of identification and differentiation. "With" — here as in the previously discussed facets of human relatedness — contains two polar concepts that remain in tension with each other, continuously informing and at the same time re-forming the other.

One is the thought (who can now avoid it?) that as human beings we are strictly part of the natural process. This is not the statement of an irreverent naturalism; it belongs to a faith that is willing to sit at table "in solidarity with beasts and plants and stones" (Barth). What could be more explicit about the human creature's essential (not only existential) being as a belonging-within-the-world than the picture we are given in the earliest creation saga: *adam* from *adamah*, human from humus? For the human creature, to be *imago Dei* means also to be *imago mundi*.[37] Imaging God is not rising above the earth, as if we were pure spirit. If there are angels, perhaps their mode of imaging God would not involve matter; but we are bodies, and our imaging of God is inseparable from our imaging of the earth. The term "Mother Earth," as has been noted, connotes certain pagan associations that may not be altogether compatible with biblical faith; but neither are they entirely incompatible, as St. Francis knew:

> Be praised, my Lord, for Brother Wind
> And for the air, cloudy and clear, and all weather!
> By which you give substance to your creatures!
> Be praised, my Lord, for our Sister, Mother Earth,
> Who sustains and governs us,
> and produces fruits with colourful
> flowers and leaves.[38]

A faith that makes such a close alliance between human and humus, and at the same time rejects the enduring temptation of a dualism that distinguishes spirit as essence from body as "tomb," could hardly consistently spurn the thought of earth's maternity. "You are dust; to dust you shall return"—these words, though they point up "the curse" on fallen existence (Gen. 3:19), are not without truth and grace. If there is an unforgettable echo of malediction in our knowledge of our human proximity to earth, and if we are ashamed of this, and like the pair in Eden hide our earthiness from our own eyes, this is not because God created us so, according to the biblical testimony, but because we sin. That is, we do not accept our being as it is fashioned and given us by our Creator, as being-with-the-ground. Pridefully, we want to rise above this affinity with our earthly source and matrix. We would be glad to elevate ourselves infinitely in order to avoid this connection entirely, an ancient sentiment poignantly described in the myth of Babel, and a modern sentiment just as pathetically enacted in our costly preoccupation with outer space.

But the pride that attempts to escape our communion with "the ground" and daily finds new ways of achieving pseudotranscendence—this pathetic quest for a place to stand outside the earth does not belong to our essential, created being. It is precisely our spoiling of the essential that is betokened in it. If in its historical pilgrimage the human race has wreaked vengeance on nature; if it has treated the earth with all the frustration of "unhappy gods" (Camus); if its *dominium* in relation to otherkind is thus more accurately described as a wrathful domination over them—all this should be attributed, not to the biblical view of how matters should stand between humanity and the rest of nature, but precisely how, in that perspective, they should not stand. In its essence, in terms of the intention of its Creator for it, the human creature is creature: creature-with-creatures. This is corroborated not only by the creational theology of biblical faith but also by its soteriology and eschatology. Again and again the Bible depicts the "righting" of the world as the overcoming of alienation between all three counterparts of human being. At base this means the humble, grateful return of human creatures to their true home within creation, alongside ("at table with") the other creatures. For we—and we alone—are the problematical element in this triad, according to the tradition of Jerusalem. It is our basic humanity, that is, our creaturehood, that we have refused. And so it is just this humanity that the redeeming God of Sinai and Golgotha wills us to accept and rejoice in: "To be a man/woman pure and simple" (Bonhoeffer).

Without apology we may conclude, then, that the fundamental emphasis in the dialectic of identification and differentiation as it relates to the humankind-otherkind relationship falls on the side of identification. At best, our distinction from the other creatures serves our participation with them in the same creaturely reality and glory, and not vice versa.

All the same, the dimension of differentiation and transcendence is also present in this relationship, biblically conceived. We cannot avoid it, nor should we attempt to do so. There is a certain pressure on Judaic and Christian faith today, coming from the good and correct concerns of all friends of the earth, to dispense with the dimension of transcendence in this relationship. But to do so is both theologically impossible (so long as one remains within the precincts of this particular theo-anthropology) and humanly, morally reprehensible. The question that responsible Christians and all human beings must ask themselves today is not *whether* there is such a thing as the human transcendence of nature but *why* there is such a thing. After all, to ask the question, or even feel the concern, is already to give evidence of such transcendence.

Those who throughout the Christian centuries have pursued the *imago Dei* along substantialist lines have advanced the human transcendence of other creatures as though it were in itself and as such a sufficient rationale, self-explanatory as well as self-evident. For this mentality, inferior beings exist both for human use and as a backdrop permitting the superiority of the human to stand out. Evolutionary theory did little to unsettle such an assumption, though it did accentuate rather more conspicuously the participatory side of the relationship.

We have already committed ourselves to a very different explanation of the dimension of differentiation and transcendence in the human. Given a relational approach to being, the human creature's distinction from the others can only be understood vocationally. That is, it is not an end in itself but the means to a greater end. Human beings are different in certain respects from other creatures because they are, so to speak, "assigned" a particular role in relation to the others in the scheme of things. This role necessitates both their firm identity with the others and their distinction from them. It now becomes our task to elaborate on this claim.

To do so, we must first introduce another set of terms that can help establish the vocational-relational basis of human transcendence. We have already noted in the discussion of the two previously treated foci of human being how the preposition *with* as it is applied to these relationships contains both an implicit "in" and an implicit "beyond." And we have also noted how each of these qualifies the other. A similar argument can be advanced, in connection with the present dimension of human relatedness, if one affirms of the human creature that it is both a natural and a historical creature. Strictly speaking, biblical religion applies the sense of history only to the human species. Remembering and hoping, with a consciousness of the past and of the future that conditions and can greatly affect our present—these are characteristics belonging uniquely to this creature. All of nature has a history; but only the human creature is historical.[39] That is to say, this creature is enabled to rise above nature (not physically, of course, but mentally and spiritually) and to consider its own and all other being from a perspective that is bound neither to the instant nor to instinct.

Quite obviously, it is this very capacity of the human spirit to transcend nature that has tempted Christian and other thinkers throughout history to single out human spirituality (especially, as we have seen, the rational and volitional dimensions of the human spirit) as the very endowments labeled "image of God" by the Priestly writer. But in doing this, they failed, for the most part, to sustain the participation/identification principle that is implicit in the creaturely being of the human; thus, at the same time that they were exaggerating human transcendence, they were robbing extrahuman creation of its proper mystery and spirituality. As a historical creature, the human being may indeed be "different"; but the difference, as history has shown with astonishing regularity, does not ensure a thing by way of valuation. "Man is not as other creatures," writes Loren Eiseley, echoing what so many have said; but then he wisely concludes the thought thus: " . . . without the sense of the holy, without compassion, his brain can become a gray stalking horror, the deviser of Belsen."[40]

The corrective to this long and ardent history of unwarranted celebration of human "superiority," however, is not to leap to an equally undialectical emphasis on the identification principle, and so to end with human beings who want to exchange their historical mode for a purely instinctual mode of being — and write books about it! Rather, the corrective is to search more diligently for the connection between the two sides of this dialectic. Why such creatures? Surely the centuries have adequately demonstrated the precarious, not to mention foolhardy, character of devising a being both natural and historical. Why, then, this difficult, almost inevitably tragic combination of nature and history, participation and transcendence, in our species? Why, among the creatures, should there be yet this one, so obviously "just a creature," a "naked ape,"[41] yet knowing itself to be creature, with all the pathos and pain pertaining to that; this being of flesh and passion, yet seeing such possibilities beyond the confines of its natural drives? Dreaming such dreams! Feeling such guilt! Yearning for such purity! Improvising such music, such cities, such evil, such good! Are we simply to take the existence of this unlikely biped as a fact and leave it there?

To do so would be most uncharacteristic of biblical faith. For the God of this tradition does not create capriciously, or merely to experience the pleasure and power of diverse creativity. Truly, the biblical God is not readily fathomed by mere human intelligence: "For my thoughts are not your thoughts, neither are your ways my ways, says the Lord" (Is. 55:8f.). Truly, a rationality that precludes paradox and mystery and "foolishness" (I Cor. 1–2) could only flounder on the sheer fact of humanity. It is no wonder that more "atheists" have been made by the contemplation of the human condition than by speculations on the divine. Yet the protagonist of that story recounted in the continuity of the Testaments, God, whose wisdom seems folly only because our wisdom is folly, does not act whimsically or even in a manner that faith must forever find irrational:

> Surely the Lord God does nothing
>   without revealing his secret
> to his servants the prophets (Amos 3:7).

We must suppose, then, that the tradition of Jerusalem posits a rationale, a *telos* (inner aim), for such an unlikely being. And we may suppose, further, that this rationale greatly exceeds the being of the human creature as such, as the end exceeds the means. For it could only be thought cruel and absurd (and all who have thought it such from Epicurus to Ivan Karamazov would be entirely justified in doing so!) to place among the mortal creatures yet another such, but one in this case having all the faculties needed to recognize its mortality. The Bible itself is honest and wise enough to permit its readers to entertain just such a thought. In Job, in certain of the Psalms, above all in Koheleth, we have expressions precisely of this typical and greatest temptation of the human creature: to think itself nothing but "a jest of God."[42] But over against this *tentatio* the scriptures of Israel and the church pose a whole spectrum of analogies, metaphors, sagas, and symbols that in their collective witness depict human being and meaning in an astonishingly elevated way — yet without ever losing sight of human creaturehood.

Not only so, but the very creaturehood of the human — its solidarity of participation in the general creaturely condition — is the ontic basis of the Bible's high teleological assessment of humanity. Take away the groundedness of the human species in the universal creaturely condition, and you may have (as in the mythological traditions of many peoples) gods and demigods in the guise of mortals, or triumphant spirits imprisoned in tenacious flesh. But you will not have beings who could live out, in the flesh and only in the flesh, the exalted calling this tradition finds to be the inheritance of the children of Adam/Eve.

VI. DOMINION REDEFINED CHRISTOLOGICALLY

We have named that calling the *imaging of God*. We have prepared the way for speaking about this and hope that some of the debris that clutters up this particular symbol has been thrown aside.

Now we must try to say what it means as it is understood in the light of the relational ontology of this tradition and in the context of a deteriorating natural environment.

Let us begin in this way. The God testified to in the Jerusalem tradition will have — within the creation itself — a being whose function is to image its Creator. Whether one turns to the biblical concept of the covenant, or to the language of holiness and priesthood, or to the idea of divine election, or to the many lesser symbols by which this creature's being and vocation are depicted in sacred Scripture, one is driven to the conclusion that the spiritual community in which this doctrinal tradition formed itself could only conceive of the deity as desiring an internally placed representative of itself.[43] That is, it could only regard humanity as a mediatorial species reflecting, within the creation, the covenant faithfulness of the Creator.

If this creature, therefore, is caused to bear the knowledge of its creaturehood, and to be in that respect "beyond" nature while remaining physically within it; if this creature is called into historicity, and so lives as a being of memory and hope and not only of instinct; if this creature is endowed with rationality and will, and is thus capable of wisdom as well as ignorance, daring as well as failure; in short, if the spirituality of this particular creature is distinct from that of its created counterparts, this by no means signifies that the tradition of Jerusalem intends to put the human creature forward as the end product of the Creator's plan. This is where the biblical doctrine of creation really does differ from some evolutionary theory. End product thinking may be Darwinian; it is not Hebraic. What the tradition of Jerusalem posits, rather, is a very different kind of *telos*. It is an end that infinitely transcends the being of the human creature, an end that the creature's peculiar being can only serve. The Westminster and other traditions correctly name this end "the glory of God." The human creature is "there" as a point of focus for the *doxa theou*. In the midst of the creation it is to image its Creator, not for its own glory but as its peculiar glory; and it is to articulate through the medium of its peculiar creaturehood the whole creation's glorification of its Creator.

But what specific content can we give to this creaturely reflection of the *gloria Dei*? To achieve concreteness for the concept, we are obliged to return to the much-misunderstood idea of human dominion. In Chapter Two above, we noted that the *imago Dei* symbol was from its inception linked with human dominion with respect to the rest of nature. What we have not yet observed—what indeed most Western religious and secular history as a whole seems not to have observed—is how the interpretation of the connection between imaging God and having dominion is altered by the confession that Jesus is Lord. I do not mean to imply that such an interpretation is inaccessible to the faith of Israel. It is accessible. For in at least this respect the God whose *doxa* is revealed "in the face of Christ Jesus" (II Cor. 4:6) is entirely consistent with the God who speaks and acts and suffers in the pages of Israel's sacred scriptures. But once a community of faith dares to affirm that Jesus is *Dominus*—that this one who is the very "image of the invisible God" (Col. 1:15) is at the same time Lord—then it is obliged not only by its faith but even by ordinary logic to apply to its understanding of the *dominium* to which humanity is called the consequences of such a confession. If "lordship" is exemplified by this Lord, then such a belief ought to transform the whole idea of human dominion within the realm of nature.

It is truly astonishing that historical Christianity made so little by way of an explicit and definitive connection between Christology and anthropology at this juncture. How could the point be missed that Christ, addressed by generation after generation of Christians as *Domine*, must be the paradigm for our entire understanding of human dominion within creation? To be incorporated into the "body" of such a Lord would have to mean, surely, to begin to emulate our Lord's mode of "having dominion." To be "conformed to his image" (the second basic theme of the New Testament's treatment of the *imago*) would have to mean to assume, with him and in him, a role more commonly associated with service than with mastery: the role of the steward.

> . . . the Christian's exemplar of this dominion is Christ. Though God has given him "a name that is above every name," his greatest glory is in "taking the form of a bondservant"; Christ's Lordship is most clearly exemplified in his stewardship. And it is a similar kind of lordship—and stewardship—as well as a similar kind of dignity and honor for which we are accountable to the Lord of the universe.[44]

This christological basis of our understanding of the *imago Dei* leads inescapably, in other words, to the conclusion that our imaging of God within the creation entails a form of *dominium* that is radically distinguishable from the manner in which the injunction to dominion in the text of Genesis 1 has been regularly received within

Christendom. If Christology is our foundational premise both for theological (*vere Deus*) and anthropological (*vere homo*) doctrine, then "dominion" as a way of designating the role of *Homo sapiens* within creation can only mean stewardship, and stewardship ultimately interpreted as love: sacrificial, self-giving love (*agape*).

> If . . . we follow the general Christian intention of abiding by the person and work of Jesus as central and decisive in directing us toward the realities of our human situation in respect to God and the world, it is shattering to contrast the Biblical notion of dominion with the opportunism of those who interpreted the Genesis mandate to "have dominion . . . over all the earth" as man's licence to exploit his natural environment. For the authority of Jesus and the understanding of his dominion grow out of his availability and service to men, expressed in patterns of caring and compassion which eventually qualify his "dominion over all the earth."
>
> We may say, then, that Biblical dominion does not masquerade in the vesture of servility in order to exert a false power over the world; it breathes humility, "lording it" over none. And inasmuch as the death of Jesus is a culmination of his life, in the sense that the life interprets the death, his ultimate authority springs from the somber glory of his cross, which, from the depths of existence, raises to dignity mankind and the world.[45]

We are confronted by a "transvaluation of values." The "lordship" of the Crucified, if seriously grasped, radically transforms our preconception of dominion, exchanging for the concept of a superior form of being one of exceptional and deliberate solidarity (being-with), and for the notion of mastery a vocation to self-negating and responsible stewardship. How could this christological critique of the human will to power have been so blatantly ignored in Christendom?

The answer is, of course, that the lordship of Christ was itself soon transmuted by imperially placed Christianity into something very different from the actual testimony to the life of the Lord given by the Bible writers. Jesus was invested with all the trappings of earthly monarchy by an adoring church—a church which, particularly in the post-Establishment situation, felt the need to present its *kurios Christos* in a manner that would simultaneously reflect and transcend the grandeur of *kurios Kaisar*. Thus the radical model of authority and majesty that Jesus as Lord actually embodied, with its intrinsic but unmistakable polemic against power, was all but lost to evolving Christendom.

Besides, the "divinity" principle in Christology so consistently displaced the humanity principle that, until the liberal approach to the question in the nineteenth century, few Christians would have considered it either possible or appropriate to think of Jesus as an exemplar of "true humanity," the *vere homo* of the Formula of Chalcedon notwithstanding. While the Middle Ages produced an *imitatio Christi* tradition of mystic spirituality that was later incorporated into aspects of Reformation piety, this must be regarded as a minority tradition. For the great majority (as can be seen from the artistic representations of the Christ throughout the centuries) Jesus Christ has functioned as the Lord, that is, a figure of unearthly majesty, power, and dominion. Not only did Christendom's *Christus* serve, therefore, to discourage human imitation of him, but also to convict human beings of their ingloriousness, their failure, and their incapacity for truly responsible service. In short, a *kurios Christos* thoroughly informed by the *theologia gloriae*.

The challenge issued to the Christian movement today by the crisis of the biosphere, namely, that it develop a more adequate theology of nature, is thus at the same time a challenge to develop a more authentic Christology. If it is true that our Christology is the ontic and noetic basis of our anthropology, as of our doctrine of God, then in order to acquire a conception of *anthropos* more conducive to the stewarding of nature, we shall simultaneously have to recover a *Christos* whose lordship is vastly different from the magisterial model preferred by empirical Christianity. Or, to state the same thing in the language of this present study: If, as our brief exposition of the New Testament's treatment of the *imago Dei* confirms, Jesus is supremely for Christians the "image of the invisible God" and the One to whose *imago* Christians themselves are "being conformed," then it is of vital importance that we recast the *pictura Christi* in such a way that it can establish in our midst a critical and positive vision of human—truly human—dominion vis-à-vis the rest of the natural order.

VII. A METHODOLOGICAL INTERLUDE

The proposal that contemporary Christians have a responsibility to "recast the picture of the Christ" is no doubt a risky one; it is certainly one that will be regarded with suspicion by every shade of biblical literalism. But it is, in fact, only a more deliberate statement of a process that has been occurring throughout Christian history. Successive ages of Christendom have always "cast their images" of Christ in forms highly influenced by the dominant assumptions of their cultures. As a matter of fact, what we regularly name "Christology" is, from a historical point of view that is only slightly skeptical of human truth claims, the evolution of a considerable variety of culturally biased images of the Christ. Some are no doubt more "graven" than others are; some are more conceptually framed, others more artistic or mythic. The classical formulation of christological doctrine given at Chalcedon in 451 C.E. is of the former variety; nineteenth-century "lives of Jesus" are mainly instances of the latter: literary or broadly artistic endeavors to actually depict Christ. One may prefer the conceptual approach (which always runs the risk of reducing the person to a theory), or one may prefer the artistic approach (which is less inclined than the conceptual to withstand the temptation of presenting Christ according to the ideals of the moment—as in many nineteenth-century "lives," where Jesus becomes a yet nobler Wilberforce). But in both of these historical examples, as well as in many others that could be listed, the prevailing values and virtues of the epochs in question, together with what were perceived as assaults against these same values and virtues, have been subtly or obviously incorporated. One does not have to claim that either Chalcedon or the liberals ignored the primary testimony to the historical Jesus, that is, the New Testament's witness to him. At the same time, a single observation makes it abundantly clear that neither these two nor any other of the major stages in the development of christological dogma were concerned exclusively or even primarily with the biblical witness.

I am referring to the fact—and twentieth-century history necessitates our calling it a fact!—that the great historical traditions of Christology have never taken the Jewishness of Jesus utterly seriously. If, as so much Christology claims for itself, the scriptural witness really had been normative for doctrine at this juncture, it would have been impossible for Christians over many centuries to offer the world a Christ/Messiah so entirely devoid of those basic assumptions, practices, and qualities of character indigenous to the Judaism that was the historic Jesus' only sociocultural context; a Christ/Messiah, indeed, who could exist for his followers as a symbol and goad of anti-Judaic sentiment! The failure of Christology in this singular respect betrays very conspicuously the excessive influence of historical, contextual assumptions in successive endeavors of the church to define this—its central doctrinal claim.[46]

And the omission is inexcusable. However, it is not without its reasons. One reason for the excessiveness of the contextual influence[47] in dogmatic teaching concerning the person and work of Christ is that it was largely unconscious and therefore an easy prey to ulterior motivation. The most influential christological decisions of the church were undertaken, after all, not only before contemporary insights into the intricacies of the human psyche but before the modern consciousness of history. We have come to know that all our articulations of theological "truth" are conditioned both by complex psychological factors and by the specific sociohistorical conditions under which we labor—our Sitz im Leben. The formulators of Chalcedonian Christology, on the contrary, could think themselves engaged in an act of permanent and universal truth telling (*theologia eterna*). They did not suffer under the impediment of historicity, of recognizing at every turn of phrase their bondage to time and place.

We cannot do this, though many in our time still attempt it. We must make our witness to the Christ with the sure and certain knowledge that it is informed from first to last by our actual situation in life, by the particularity of our individual and corporate needs, by our class, our race, our sex, our economic status, our language world, our hopes and anxieties, and so forth. For us, therefore (when we are wise), there is the constant awareness that our witness has only a temporary veracity, if any; that in spite of our sinful will to extend our influence beyond the limits of our age and place, the most that we can aim for is the engagement of the particular context in which we live, move, and have our being-with.

Yet what is from one perspective a limitation is from another a possibility, and one that was not open to our theological forebears. For if, freeing ourselves through this same historic consciousness from a questionable kind of dependence on the past and an even more questionable bid for the immortality of our own ideas, we are really able to focus on and engage our own *hic et nunc*, then—for all its temporariness—whatever veracity our witness does acquire, it will be more to the point as witness than so much of the conventional doctrine of the ages. This is doctrine that, under the guise of absolute truth, has served to insulate many from the realities of their here-and-now.

In short, may we not use the awareness of our radical temporality to advantage? In the attempt to "recast the biblical picture of our Lord" in a way that can establish for today a critical paradigm for the character of the *dominium* for which he stands, we may, for one thing, be entirely honest about the relationship between text and context. That is, we know—and may allow ourselves quite deliberately to know—that many of the concerns that we must bring to our christological reflections are concerns about which neither the historical Jesus himself nor those who recorded his story could ever have given a passing thought. An obvious example is that "fact" to which I referred in the foregoing discussion: the omission from Christology of Jesus' Jewishness. The writer of the Gospel of Matthew, for example, cannot be expected to have anticipated fully the extent to which the anti-Jewish statements sprinkled throughout his account would contribute to a climate of opinion that eventually led to the railway platform at Buchenwald. Yet we not only can and may, but we must bring this dreadful knowledge to our christological reflection. To avoid it would be at least as irresponsible on our part as it would have been for the Matthean writer to avoid, in his protochristological reflections, any mention of the Christian discontinuity with Israel.

Or again, no New Testament writer knew or could have known of the proliferation of "churches" in the modern world, with their enormous variety in christological, missiological, liturgical, and other doctrines and practices; or of the imperial status of the Christian religion throughout most of its history to date; or of the character of contemporary warfare and its mandatory revision of the whole concept of the just war, and so forth. These authors did not even know the most rudimentary scientific facts that we simply take for granted—the roundness of the earth, the force of gravity, the second law of thermodynamics. Yet all of these data have implications for our christological meditation and formulation. To ignore them is as foolish as it would be to assume, as sectarian Christians frequently try to do, that all such data were already fully anticipated by the Bible writers, since they were in any case only amanuenses for a heavenly finger.

Responsible Christology cannot follow the path of the kind of "orthodoxy" (more properly designated antiquarianism) that satisfies itself with established christological formulae of the past; for Christ is Lord of the present and future too! Nor can it pretend, on the other hand, that the biblical material already contains, openly or implicitly, all the data that christological reflection requires. For Jesus was a historical person, and obedience to Christ is obedience in time. There is, however, another way. Faith—which is not faith in the Bible but in the living Lord—may and must believe that the Christ to whom the Bible bears witness is both wise enough and expansive enough to entertain, from our vantage point in time and space, questions and concerns that the biblical witness to him does not and could not in itself anticipate. In other words, we may and must confidently assume that our contextual problematic will be able to evoke from the text, when it is thoughtfully and prayerfully studied by the church in the power of the divine Spirit, a testimony to the Christ that can and does address our historical moment. This testimony may not be said to be explicitly present in the text, to be sure; but given what *is* in the text, the context out of which we ourselves approach the text may, if it is sufficiently articulated in us, draw from the text a witness that is no longer "dated" but entirely pertinent to our situation.

The only thing in this procedure that is different from the common approach of past exegetical/theological interpretation is our necessary consciousness of what is involved in this hermeneutic. The truth is, Christology has never been the mere knowledge and acknowledgment of the biblical witness to Jesus as the Christ. It has always been a combination of biblical study or recollection and speculative thought heavily informed by the contextual realities of the interpreters. The fact that the role (unconscious or unacknowledged) of the contextual dimension in past christological formulations has been excessive does not mean that we should now eschew christological reflection that goes beyond the most "scientific" exegesis of Scripture. In any case, that alternative does not exist, since part of the historical as well as the scientific consciousness that we have imbibed informs us that such "objectivity" with respect to the scriptural witness is neither possible nor desirable; moreover, if we are disciples of a Lord who is in some real sense contemporary to us, a Christology that refused a priori to consider the presence of the Christ in the midst of our historical present, with its particular crises, would be a contradiction in terms.

Instead of substituting exegesis for theology, then, we must allow contemporaneity—for all its imprecision and diversity—to enter fully into our christological and soteriological reflections. And we may guard against the excessive influence of this contextual dimension by frankly recognizing the existential genesis of the problems that we bring to our meditations on the meaning of the

Christ. There is, then, no question but that the biblical witness to Jesus as Christ is normative for Christology. We are not at liberty to construct a Christ out of our own untrammeled entelechy, based simply on our present needs as individuals and societies. We are not, for instance, at liberty to offer the message about Christ as though in its biblical form it were already apprised of present-day problems of the environment. Methodologically, the question is not whether the historical Jesus or those who recorded his words and deeds had been able to anticipate the twentieth-century need for a critical theology of nature. Rather, the question is whether the picture of Christ that we *are* given in the scriptures of Israel and the church is comprehensive and penetrating enough to "speak to" realities and concerns that under the conditions of history could not have been experienced by the biblical authors themselves.

To bring the matter to the point of our immediate concern: As a generation of Christians who obviously feel the need to acquire an understanding of the human-to-nature relationship that avoids some of the dangers of our Christian/Western past, may we, still adhering to the *sola Scriptura* of the Reformation, expect to discern in the Christ to whom this Scripture bears its unique and indispensable witness some concrete guidelines for our search? Without reading into the gospel records counsels that are not there and could not be there, and without making of Jesus either a St. Francis or a contemporary environmentalist, may we nevertheless look to this literary source and norm of our faith for an *imago Christi* that really does address our need for a better conception of the role of *Homo sapiens* within the natural order?

The response to this question that has been assumed in the foregoing is an affirmative one. The affirmation is based on two closely related claims: First, on the general conception of the nature of being that informs the tradition of Jerusalem, and, because it conceives of all being relationally, implies even when it does not always specify a relational conception of nature. Second, it is based on the characterization of *dominium* that is expressed through the biblical witness as a whole and made explicit in the person of Jesus. This exemplification of human dominion provides a critique of triumphalist anthropologics and at the same time offers an alternative model of the nature of dominion, which can and must be applied in our time to the relationship of the human with the nonhuman creation. Thus while the biblical testimony may not speak directly to our quest for an ecologically responsible theology of nature, it does present foundational beliefs that in the last analysis are more significant for that search than explicit ethical directives could have been.

VIII. IMAGING GOD/STEWARDING EARTH

"Let us make man in our image, after our likeness; and let them have dominion. . . . " Reading that ancient statement christologically (which to Christians who have renounced Marcionism must mean reading it in the full light of the theoanthropology of Israel), we are no longer tempted to anthropocentric hubris, as if we were being compared and contrasted with lesser creatures over whom we, like gods stalking the earth, might display our vain omnipotence. He whom we call *Dominus*, to whose *imago* we are being made conformable by a will not yet identical with our own, has taught and is teaching us to hear these words in a different way. As he represents for us a transvaluation of almost every other value our frenetic society teaches us to cherish — the values of possessing things, of achieving mastery, of acquiring preeminence among our peers, of winning — so with the same disconcerting logic he pulls us back from the false ambition of being nature's "lords and possessors" (Hobbes). A Lord who serves does not beget disciples who act like lordlings! "The rulers of the Gentiles lord it over them. . . . It shall not be so among you" (Mt. 20:25).

"Let us make man in our image, after our likeness; and let them have dominion. . . . " The One whom we, like so many tiny mirrors within the great light and dark of the creation, are to image is not *any* sort of being or principle to which the name of deity could be given. Looking over the history of our species and contemplating the bloody role of so much religion still today, we know all too well what the name of deity regularly stands for. The great bulk of the gods we have made in *our* image have one thing in common: the thirst for power. When they are called Moth and Moloch and Ba'al, we know that they are out for sheer supremacy; they want to consume us and our children — or to make of us the consumers of others. Unfortunately, we are not so clever about recognizing these power-hungry gods of human devising when they are named "Almighty God" or "dear heavenly Father" or . . . "Jesus Christ"! We hear these pious pseudonyms uncritically, assuming that the name alone suffices. But it should be said of these "Christian" gods as well as of the others: "By their fruits ye shall know them." How many meek souls has the "dear heavenly Father" consumed in his wrath? It is no wonder that when the devil appeared to Martin Luther, tempting him to hold onto a triumphalist gospel and an imperialist church, he showed up in the form of the crucified Christ! When we allow our theology, our Christology, and our pneumatology to be informed primarily by the power principle, can we really expect our anthropology to be informed by humility and service and love? "Be imitators of your father which is in heaven. . . . " And what if the "father in heaven" is Moloch in disguise?

But the one who is represented in Scripture as determining to make beings "in *our* image, after *our* likeness" is not Moloch, and not the "Almighty God" of imperial Christendom either. Power is not the name and the game of this God. Well, there may be power there —who will doubt that? But it is "weak" power, because it is the power of love.[48] It is the power of one who will not assert the will to be apart from the will to be-with the beloved. From the perspective of the power ideals of peoples and kingdoms seeking dominion wherever and however they can, it is a pathetic power, this omnipotence of the Crucified! What can the powerful of this world make of the dominion of a weeping Lord, a shepherd who lays down his life for the sheep, a donkey-riding king mocked, judged, and executed by the powers that were? And what would it mean for us to image the dominion of such a "king" in our life with the inarticulate creation?

There can be no exhaustive answer to that question, and above all, no hasty answer. In a real sense, the most important thing that could happen to Christianity in this connection would be to have to live with the question, to wait with the question. Without that waiting, we shall not know that it is no mere academic question; it is no question for which, with our long-established reputation for answering everything, we might find "an answer" without too much inconvenience to ourselves.

At any rate, the question is not put to us in an objective manner, politely, by a world desiring earnestly to know "the religious perspective" on nature. The question is flung at us, at our tradition, at our belief system. We stand accused. We are on trial. There are angry people in the court, and even the kindest amongst them are asking for an explanation—whether we might have said or done differently.

 . . . ecologists now call upon Christian theologians to change the old image of "subdue the earth." The history of the various religions' attitudes towards nature shows that no tradition has been a simon-pure friend of the earth, but it is Western technology that has set in motion the forces of modern pollution, and behind Western technology one finds an anthropocentrism that sees nature more exploitatively than Eastern systems do. Perhaps it can expand its sense of stewardship into an equivalent of a Taoist reverence for nature's Way, a Buddhist reverence for nature's Dharma. Until it starts along this path, however, many ecologists will consider biblical religion a foe of the earth, a blind guide that has helped bring spaceship earth close to ditching.[49]

It is tempting for Christians to become defensive in the face of this accusation, but it is better (not only wiser, but also more honest) to begin, as we have done in Chapter One, in a spirit of contrition, and to conduct ourselves as people who are becoming somewhat aware of their sins, particularly of their sins of omission.

What have we omitted in our understanding of the relationship between human being and extrahuman nature? Not with the thought of being exhaustive, but by way of suggesting a direction, I shall name three areas in which we have been negligent: the sacrificial element in the stewarding of nature; the preservational dimension in the stewardship of other forms of life; and the recognition of the spiritual element in matter.

The Sacrificial Element in the Stewardship of Nature. If dominion is defined for Christians by Jesus, then we cannot avoid the sacrificial element in the imaging of God into which, as Jesus' "body," we are being incorporated. Here and there during the last few decades, we have begun to recognize the implications of the theology of the Cross for the church: to be the church is to be a pilgrim people, to bear the marks of the Crucified, to enter into the pain of the world, especially of the world's victims. But where this teaching has been taken seriously in its application to this world (which is still unfortunately the exception to the rule), it has on the whole limited itself to the sacrificial life of the people of God in relation to other people.

Does the theology of the Cross have application for our way of being with the nonhuman creation as well? Are there, for instance, occasions when as human beings who are undergoing the *conformitas Christi* we are called to put other species and their survival before our own? We live in a society whose way of life has greatly accelerated the disappearance of plant and animal species and depleted the earth's natural resources. Not only are we a meat-eating people who consume far more calories daily than we need and waste untold quantities of the food prepared for us, but our system of production itself is sinfully extravagant. As long as it could be assumed that *Homo sapiens* belongs to an entirely different order of creation, raised to near-divinity by its special "endowments"; and as long as Christianity could seem not only to confirm this hierarchical conceptualization of life but even to be its spiritual and intellectual foundation — then the only truly serious question for faith was its responsibility for the survival of other human beings. But if the human species is to be regarded as serving an end greater than itself; and if to serve this end it exists in continuity and ontic solidarity with the other creatures of God; and if with respect to those other creatures it is called to behave with the kind of compassion and care revealed in Jesus as the Christ — then the survival of the others can no longer be a matter of indifference for Christians.

Certainly, the mere use of the others is ruled out. Grave questions are to be raised about the manipulation of other species through scientific and technical means. Above all, a dominion defined by sacrificial love will put this question to all within earshot of such a gospel: Can we be content with a social system that expects sacrifice only on the part of nonhuman species? And not only the sacrifice of individual members of these species, but of whole species — one per week? Is it really essential to our life that all these others must be sacrificed on the altar of our well-being? Do we really need newspapers, weekend editions of which consume hundreds of acres of prime forest? Is the quality of our life dependent on confronting, in our local supermarket, whole aisles filled with soaps and cleaning fluids bearing a hundred different brand names — products whose manufacture and use are polluting whole waterways and killing off ancient forms of life? Is "the great American steak religion" (Lappe) indispensable to our health of body and mind and soul? If we are tempted — for whatever reasons — to answer in the affirmative, we should consider what comes of a very large portion of what we claim absolutely to need — waste!

> Some idea of the magnitude of the problem can be gained from the calculation that North Americans throw away enough solid waste each year to build a wall 75 feet wide and 200 feet high along the Canada-U.S. border.[50]

To be sacrificed so that another might live — that is a logic Christians can perhaps understand; but to end up in the garbage, half-eaten, "almost new," the victim of built-in obsolescence?

Tolstoy wrote a famous short-story entitled "How much land does a man really need?" It is the kind of question that providence has been writing over Western civilization for a century. How much of "nature" is really needed to sustain human nature — to ensure a truly *human* life? There have been and still are societies that seem eminently human and do not require all of this, are perhaps human because they do not. They are not all that remote either. Here and there, where it has not been utterly demoralized by Euro-American patterns, the culture of the native peoples of this continent still provides living examples of being-with-nature that are perhaps more Christian than the "Christianity" that has decimated and demoralized those peoples. An ironic and painfully instructive illustration of the distinction between European and indigenous Canadian attitudes toward nature is provided — unintentionally — in the following excerpt from a 1913 primary school history text. The paragraph is headed "The Indians," a paragraph being all that this phase of Canadian history apparently warranted:

> All Indians were very superstitious, having strange ideas about nature. They thought that birds, beasts, and reptiles were like men. Thus an Indian has been known to make a long speech of apology to a wounded bear. They thought, too, that in lakes, rivers and water falls dwelt the spirits of living beings, and they strove to win the favour of these by means of gifts.

The author (presumably a Christian and therefore a believer in the divine Incarnation) goes on at once to link these "strange ideas" about nature with the religion of the native peoples:

> The Indian's idea of a Supreme Being was not a high one. When he tried to think of the One who made the world, he brought Him down to the level of a man. The Indian had no word to express the idea of God; the word Manitou meant anything which he thought of as having more than human power.

The little entry concludes with an oddly contradictory observation: "Such were the people whom the pioneers of our own race found lording it over the North American continent. [Considering the information immediately preceding this that the Indian population of the country was very sparse considering its geographic size, the term 'lording it over' seems somewhat out of place. But then the author proceeds, apparently without the benefit of self-knowledge, to designate the fate of these poor natives at the hands of those who really knew something about 'lording it over' their environment.] In his dealings with these intruders the Indian displayed two very marked characteristics: a love of freedom and a spirit of revenge. This untamed savage of the forest could not bring himself to submit to the restraints of European life; so, as the newcomers pushed inland from the Atlantic, he withdrew farther and farther west rather than part with his beloved freedom."[51]

Humbly reconsidered, the history and ways of the first peoples of this continent could still perhaps teach us something about the reciprocity of being—about being-with-nature. We are not, I think, in the desperate position of a species that is asked to sacrifice its existence for the survival of other species (though some of the more romantic of contemporary environmentalists appear to indulge this fantasy); but we are, certainly, in the position of a species that is asked to sacrifice much of what it evidently regards as being essential to its "way of life" for the sake of the others. But here too the saying is true that whoever loses his life shall find it. For it is by now evident not only that we shall jeopardize our own survival as a species through the befoulment of our environment, but that our survival shall be less than truly human if we are unable to discover a cooperative solidarity with other forms of life.

Stewardship as Participation in the Divine Preservation of Creation. The positive side of self-sacrifice is the preservation of the other. Jesus did not give up his life as if the renunciation of life were a good in itself (though some articulations of atonement theology come close to suggesting such a thing). Rather, he "lay down his life for his friends." There is here no celebration of life-denial, or even an ethical asceticism that intends to bridle the life force. Jesus' death is motivated by his quest for life, the life of those with whom he has made common cause. "I came that they might have life, and have it more abundantly."

It could hardly be otherwise, given the theology (doctrine of God) that the soteriology of the New Testament is obliged to presuppose as long as it maintains its Hebraic roots. The divine dominion of the world that expresses itself ultimately in the cross of Christ is a dominion that serves. Its object is the preservation of life. That is why it has always been impossible for any theology that took seriously the biblical witness to the divine sovereignty to separate it from the belief in divine providence (*providentia Dei*). God does not rule the universe (heteronomously) for his own sake, as One who has determined to exercise an absolute monarchy, come what may! God is "master of the universe" for the sake of the universe. In other words, God's sovereignty is a function of God's love. If God exercises dominion in the world, it is in order to preserve the creation against forces intrinsic to itself that, without this preservative work, would become destructive. Creation is not a once-for-all act, according to this tradition; once begun, the creative process must be purposely and continuously fostered (*creatio continua*).

All of this assumes that the creation is eminently worth conserving. So much is this an assumption in the tradition of Jerusalem that it is hardly necessary for our primary sources to belabor the point. Against all the isolated texts (e.g., I Jn. 2:15f.; Jas. 4:4) that can be adduced by those who would claim the contrary, it must always be pointed out that a religious tradition in which the energies of God are focused on the world as insistently as is the case with biblical faith can scarcely be thought otherworldly. Not only is this tradition not negative or neutral about this world; it presents us with the astonishing spectacle of a deity who is in love with the world. Its *Theos* is geocentric! The God whom it glorifies, as such glories in creation:

> May the glory of the Lord endure forever,
> may the Lord rejoice in his works.
>
> (Ps. 104:31)

Herein lies the reason that it cannot be claimed on the grounds of this tradition that the necessary corrective to an anthropocentric theology and ethic is an enhanced theocentrism. God's own glory being inseparable from the glory of what God has made, rightly to glorify God is at the same time to become newly conscious of the glory of God's creation. The simultaneity of faith's awareness of divine and created glory is repeatedly expressed in the Scripture:

> 'Holy, holy, holy is the Lord of hosts;
> the whole earth is full of his glory.'
>
> (Is. 6:3)

It is the subject of the angelic song heralding the birth of the Christ:

> Glory to God in the highest,
> and on earth peace among men
> with whom he is pleased.
>
> (Luke 2:14)

To glorify God is to be engaged in a concrete spirituality that refuses to draw marked distinctions between sacred and secular, contemplation and deed, theology and ethics. For this tradition, a theocentrism that does not contain a concomitant geocentrism is unthinkable; and if some forms of Christianity have indeed erred on the side of a too exclusive anthropocentricity, this is not to be judged as totally unwarranted but rather as an exaggeration of the Bible's own theo-anthropology. As Irenaeus said, "The glory of God is humanity fully alive."

Indeed, if we faithfully follow the lead of the relational ontology that informs this religious tradition, we shall have to conclude that centering faith exclusively in any one of the three counterparts of our being would constitute a misapplication of the tradition. A faith that is theocentric is at the same time anthropocentric and geocentric. These are not to be regarded as alternative foci for the believing community but as interdependent spheres of faith's concentration. For it would be impossible for a faith that concentrates on this God to avoid what this God is concentrating on.

The preservational dimension of biblical theology is thus not just one dogmatic theme among others; it is in a real sense the gospel *in nuce*. This gospel opens us to the contemplation of a God bent on the healing and fulfillment of creation. And rightly to contemplate this preserving God—rightly to glorify God—is to be made participants in God's own preserving work. We image God as we are incorporated through grace and faith into the preservational dominion of God in the world. Or, to state the same thing in other words, we mirror the sovereignty of the divine love in our stewardship of earth.

This lifts Christian stewardship well beyond the confines of a pragmatic ethic. The motivation for our stewardly acts of preservation, as Christians, is not merely utilitarian (as when, for example, it is said that human beings need to preserve forests because we ourselves, or future generations of our kind, are going to need the forests). Rather, as preservers and conservers of all life, we have our commission as a sacred trust that inheres in our new identity—or, more accurately, this old identity into which we are newly born through grace and repentance. We are preservers because the creation is intrinsically good, and we are being delivered from the kind of egotism that is able to find goodness only in what is useful to ourselves.

"Until men come to believe in their hearts that all life is held in trust from God . . . there can be no valid ethical reason why we should owe a duty to posterity. Once it is believed that men hold their dominion over all nature as stewards and trustees for God, then immediately they are confronted by an inalienable duty towards and concern for their total environment, present and future; and this duty towards environment does not merely include their fellow-men, but all nature and all life." [Hugh Montefiore]. Dr. [René] Dubos speaks in very similar terms: "We must now take to heart the biblical teaching 'The Lord God took the man and put him into the Garden of Eden to dress it and to tend it. . . . ' This means not only that the earth has been given to us for our enjoyment, but also that it has been entrusted to our care. Technicized societies thus far have exploited the earth: we must reverse this trend and learn to take care of it with love."[52]

"Man," counsels Dostoevsky's Father Zosima, "love the animals. . . . Do not pride yourself on your superiority to the animals, they are without sin."[53] Only when human pride has been chastened by the knowledge of our distortion of our own creaturely status is it possible for us to have some share in God's own joy in the creation. When self-preservation gives way to the preservation of a world that is larger than self and larger than our own kind, we may begin to image God's dominion in our stewardship of that world.

Recognizing the Spiritual Element in Matter. The corollary of the statement that human being is being-with-nature is the recognition that nature, from its side, has a capacity for relatedness.

Earth's relationship to men is not that of a dead mass to living beings; the earth is partner in a covenant relationship which is not invariably dominated from the human side. . . . Man and earth are a psychic community; they are the constituents of personal life.

"If my land has cried out against me,
　and its furrows have wept together;
if I have eaten its yield without payment,
　and caused the death of its owners;
let thorns grow instead of wheat,
　and foul weeds instead of barley." (Job 31:38–40)[54]

A theology that takes seriously the relational character of all that is

cannot conceive of "the material world" as though it were totally devoid of spirit—as though it were simply "it"! Martin Buber was not
giving vent to a cryptic nature-romanticism, but was accurately
deducing the implications of this relational ontology of our tradition
when he insisted on the "thou" quality of nature.

> I consider a tree.
> I can look on it as a picture. . . .
> I can perceive it as movement. . . .
> I can classify it in a species. . . .
> I can dissipate it and perpetuate it. . . .
> In all this the tree remains my object. . . .
>
> It can, however, also come about, if I have both will and grace,
> that in considering the tree I become bound up in relation to it.
> The tree is now no longer It. I have been seized by the power of
> exclusiveness.
>
> To effect this it is not necessary for me to give up any of the
> ways in which I consider the tree . . . structure, colors and
> chemical composition. . . .
>
> The tree is no impression, no play of my imagination, no
> value depending on my mood; but it is bodied over against me
> and has to do with me, as I with it—only in a different way.[55]

Why is it that Christians, particularly Protestant Christians,
have so seldom felt or expressed this strange mystery and "power of
exclusiveness" in all that is? It has frequently been remarked, of
course, that Protestantism generally is peculiarly one-dimensional.
Few among us seem capable of finding spirit and mystery even in
other human beings. But the typical Protestant, especially the male
of the species, is actually embarrassed by any discussion of the world
in sacramental terms. This mentality views venturing out beyond
the safe bounds of utilitarianism and the "thingification" of nature
with great suspicion. One may grant that this suspicion is due in part
to the antithetical phenomenon—also visible in the Protestant
ethos—of an affected sentimentality with regard to the natural
world. Still, should one not wonder that a religion has come to be
on the face of the earth that, in contradistinction to the great majority of human religions, is able to view worldly life as such, including
its own life, in so detached a manner?

This is to be explained partly by the marriage of Protestantism
with the spirit of modernity. After all, the two grew up together!
Capitalism gave us the final statement of the illusion of possession,

and empiricism enabled us to regard and analyze "things" as though they had no soul, no *nephesh*.[56] Yet it is ironic that, while so many Protestants languish in a state of incipient naturalism, significant numbers of those who are the tutored inheritors of the "scientific" approach to reality that was engendered by modernity have redis-covered the numinous. They have, as it were, gone far enough into the heart of *matter* to discern spirit.[57] One of these latter writes:

> I have had the vague word "mystic" applied to me because I have not been able to shut out wonder occasionally, when I have looked at the world. I have been lectured by at least one member of my profession who advised me to "explain myself" — words which sound for all the world like a humorless request for the self-accusations so popular in Communist lands.[58]

The same author calls nature "the one great hieroglyph."[59]

The Protestant ascription of mystery to God tended, together with the impact of modern secularity, to rob God's creation of its mystery. But there was an older Protestantism that did not take that route and, wherever it has been imaginatively grasped, has con-tinued to engender *Ehrfurcht vor dem Leben* ("awe before life" or "reverence for life").[60] I mean the Protestantism of Luther. It would be a good thing if Protestants reared on the leavings of a rationalized Calvinism and a pragmatized Wesleyanism could return to the class-room at Wittenberg. Luther, for reasons that are as obscure as they are fascinating, never was touched by the bug of humanism that stung both Calvin and Zwingli, and introduced strangely un-Lu-theran nuances into the Lutheran reform through the ministrations of Philip Melanchthon. I suspect that Luther was utterly perplexed by Erasmus. For while he was infinitely beyond the superstitions of late medieval ecclesiastical life, Luther remained at heart a mystic. He found the more "reasoned" approaches of his associates flat, though he perhaps admired Master Philip, as intuitive persons often admire the more meticulous. In the famous colloquy at Marburg, he had, one guesses, no idea of what Huldreich Zwingli was talking about. It was, I think, one of those conversations where the words of each fly past the other. For Zwingli, the more Modern man, bread was bread; for Luther, bread — even in its unconsecrated state — was brimful of theological meaning, was "our daily bread"! *Finitum capax infiniti*. Nature does not resist grace, only human nature does. And above all, human nature at its most promethean, its most "rational," its most willful.

Having followed the rationalist and voluntarist dimensions of the Protestant Reformation into the labyrinthine darkness of the technological society, we are perhaps at last in a position to reconsider Protestantism's mystical roots — and thus the submerged forms of Catholic Christianity as well, such as that of Francis. One thing seems clear: we shall not be ready to assume a different posture over against the natural order until we have explored the capacity of matter for spirit, that "Spirit and matter are not dichotomized but are the inside and outside of the same thing."[61] We can envision our existence as being "with" nature only if we are able to think that nature, from its side, is capable of being "with" us — though "in a different way" (Buber).

IX. HOMO LOQUENS: REPRESENTATIVE CREATUREHOOD

The rabbinic tradition of Israel recounts a tale about the creation of the world. Having completed creating everything in five days, the Creator asked one of the attending angels whether anything were still missing. The angel answered that everything was, of course, perfect, as one might expect of God's own handiwork. "Yet perhaps," the angel ventured, "perhaps one thing could make this already perfect work yet more perfect: speech, to praise its perfection." God thereupon approved the angel's words and created the human creature.

In this creature the inarticulate (though never silent) creation becomes articulate. In this creature the creation, which goes quietly on its way, following by pattern and instinct its God-given destiny, finds a voice. Here the perfection God has made rises to give utterance to itself — in language, but also in song, in art, in symbol; in words, but also in the complex and interwoven thoughts behind the words; in concepts, but also in story, and in the music that begins where conceptualizing must leave off. In this creature the speaking God, *Deus loquens*, locates a counterpart within the *saeculum*, a speaking animal. Here the creation gathers itself and addresses the One whose glorious Word brought it into being, word answering Word.

But this is the point: the speaking creature does not answer for itself alone. It is the whole creation that finds a voice in *Homo loquens*. The creation that, quite apart from this work of the sixth day, is already perfect! Now this perfection grows vocal. It cannot contain itself. Like the prophet Jeremiah, it must let the word be formed. All being finds its voice in the human. This creature, which on the one hand mirrors God's care for all God's creatures, now turns again to its Creator and speaks representatively for them all.

And when it is being true to itself and to all of those whose priest it is, there is only one thing that it ultimately expresses — though with infinite variations on the theme. And that one thing is *gratitude*.

"I have been fortunate in many ways," says a great scientist of our time, now an old man, in what can be accounted a modern psalm of thanksgiving:

> I have been fortunate . . . and have been able to see many wonders of the world. I like everything about the world. . . . I like the mesons and the hadrons, and the electrons and the protons and the neutrons; and the atoms, the molecules; the microorganisms, the plants and animals; the minerals: the zunyite and cuprite, the pyrite and marcasite and andalusite, and all the other minerals; the oceans and the mountains, and the forests; the stars and the nebulae and the "black holes" out there; the "Big Bang" eighteen billion years ago. I like all of it.
>
> I like satisfying my intellectual curiosity. As a scientist I have been fortunate to have been aware of what has been done during the last seventy-eight years. Every month I read about something new and interesting about the universe that some scientist has discovered. Such as what it was that caused the extinction of the dinosaurs sixty-four million years ago. It is really wonderful, the world, and one wonderful part about it is that there are sentient beings here who are able to appreciate the wonders of the world, to understand them!
>
> So I feel that we have a duty to try and prevent the nuclear war, to reverse this situation. I believe that it can be done. Otherwise I wouldn't be here. Why should I waste my time if the effort is not going to be successful? I might as well be enjoying myself, making some quantum mechanical calculations! So I really believe that we can win out, that we can stop this irrational trend to our self-destruction.[62]

Notes

INTRODUCTION

1. *Who Is Man?* (Stanford: Stanford University Press, 1968), pp. 7–8.

2. They also eat " . . . 250,000 pounds of lobster, four million pounds of bacon, 170 million eggs, 12 million chickens, 1.2 million bushels of potatoes, 11,465 miles of licorice twists, 95 tons of sardines, 6.5 million gallons of popcorn, 400,000 gallons of canned corn, 90,000 bushels of fresh carrots, 1.7 million pounds of cheese, 19 million gallons of milk, 1.5 million pounds of lard and 23 million gallons of soft drinks.

"They distribute their remaining wealth to the tune of $40 million for prostitution, $12,000 on dental floss, $700 million on entertainment and recreation in general, $2.5 million on washing their cars, $40 million on automobile repairs, $200 million on advertising, $14.3 million on lottery tickets, and $165 million on charity." Statistics quoted from a book by Tom Parker, *In One Day: The Things Americans Do*, published by Houghton Mifflin; quoted in *The Toronto Globe and Mail*, 10 January 1985.

3. Frances Moore Lappe, *Diet for a Small Planet* (rev. ed.; New York: Ballantine Books, 1975). Note that the figure, seven pounds of feed for one pound of meat, includes the (relatively) high "converters," especially poultry. With beef the figure is much more startling: "Today an average steer is able to reduce sixteen pounds of grain and soy to one pound of meat on our plates. The other fifteen pounds? It becomes inaccessible to us, for it is either used by the animal to produce energy or to make some part of its own body that we do not eat (like hair), or it is lost entirely in manure." (All references are taken from Part I of Ms. Lappe's study, provocatively entitled "Earth's Labor Lost," pp. 3ff.)

4. The reference is to the famous prayer of Reinhold Niebuhr: "Give me the serenity to accept the things that cannot be changed, the courage to change what can be changed, and the wisdom to know the difference between them."

5. *God's Unfolding Purpose* (Philadelphia: Westminster Press, 1957), p. 23.

6. Joseph Sittler, "A Theology for Earth," *The Christian Scholar*, 37 (Mar. 1954):369.

7. George P. Grant, "The Computer Does Not Impose on Us the Ways it Should be Used," in *Beyond Industrial Growth*, Abraham Rotstein, ed. (Toronto: University of Toronto Press, 1976), p. 131.

8. The distinction is Ulrich Simon's in *Sitting in Judgement 1913–1963: An Interpretation of History* (London: S.P.C.K., 1978), p. 69.

9. Philadelphia: The Westminster Press, 1981, p. 12.

10. *The McGill Daily*, 11 February 1985.

11. The Canadian Broadcasting Corporation's *Ideas* series devoted three programs to "The Rise of the Citizen Scientist" in January 1985; see CBC *Radio Guide* (Jan. 1985):27.

12. *The Two Cultures: And A Second Look*, an expanded version of *The Two Cultures and the Scientific Revolution* (Toronto: New American Library of Canada Limited, A Mentor Book, 1964), p. 27.

13. Quoted by Richard E. Wenz in "The American Spirituality of Loren Eiseley," *The Christian Century* (Apr. 25, 1984):430.

14. The names of persons like René Dubos, Paul Ehrlich, Barbara Ward, K. E. F. Watt, Michael Polanyi, E. F. Schumacher, Barry Commoner, Robert Lifton, Linus Pauling, and many others come to mind.

15. Reinhold Niebuhr, *The Nature and Destiny of Man*, I (New York: Charles Scribner's Sons, 1953), 16–17.

16. *Political Theology*, trans. John Shelley (Philadelphia: Fortress Press, 1971), p. 89.

17. See Allen O. Miller, ed., *Christian Declaration on Human Rights* (Grand Rapids: William B. Eerdmans Publishing Company, 1977).

18. Fully 80 percent of all trips in Canada are made by automobile, and Canadian cars (according to the CBC) pollute three times as much as do U.S. cars.

19. See *Consumer Society Notes*, 1 (Dec. 1975):2 (published by the Science Council of Canada).

20. The Canadian figures are less impressive. According to the United Church *Observer* (new series, vol. 48, no. 8, 20), "A poll taken recently in Canada, asking over 1000 people if organized religion was a relevant part of their lives, found that only 44 percent replied 'yes.' That is down four percent from six years ago, when a similar poll was conducted. The same poll asked people if they had attended church or synagogue in the last seven days: 36 percent said yes." At the same time, "belief in God" is still high in Canada: 87 percent according to the Montreal *Gazette* of Sept. 12, 1985.

21. *U.S. News and World Report* (November 4, 1985):70.

22. In this connection, see Reinhold Niebuhr, *Moral Man and Immoral Society* (New York: Charles Scribner's Sons, 1932/1960), ch. III.

23. The religious right on this continent has grasped this necessity in a way that more liberal Christian bodies have not. But because the right champions "old-fashioned belief" as a weapon against the present rather than a way of engaging present problems, it both fails to achieve the potential of prophetic faith for producing a genuinely political theology, and ends by providing religious sanction to reactionary social forces that are partly responsible for the problems in question.

24. *The Steward: A Biblical Symbol Come of Age* (New York: Friendship Press, 1982).

25. Paul Ricoeur, *History and Truth*, trans. Charles A. Kelbley (Evanston: Northwestern University Press, 1965), p. 110.

CHAPTER ONE

1. *Ethics*, ed. Eberhard Bethge (London: S.C.M. Press, 1955), p. 332.

2. *The Arms Race Kills: Even Without War*, trans. Gerhard A. Elston, (Philadelphia: Fortress Press, 1981), p. 26.

3. "It is in the modern technological civilization — in the West and more particularly in the United States — that the difficulties have become most acute" (Claude Y. Stewart, *Nature in Grace* [Macon, GA: Mercer University Press, 1983], p. 40).

4. Allan Boesak's speech at the 75th Anniversary Conference of the National Urban League, Washington, D.C. on July 23, 1985, is in its totality a moving documentation of the hope of so many Christians and others in Third World contexts that within this First World they might hear echoes of their own struggle for liberation against forces that are backed — or at least not seriously challenged — by our own societies and their institutions.

5. "Many of the deepest roots of America's dilemma before nature are religious . . . " (Paul Santmire, quoted by Stewart, *Nature in Grace*, p. 40).

6. This essay first appeared in written form in *Science*, 155 (Mar. 10, 1967):1203–1207.

7. Frank Fraser Darling, Reith Lecture #3, 1969; reprinted in *The Listener*, Nov. 27, 1969.

8. *Ecology and Human Liberation: A Theological Critique of the Use and Abuse of Our Birthright* (Geneva: a W.S.C.F. book, vol. III, no. 1, 1973, serial no. 7), p. 19; see also John B. Bennett, "On Responding to Lynn White: Ecology and Christianity," *Ohio Journal of Religious Studies* 5, 1 (Apr. 1977):71ff.

9. *Lighten Our Darkness: Towards an Indigenous Theology of the Cross* (Philadelphia: Westminster Press, 1976).

10. I am in full agreement with the conclusion reached by H. Paul Santmire in a recent article, "The Liberation of Nature: Lynn White's Challenge Anew" (*The Christian Century*, 102 [May 22, 1985]:530ff.). Santmire writes: "Although White has raised a number of sharp historical questions, few of which have been fully blunted by his critics, the deepest significance of his thesis seems to lie not so much in what it describes as in what it prescribes or envisions: the end of the theological legitimization of any structure of domination; the challenging of all master–slave relationships; the final inclusion of all creatures of nature within the realm of grace; the normative vindication of St. Francis and his life story; and the adoption of

the Pauline theology of universal liberation that Francis so compellingly exemplified. Thanks largely to Lynn White, the liberation of nature is now unavoidably before us as a theological theme."

11. The criticism predates White's article. Claude Stewart notes: "The view, which was the academic fashion during the sixties, that the blame for the desecration of nature in the West is to be attributed to the Judeo-Christian tradition, appears to have been promulgated around 1950 by the Zen Buddhist scholar Daisetz Susuki. But it was Lynn White's article which gave the thesis notoriety" (*op. cit.*, p. 16.).

12. *Doing Theology in a Revolutionary Situation* (Philadelphia: Fortress Press, 1975), p. xxvi.

13. Christopher Derrick, *The Delicate Creation: Towards a Theology of the Environment* (Old Greenwich, Conn.: The Devin-Adair Company, 1972), p. 74.

14. Lynn White Jr. himself believed this to be the appropriate route. He proposed that Christians and Westerners influenced by biblical religion consider, as an alternative to the mastery of nature, the Christian model embodied by Francis of Assisi. See n. 10 above, and Claude Y. Stewart's discussion of White's proposal, in *Nature in Grace*, pp. 17ff.

15. For another discussion of Christian attitudes toward nature, see John Carmody, *Ecology and Religion: Towards a New Christian Theology of Nature* (New York: Paulist Press, 1983), esp. ch. 8, pp. 116ff.

16. A careful and provocative treatment of the theology of nature in both Testaments is offered by H. Paul Santmire, *The Travail of Nature: The Ambiguous Ecological Promise of Christian Theology* (Philadelphia: Fortress Press, 1980). More detailed discussion of this is given in the final chapter of the present study, pp. 167ff.

17. Santmire, *Travail*; J. Christiaan Beker, *Paul the Apostle: The Triumph of God in Life and Thought* (Philadelphia: Fortress Press, 1980).

18. Santmire, *Travail*, pp. 212–215.

19. In quoting Paul in this connection, I do not wish to challenge the thesis of Santmire, who (with Beker) finds Paul compatible with an ecological and "somatic" interpretation of salvation as distinct from the spiritualistic bent of Johannine and other New Testament literature. My purpose here is simply to establish that the language of Scripture frequently suggests a negative impression of the world as such.

20. Hal Lindsey, champion of the idea of "the Rapture"—a bodily ascension of true believers into heaven, just before the final tribulation that obliterates all life on earth—concludes his book on the subject with these words: "Although I grieve over the lost world that is headed toward catastrophe, the hope of the rapture keeps me from despair" (*The Rapture* [Bantam Books, 1983]: p. 176). See my *Christian Mission: The Stewardship of Life in the Kingdom of Death* (New York: Friendship Press, 1985), 2nd meditation, part 3: "The Religion of Death Behind the Politics of Death," pp. 36ff.

21. Christopher Derrick uses the idea of Manichaeanism to describe the attitude that says we are trapped in an evil world. He thinks this may even be majority opinion. "The Manichaeans — strictly so called — flourished chiefly in the fourth century: for a time they held the allegiance of the great St. Augustine, and he never entirely shook off their influence. But there is a great deal in common between their view of life and that held by the second-century Gnostics, the medieval Catharists and Albigensians, and the countless similar groups that emerge at intervals in the light of history. . . . Throughout much of European history, such groups constituted a substantial religious underworld. . . .

"Manichaeanism (in our broader sense of the word) has thus been present, as an alternative and rival to official Catholicism, throughout practically the whole history of the Christian West — at least, up to the time of the Reformation. . . .

"De-mythologized, the Manichaean view of the universe starts off with something very simple and familiar — the sense of living in a hostile environment; the vague nostalgic feeling that we are not really at home here, but belong elsewhere; the experience of this world as an alien place into which man has strayed and from which he may find his way back home to the other world of his origin"(*The Delicate Creation*, pp. 35ff.).

22. *The Story of a Soul*, trans. John Beevers (Garden City, NY:Image Book Edition, 1957), p. 154.

23. *Ibid.*

24. *On the Imitation of Christ*, trans. Abbott Justin McCann (New York: New American Library, a Mentor Religious Classic, 1957), pp. 58–59.

25. *Ibid.*, pp. 44–45.

26. *Christian Faith: An Introduction to the Study of the Faith*, trans. Sierd Woudstra (Grand Rapids: Eerdmans Publishing Company, 1979), pp. 499–500.

27. *Interpreter's Dictionary of the Bible: An Illustrated Encyclopaedia* (New York: Abingdon Press), p. 857.

28. Students of the New Testament especially (one thinks of Krister Stendahl, James Barr, E. P. Sanders, and others) have helped us appreciate the Judaic background of the Gospels and Epistles, which are still read by the majority of Christians under the influence of essentially non-Hebraic and often blatantly anti-Hebraic preconceptions, such as the inferiority of matter, the soul's "immortality," the utter vanity of historical existence, etc.

29. Sensitive Christian thinkers such as Reinhold Niebuhr, Franklin H. Littell, Robert McAfee Brown, and many others have themselves been deeply altered in their perception of the faith through their meditation on the Christian causation of the Holocaust. This meditation achieves a particularly poignant as well as scholarly summation, in my view, in Rosemary R. Reuther's *Faith and Fratricide: The Theological Roots of Anti-Semitism* (New

York: The Seabury Press, 1974), with a fine introduction by Roman Catholic theologian Gregory Baum.

30. See Philip Culbertson, "The Pharisaic Jesus and His Gospel Parables," *The Christian Century* 102, 3 (Jan. 23, 1985):74ff. The author concludes his article with these words: "Christians have only begun to understand the import of the scandalous particularity of Jesus' Jewishness, and the material remains extremely difficult to preach in local congregations. But if the church is to proclaim its understanding of God's revelation in Christ, the Prince of Peace, in a manner which does not promote bitterness and hatred, persecution and pogrom, then it must learn to let Scripture speak for itself as a Jewish document. God humbled himself in Christ, taking the form of a Pharisaic Jew, teaching an exciting renewal of the covenant between God and his bride, his vineyard Israel. The Christian tradition's anti-Jewish motif perpetuates violence against the choices God made in the Incarnation."

31. In this connection, see John Carmody's discussion "Traditional Theological Doctrines," in *Ecology and Religion*, pp. 100ff.

32. Berkhof, *Christian Faith*, p. 503.

33. *Ibid.*

34. Berkhof provides a suggestive discussion of these "exceptions" (*Ibid.*, pp. 503ff.).

35. Ed. John Macquarrie (London: S.C.M. Press, 1967), the article on "Worldliness," pp. 363–364.

36. London: S.C.M. Press, 1966, p. 459.

37. I should like to distinguish the "symbolic figure" from merely prominent persons, whether in ecclesiastical government, theology, or other areas of Christian endeavor. By symbolic figure I mean what other ages may have meant by "saint," i.e., a person in whom the special genius of the faith as it expresses itself concretely with a given historical context is particularly luminous.

38. Quoted by Vernon Sproxton in *Teilhard de Chardin* (Naperville, IL: S.C.M. Book Club, 1971), p. 46.

39. *Christian Faith*, p. 500.

40. See Harvey Cox, *The Secular City* (New York: The Macmillan Co., 1965).

41. *Is It Too Late? A Theology of Ecology* (Beverly Hills: Bruce, 1971), p. 122. "Secular atheism," writes Cobb, "is involved in the technological attitude. It is suited to the efficient achievement of arbitrary ends. The ends are usually set by a society that is still largely humanistic or nationalistic. . . . We cannot return to humanism even though it continues to be pervasively influential. Its internal instability is now too obvious. In any case, its separation of man from his world is just what we do not want. We need a new, inclusive commitment that will direct our concern to the subhuman world as well as to man, and that will guide and sustain intelligent action through thick and thin" (pp. 122–123).

42. As Barth in all of his writings has insisted, atheism means literally *a-theos*: being-without-God. It should not, therefore, be assumed that it always takes the militant and bragging form associated with its nineteenth-century American advocates like Robert Ingersoll. In fact, in our time atheists show up more consistently in the guise of those who are mourning the loss of the transcendent dimension.

43. Since religion is the opiate of the people, Marx went on to say, "the abolition of religion as the illusory happiness of the people is required for their real happiness." ("Contributions to the Critique of Hegel's Philosophy of Right," in *On Religion*, 2nd ed. (New York: Shocken Books, 1967), p. 42.

44. Before the Oxford Union on June 19, 1985, defending the proposition: "This house believes that current economic policy has been socially divisive."

45. *Christian Faith*, p. 505.

46. Certainly in this respect at least, process theology offers a viable and evocative alternative to the tradition. See Cobb's discussion of Whitehead's "ecological philosophy" in *Is It Too Late?* (esp. pp. 111–115).

47. *Christian Faith*, p. 506.

48. This is also the argument presented by Gordon Kaufman in his *Theology for a Nuclear Age* (Philadelphia: Westminster Press, 1985): " . . . in the religious eschatology of the West the end of history is pictured quite differently than we today must face it. For it is undergirded by faith in an active creator and governor of history, one who from the beginning was working out purposes which were certain to be realized as history moved to its consummation. The end of history, therefore—whether viewed as ultimate catastrophe or ultimate salvation—was to be God's climactic act. A consummation of this sort was something that the faithful could live with—even look forward to with hope—for it would be the moment when God's final triumph over all evil powers was accomplished.

"In contrast, the end of history which we in the late twentieth century must contemplate—an end brought about by nuclear holocaust—must be conceived primarily not as God's doing but as ours" (pp. 3–4).

Commenting on Kaufman's statement, John Coleman Bennett writes: "An end of history that humanity brings on itself would produce such intense human suffering on so vast a scale that it is the height of callousness to try to belittle it. More important, when we consider how short the conscious history of humanity has been, how short the period of its spiritual, moral and cultural achievements on this planet, a self-inflicted early end of the human adventure would be an unbelievable tragedy. *It would be a defeat of God's own purposes*." (From a paper delivered to the American Academy of Religion meeting at Anaheim, California, Nov. 1985 (italics added). An earlier version of Professor Bennett's paper appeared in *The Christian Century* 102, 19 (May 29, 1985), under the title "Divine Persuasion and Divine Judgment." The expanded version presented at Anaheim was entitled "Christian Hope in the Face of the Possibility of Nuclear War.")

49. Carmody, p. 150.

50. *Ibid.*, p. 132.

51. This is the stand that has been taken, for instance, by the Moderamen of the Reformed (Calvinist) Church in West Germany. To declare something a *status confessionis* is to say that it is implicit within the Christian confession of belief in God.

52. The theme of the Sixth Assembly of the World Council of Churches, meeting in Vancouver in 1985, can sound innocuous and simply "pious" unless the last three words are emphasized.

53. Global theology should not be understood as antithetical to contextual theology. It is not as if one had a choice between being concretely engaged with our own immediate sociohistorical milieu or, on the other hand, being concerned for "the whole earth." It is a matter of both/and—and the one through and because of the other. Faith's world-consciousness prevents contextualized theologies from becoming mere religious situationalism; and the fact that I must be intimately involved with "my own" (e.g., with Quebec, Canada, the First World, etc.) prevents my more global orientation from degenerating into the kind of universalism that has no particular focus and therefore functions, in all likelihood, as a theoretical escape from the world. (See my article "On Contextuality in Christian Theology," *Toronto Journal of Theology* 1, 1 (Spring 1985):3ff.

54. Sittler, "A Theology for Earth," p. 374.

55. E.g.: "How much more are we bound to call God the founder of nature; for he does not create from material which he himself did not make. . . . And if he were to withdraw what we may call his constructive power from existing things, they would cease to exist; just as they did not exist before they were made" (*The City of God* [Penguin Press], bk. xii, ch. 26, 506).

56. E.g.: "In short it [the carnal mind] imagines that all things are sufficiently sustained by energy divinely infused into them at first. But faith must penetrate deeper . . . it must infer that He is also a Governor and Preserver . . . by special providence sustaining and cherishing all things which He has made . . . even to the sparrow" (*Institutes of the Christian Religion*, bk. I, ch. xvi).

57. *Ibid.*, bk. III, ch. xxi.

58. See Paul Tillich, *Systematic Theology*, vol. II (Chicago: University of Chicago Press, 1951), 83–86, as well as other references throughout this work.

59. *A Theology for the Social Gospel* (New York & Nashville: Abingdon Press, 1917), p. 179. In another place, Rauschenbusch writes: "Every human life is so placed that it can share with God in the creation of the Kingdom. . . . The kingdom is for each of us the supreme task" (*ibid.*, p. 141). Shailer Matthews, in *The Social Teaching of Jesus* (New York: Macmil-

lan, 1906, p. 181), writes: "If now, we attempt more positively to set forth those primary forces upon which Jesus counted for the accomplishment of his ideals we are forced back upon his fundamental conception of the nature of men. Jesus trusts in the inherent powers and capacities of the race . . . men with whom he associated and out of whom he hoped for his kingdom."

In a similar vein, the Canadian founder of the socialist party, the C.C.F. (later the N.D.P.), J. S. Woodsworth, a Methodist minister and theologian, writes: "If Christianity would now add its moral force to the social and economic forces making for a nobler organization of society, it could render such help to the cause of justice . . . as would make this a proud page in history" (*My Neighbour* [Toronto: Clark Stephenson, 1911], p. 335).

60. See Grant's *Philosophy in the Mass Age* (Toronto: The Copp Clark Publishing Company, Ltd., 1966).

61. See Sydney E. Ahlstrom, *A Religious History of the American People* (Garden City: Image Books, 1975), I, 34; Sydney E. Mead refers to the idea of inevitable progress that gripped the U.S.A. in the nineteenth century as standing on "a teleological escalator" (*The Lively Experiment: The Shaping of Christianity in America* [New York: Harper and Row, 1963], p. 145).

62. See Reinhold Niebuhr, *The Irony of American History* (New York: Charles Scribner's Sons, 1952), esp. ch. 4, "The Master of Destiny." Niebuhr writes: "Among us, as well as among communists, an excessive voluntarism which finally brings human history under the control of the human will is in tentative, but not in final, contradiction to a determinism which finds historical destiny favorable at some particular point to man's assumption of mastery over that destiny" (p. 72).

63. John Cobb, *Is It Too Late?* p. 35.

64. *Ibid.*, p. 33.

65. Eberhard Jüngel, *God as the Mystery of the World*, trans. Darrell L. Guder (Grand Rapids: Eerdmans, 1983).

66. See my memorial lecture, "John Wyclif: The Reformation That Did Not Come Off . . . Yet!" given at Wycliffe College, University of Toronto, Nov. 1984 (to be published).

67. "Autonomy and heteronomy are rooted in theonomy, and each goes astray when their theonomous unity is broken. Theonomy does not mean the acceptance of a divine law imposed on reason by a highest authority; it means autonomous reason united with its own depth. In a theonomous situation reason actualizes itself in obedience to its structural laws and in the power of its own inexhaustible ground. Since God (*theos*) is the law (*nomos*) for both the structure and the ground of reason, they are united in him, and their unity is manifest in a theonomous situation" (Tillich, *Systematic Theology*, vol. I, 85).

68. Trans. Ronald Gregor Smith (Edinburgh: T. & T. Clark, 1937 etc.), p. 7.

69. Feminist theology has explored the nuances of this association of

sin with "the flesh" much more rigorously and imaginatively than has been done in the past, even by very perceptive male theologians. See, e.g., Rosemary Radford Ruether, *Sexism and God Talk: Toward a Feminist Theology* (Boston: Beacon Hill Press, 1983), esp. ch. 3, "Woman, Body and Nature: Sexism and the Theology of Creation."

70. *Ibid*, see the introduction, pp. 14–15.

71. See his book by this title (New York: Harper and Row, 1973).

72. It was, I think, Rachel Carson's *The Silent Spring* (Boston: Houghton Mifflin, 1962) that signaled for many in North America the beginnings of this new consciousness.

73. The counterculture of the 1960s and early 1970s has in important respects influenced all of us, even though as a movement it now seems a rather pathetic or failed attempt to stem the tide of a burgeoning and dehumanizing technocratic society.

74. Robertson Jeffers, "Signpost," in *Not Man Apart: Lines from Robertson Jeffers* (Sierra Club: Balantine Books, 1970), p. 100.

75. See "Canada's Vanishing Forests," *MacLean's* 98 (Jan. 14, 1985): 36ff.: "Last year, the Science Council of Canada declared: 'We have allowed the forests to degenerate to a dangerous point. We have been felling, selling and shipping timber for so long that today a $23-billion industry is facing economic stagnation' " (p. 37).

CHAPTER TWO

1. See his *Dynamics of Faith* (New York: Harper & Bros. Publishers, 1957), ch. III ("Symbols of Faith").

2. Macquarrie believes that Tillich's distinction between sign and symbol does not hold in the English language because we sometimes use the term "sign" to refer to intrinsic connections between things, which Tillich reserves for the meaning of the symbol (Macquarrie's example: "Clouds are a sign of rain"). I confess to find this a rather strained argument, and rather believe that Tillich's distinction makes eminent sense both in English and in German. (See *Principles of Christian Theology* [London: S.C.M. Press, 1966], p. 123.)

3. David Cairns, *The Image of God in Man* (London: S.C.M. Press Ltd., 1953), pp. 73ff. For example, Irenaeus uses the Eucharist to illustrate, against the Gnostics, that the flesh is also graced: "For when the mixed cup and the bread that has been prepared receive the Word of God, and become the Eucharist, the body and blood of Christ, and by these our flesh grows and is confirmed, how can they say that flesh cannot receive the free gift of God, which is eternal life . . . ?" (*Library of Christian Classics*, vol. I, *Early Christian Fathers*, ed. and trans. Cyril C. Richardson [Philadelphia: The Westminster Press, 1953], p. 388).

4. *History and Truth*, trans. Charles A. Kelbley (Evanston: Northwestern University Press, 1965), p. 110.

5. James Russell Lowell (1819-1891), "Once to Every Man and Nation."

6. See Harvey Cox, *God's Revolution and Man's Responsibility* (Valley Forge: The Judson Press, 1965), pp. 8-9.

7. *Christian Faith*, p. 180.

8. E.g., Anders Nygren, *Agape and Eros*, trans. Philip S. Watson (Philadelphia: The Westminster Press, 1953), vol. I, 230.

9. See G. von Rad's article on the image of God in the Old Testament, in *Theologische Wörterbuch zum N.T.*, vol. II, 387-390; and W. Eichrodt, *Theologie des alten Testaments*, II, 58. Both authors are cited by D. Cairns, *Image of God*, pp. 18ff.

10. Calvin writes: "There is no small controversy concerning 'image' and 'likeness' among expositors who seek for a difference, whereas in reality there is none, between the two words; 'likeness' being only added by way of explanation. In the first place, we know that it is the custom of the Hebrews to use repetitions, in which they express one thing twice. In the next place, as to the thing itself, there is no doubt but man is called the image of God, on account of his likeness to God. Hence it appears that those persons make themselves ridiculous who display more subtlety in criticising these terms, whether they confine *zelem*, that is 'image' to the substance of the soul, and *demuth*, that is, 'likeness,' to its qualities, or whether they bring forward any different interpretation. Because when God determined to create man in his own image, that expression being rather obscure, he repeats the same idea in this explanatory phrase, 'after our likeness'; as though he had said that he was about to make man, in whom, as in an image, he would give a representation of himself upon him" (*Institutes*, bk. I, ch. xv, trans. John Allen [Philadelphia: Presbyterian Board of Christian Education], I, 207).

11. *Adversus Haereses*, pp. 385ff.

12. *Summa Theologica*, Part I, Ques. 93, no. 9 (*Basic Writings of Saint Thomas Aquinas*, ed. Anton C. Pegis [New York: Random House, 1945] vol. I, 899ff.).

13. Berkhof, p. 179.

14. New York: Abingdon Press, 1952, vol. I, 484.

15. Socinian beliefs are traced to the contemporary of the Reformers, Lelio Francesco Maria Sozini (1525-62), the Polish "Unitarian" whose doctrine of God was questioned by the Geneva reformers but finally approved by Bullinger. The principles of Socianism were stated in the Racovian Catechism, drawn up at Racow in southern Poland in 1605.

16. See G. C. Berkouwer, *Man: The Image of God*, trans. Dirk W. Jellema (Grand Rapids: Eerdmans, 1962), pp. 70ff.

17. *Church Dogmatics*, III, 1, trans. J. W. Edwards *et al.* (Edinburgh: T. & T. Clark, 1958), pp. 183f.

18. *Ibid.*

19. Berkouwer, pp. 73-74.

20. Claus Westermann, *Creation*, trans. John J. Scullion, S.J. (Philadelphia: Fortress Press, 1974), p. 58.

21. Barth, p. 183.

22. Westermann, p. 56.

23. *Ibid.*, pp. 56–57.

24. David Cairns (*Image of God*, p. 32) identifies a third N.T. usage, namely the application of the symbol to humanity in general, as in the O.T. He himself acknowledges, however, that this is marginal. The most direct reference, and it is oblique, is James 3:9. The idea that human being as such is intended to image God is, however, implicit in the second usage of the term in the N.T., as I shall attempt to show.

25. The most significant references are: Rom 8:29; I Cor. 11:7, 15:49; II Cor. 3:18, 4:4; Col. 1:15, 3:10; Heb. 1:3. In the course of the discussion, I will refer to some of the related passages as well.

26. From Moule's commentary on Colossians in *Peake's Commentary on the Bible*, rev., ed. Matthew Black (London: Thomas Nelson & Sons Ltd., 1962), p. 991.

27. Eduard Lohse, *A Commentary on the Epistles to the Colossians and to Philemon*, trans. William R. Poehlmann and Robert J. Karris (Philadelphia: Fortress Press, 1971), p. 3.

28. *The Second Epistle of Saint Paul to the Corinthians*, trans. A. W. Heathcote and P. J. Allcock (London: The Epworth Press, 1967), p. 30.

29. *Calvin's Commentaries: The Epistle of Paul the Apostle to the Hebrews and the First and Second Epistles of St. Peter*, trans. William B. Johnston, ed. David W. Torrance and Thomas F. Torrance (Grand Rapids: Eerdmans, 1963), p. 8.

30. Karl Barth, *The Epistle to the Romans*, trans. Edwyn C. Hoskyns (New York: Oxford University Press, 1933), p. 323.

31. Lohse, p. 143.

32. Jean Héring, *The First Epistle of Saint Paul to the Corinthians*, trans. A. W. Heathcote and P. J. Allcock (London: Epworth Press, 1962), p. 179.

33. *Calvin's Commentaries: The First Epistle of Paul the Apostle to the Corinthians*, trans. John W. Fraser, ed. David W. Torrance and Thomas F. Torrance (Edinburgh: Oliver and Boyd, 1960), p. 341.

CHAPTER THREE

1. For interesting historical treatments of the symbol, see David Cairns, *The Image of God in Man*; G. C. Berkouwer, *Man: The Image of God*; and for earlier sources, Jacob Jervell, *Imago Dei: Gen. 1.26f. im Spätjudentum, in der Gnosis und in den paulinischen Briefen* (Göttingen: Vandenhoeck & Ruprecht, 1960).

2. New York, Charles Scribner's Sons, 1950.

3. *Ibid.*, p. 250.

4. I find myself in disagreement with Ramsey, who writes that "most of the decisive and distinctive Christian interpretations of man have been of [the relational] sort" (*ibid.*, p. 255). This judgment is obviously influenced by his insistence that Augustine belongs in the relational school. I shall question that interpretation in the course of this discussion. However, even if some aspects of Augustine's treatment of the *imago* suggest the relational dimension, I would argue that while there have been powerful renditions of that interpretation in the history of Christian thought, the more substantive conception of the *imago* has dominated in both popular and more scholarly circles of Christian belief (cf. n. 22 below).

5. Cambridge, At the University Press, 1941, p. 44.

6. L. Harold DeWolf, *A Theology of the Living Church* (New York: Harper & Bros. Publishers, 1953), pp. 205ff.

7. Berkhof, p. 179.

8. Cairns, p. 110.

9. *Adversus Haereses*, IV, 4, 3.

10. *Protepticus*, 124, 3.

11. *De Incarnatione*, 3.

12. *De Trinitate*, XIV, 4.

13. Cairns, p. 110.

14. *Summa Theologica*, Ques. 93, Art. 2.

15. *Ibid.*, Ques. 93, Art. 6.

16. *Ibid.*, Ques. 94, Art. 1.

17. Handley C. B. Moule, *Outline of Christian Doctrine* (London: Hodder and Stoughton, 1905), pp. 157–58.

18. *God's Image in Man: And Its Defacement in the Light of Modern Denials* (London: Hodder and Stoughton, 1905), pp. 56–57.

19. *Ibid.*, p. 156.

20. Edinburgh: T. & T. Clark, 1888, vol. V, 79–80.

21. *Systematic Theology*, Vol. II (London and Edinburgh: Thomas Nelson & Sons, 1872), 97ff.

22. As previously noted, Paul Ramsey attempts to locate Augustine among those who develop the theology of the image of God in relational terms (he names Augustine along with Kierkegaard and Barth). The argument is not very convincing, however; for while Augustine certainly had a more dynamic sense of both the divine and the human than did later Schoolmen, his primary use of the *imago* symbol is in his discussion of the Trinity, where he shows that a "vestige of the Trinity" is found in human being, namely, in the faculties of memory, intellect, and will (see Ramsey, pp. 255ff.).

23. *Church Dogmatics*, vol. III (*The Doctrine of Creation*), part 1, ed. G. W. Bromiley and T. F. Torrance (Edinburgh: T. & T. Clark, 1958), 184.

24. *Ibid.*, pp. 184–185.

25. *The Image of God in Man*, pp. 121ff.

26. For example, commenting on the prologue of John's Gospel, Luther becomes conscious of his growing disagreement with Augustine over the interpretation of the sentence, "And the life was the light of men" (v. 4). There are, he notes, many speculations about this statement, linking it with the divine image. But "these are all human, Platonic, and philosophical thoughts, which lead us away from Christ into ourselves; but the Evangelist wishes to lead us away from ourselves into Christ." The Johannine writer, he insists, is really speaking about "the true light of grace in Christ, and not the natural light" of reason. But at this point he becomes aware of Augustine's possible divergence from his interpretation. At first Luther protests that he does not disagree with the Bishop of Hippo: "But let no one accuse me of teaching differently from St. Augustine, who interpreted this text to mean the natural light. I do not reject that interpretation and am well aware that all the light of reason is ignited by the divine light. . . . But this interpretation is out of place in this connection, because only the light of grace is preached here." And then: "St. Augustine was only a man, and we are not compelled to follow his interpretation. . . . " And finally: "O, that this interpretation, that reason has a natural light, were rooted out of my heart. How deeply it is seated there. . . . The Platonic philosophers with their useless and senseless prating first led Augustine to his interpretation. Augustine then carried us all with him" (*Church Postil Sermons*, trans. John Nicholas Lenker (Minneapolis: Lutherans in All Lands Co., 1905), vol. I, 192ff.).

27. "True theology is practical, and its foundation is Christ, whose death is appropriated to us through faith. . . . Accordingly speculative theology belongs to the devil in hell" (*Luther's Works*, ed. Jaroslav Pelikan [St. Louis: Concordia Publishing House, 1972], 54, 22).

28. Joseph Sittler, "Ecological Commitment as Theological Responsibility," *Zygon: Journal of Religion and Science* 5 (1970):174.

29. Hence, though he rejected the Zwinglian symbolic interpretations of the Eucharist, Luther could not retain the conventional transubstantiational theology of Rome either, which equated the elements themselves with grace, substantially conceived as "the medicine of immortality."

30. In a moving piece written near the end of his life, Luther reviews his "conversion" on the basis of his relationship to the word "righteousness": "I had indeed been captivated with an extraordinary ardor for understanding Paul in the Epistle to the Romans. But up till then it was . . . a single word in chapter 1 (:17): 'In it the righteousness of God is revealed,' that stood in my way. For I hated that word 'righteousness of God', which, according to the use and custom of all the teachers, I had been taught to understand philosophically regarding the formal or active righteousness, as they call it, with which God is righteous and punishes the unrighteous sinner.

"Though I lived as a monk without reproach, I felt that I was a sinner before God. . . . I did not love, yes, I hated the righteous God who punishes sinners, and secretly, if not blasphemously, certainly murmuring greatly, I was angry with God, and said, 'As if, indeed, it is not enough that miserable sinners, eternally lost through original sin, are crushed by every kind of calamity by the law of the decalogue, without having God add pain to pain by the gospel, and also by the gospel threatening us with his righteousness and wrath!' Thus I raged with a fierce and troubled conscience. Nevertheless, I beat importunately upon Paul at that place, most ardently desiring to know what St. Paul wanted.

"At last, by the mercy of God, meditating day and night, I gave heed to the context of the words, namely, 'In it the righteousness of God is revealed as it is written, "He who through faith is righteous shall live." ' There I began to understand that the righteousness of God is that by which the righteous live by a gift of God, namely by faith. And this is the meaning: the righteousness of God is revealed by the gospel, namely, the passive righteousness with which merciful God justifies us by faith, as it is written, 'He who through faith is righteous shall live.' Here I felt that I was altogether born again and had entered paradise itself through open gates. . . .

"And I extolled my sweetest word with a love as great as the hatred with which I had before hated the word 'righteousness of God' " (*Luther's Works*, vol. 34, 336–337).

31. I am thinking in particular of the traditions of mysticism, especially, of course, of the German mystics like Tauler and Eckhart, on whom Luther depended so heavily. Mystical faith, as distinct from the more philosophical (scholastic) forms that dominated during the Middle Ages and again in seventeenth-century Protestant orthodoxies, presupposes relationship with the Divine as the "given" of all faith-categories.

32. *The Image of God in Man*, p. 125.

33. So utterly lost is the image of God through the Fall that, says Luther, "When we now attempt to speak of that image, we speak of a thing unknown; an image which we have not only never experienced, but the contrary of which we have experienced all our lives, and experience still. Of this image therefore all we now possess are the mere terms — 'the image of God'! These naked words are all we now hear, and all we know" (*Luther's Works*, "Lectures on Genesis 1–5," ed. Jaroslav Pelikan [St. Louis: Concordia Publishing House, 1958], 1, 63).

34. It *is* absurd, of course, if it is taken to mean that the human being by "falling" loses or has lost the quintessence of humanity, so that one could no longer say of postfallen *anthropos*: this is a human being. Unfortunately, the admixture of *imago*-theology with hamartiology — especially with the idea of "total depravity" — has greatly confused the issue; and it does not help the matter that Luther himself, among others, could sometimes cast his discussion of the loss of the image of God in language suggestive of a lost substance, the "stuff" of real humanity, of which existing, sinful creatures had

been totally deprived. Thus he is frequently heard, even by persons fundamentally sympathetic to his point of view, as if he were denying any semblance of essential humanity in fallen creatures. For instance, Reinhold Niebuhr appears to have understood Luther in this way when, pointing to what he sees as an inconsistency in Luther's theology of the *imago*, he wrote: "Though Christian theology has frequently expressed the idea of the total depravity of man in extravagant terms, it has never been without witnesses to the fact that human sin cannot destroy the essential character of man to such a degree that it would cease being implied in, and furnishing contrast to, what he had become. It is not surprising to find this emphasis in Thomas Aquinas, who does not hold to a doctrine of total depravity. Yet even Luther, who believes that nothing but the name of the "image of God" is left to sinful man, animadverts upon the significance of man's uneasy conscience, a phenomenon that can be understood only as the protest of man's essential nature against his present state" (*The Nature and Destiny of Man*, vol. I: *Human Nature* [New York: Charles Scribner's Sons, 1953], 267).

35. *Luther's Works*, vol. I, 60.

36. *Ibid.*, p. 61.

37. *Ibid.*, p. 63.

38. *Cairns*, p. 144.

39. John Calvin, *Commentaries on the First Book of Moses Called Genesis*, vol. I (Edinburgh: Calvin Translation Society, 1847), 93.

40. *Ibid.*, p. 94.

41. *Ibid.*

42. *Institutes of the Christian Religion*, trans. John Allen (Philadelphia: Presbyterian Board of Christian Education, n.d.) vol. I, bk. 1, ch. XV, no. 5, p. 210.

43. *Commentary on the First Book of Moses Called Genesis*, p. 94.

44. *Institutes*, vol. I, 210.

45. *Ibid.*, pp. 210–211.

46. *Ibid.*, p. 214.

47. *Ibid.*, p. 208.

48. *Ibid.*

49. *Ibid.*

50. Grand Rapids: Eerdmans, 1957, p. 36.

51. *Ibid.*, p. 91.

52. *Basic Christian Ethics*, p. 255.

53. Calvin, *Institutes*, vol. I, 208.

54. Brunner's treatment of the *imago Dei*, especially in his *Man in Revolt: A Christian Anthropology* (London: R.T.S.: Lutterworth Press, 1939, trans. Olive Wyon, esp. chs. V and VI), is a neglected but very provocative one. It is one of the more consistent statements of the meaning of the *imago* in relational terms, and one that takes with full seriousness the New Testament's exegesis of the Hebraic phrase. It is, of course, cast in Brunner's spe-

cial language of "response": "Man is destined to answer God in believing, responsive love, to accept in grateful dependence his destiny to which God has called him, all his life. Thus here we are concerned not with an 'image' and a 'reflection' but with a 'word' and an 'answer'; this is the exposition which the New Testament gives of the Old Testament story of Creation, the idea of the *Imago Dei*. The intrinsic worth of man's being lies in the Word of God, hence his nature is: responsibility from love, in love, for love" (pp. 98–99).

55. *Basic Christian Ethics*, p. 259.

56. *Works of Love* (Princeton, NJ: Princeton University Press, 1946), p. 52.

57. Even Luther compares her to the moon in relation to the sun, and this on the basis of the Pauline comparison that while the male is the image of God the female is the "glory" of the male (I Cor. 11:7).

58. See George A. Lindbeck, *The Nature of Doctrine: Religion and Theology in a Postliberal Age* (Philadelphia: Westminster Press, 1984). Lindbeck's discussion of propositionalism is illuminating. He writes that "the conceptual difficulties involved in traditional propositional notions of authoritative teaching have contributed to discrediting the whole doctrinal enterprise" (p. 78).

59. See above, p. 102–103.

CHAPTER FOUR

1. *Outline of the History of Dogma*, trans. Edwin Knox Mitchell (Boston: Beacon Press, 1957), p. 558.

2. *Church Postil Sermons*, vol. I, 10–11.

3. "Ecological Commitment as Theological Responsibility," *Zygon: Journal of Religion and Science* 5 (1970):174.

4. *Ibid.*

5. George Steiner, "The House of Being," *Times Literary Supplement*, 9 October 1981, p. 1143.

6. George Steiner, *Heidegger* (Glasgow: Fontana/Collins, 1978), p. 42.

7. *Ibid.*, p. 81.

8. *Ibid.* And see Martin Heidegger, *Being and Time*, trans. John Macquarrie and Edward Robinson (London: S.C.M. Press, Ltd., 1962) p. 308. There are many aspects of Heidegger's discussion of being that are related to our present enterprise — including such expressions as *Untereinandersein* (being-among-one-another), *Sein bei* (being alongside), *Für-einandersein* (being-for-one-another), *Alleinsein* (being alone), *Mit-dabei-sein* (being "in on it" with someone), etc. However, since the interpretation of the analysis of this important philosopher is itself a complex and engrossing task, I cannot attempt more than an allusion to him in the present context.

9. Bruce C. Birch, "Old Testament Foundations for Peacemaking in the Nuclear Age," *The Christian Century* 102, 38 (Dec. 4, 1985):1115.

10. Barth, *Church Dogmatics*, III, 1, ed. G. W. Bromiley and T. F. Torrance (Edinburgh: T. & T. Clark, 1958), Sec. 41, 3, "Covenant as the Internal Basis of Creation" (pp. 228ff.).

11. *Church Dogmatics*, II, 1, ed. G. W. Bromiley and T. F. Torrance (New York: Charles Scribner's Sons, 1958), 283–284. The entire section of ch. VI in which this quotation appears is pertinent to my argument here.

12. In the light of the contemporary dialogue between Christians and Jews, and especially among Christians who are seeking to reestablish their theological roots in the faith of Israel, it is necessary to ask whether the "stumbling block to the Jews" is really the cross, as Paul suggests (I Cor. 1:23). Inasmuch as the Cross represents the divine participation in the human condition (God-with-us "in the fullest possible way"), it is surely not more than an extension of the theology of the Old Testament, which depicts Yahweh-God — as one might almost say — already on the road to Calvary. The cross that was eventually raised there was certainly present long before "in the heart of God" (H. Wheeler Robinson). The "logic of the cross" (Reinhold Niebuhr) belongs to the faith of Israel as much as it does to the Christian faith, and in fact the source of the Pauline and Lutheran *theologia crucis* is certainly the prophetic traditions of Israel. One must ask today, then, whether the real stumbling block to Judaism is not, rather, a consequence of the translation of the relational categories belonging to the tradition of Jerusalem into the substantialist categories of Athens, especially as this translation relates to the doctrine of the Trinity, Christology, and soteriology.

13. The principle of identification is so undialectically applied in some Anglo- and Roman-Catholic ecclesiology that it becomes virtually impossible for the church to engage in creative self-criticism. Quoting with approval St. Robert Bellarmine, Pope Pius XII in the famous encyclical, *Mystici corporis Christi* (*cf. The Wisdom of Catholicism*, ed. Anton Pegis [New York, The Modern Library, 1955], p. 794) states: "This naming of the Body of Christ is not to be explained solely by the fact that Christ must be called the Head of His Mystical Body, but also by the fact that He so sustains the Church, and so in a certain sense lives in the Church, that it is as it were another Christ." Such a substitution of unity for "community" ends "by denying in principle and as a matter of logical necessity all possibility of appeal beyond the actual historically developing society to the eternal God made known in Christ . . . " (Leslie Newbiggin, *The Reunion of the Church* [New York: Harper & Bros., 1948], p. 56). It is certainly such a denial that liberationists and others within the Catholic community today are struggling to correct.

14. In employing the term "communion" throughout this chapter, including the chapter head, I fully intend to draw the reader into eucharistic

reflections, though not in a narrow sense. What we name Holy Communion has of course many levels of meaning; but one of them is certainly the fact that it functions as a ritual enactment of the new being-with that is enabled through the grace of God in Christ.

15. "Ecological Commitment as Theological Responsibility," pp. 177-178.

16. The "first science" was of course named *metaphysics*; "ontology" was "coined by scholastic writers in the seventeenth century" and finally "canonized by Christian Wolff (1679-1754)" (Alasdair MacIntyre, in *The Encyclopedia of Philosophy*, Paul Edwards, editor in chief, [New York: The Macmillan Company & The Free Press, 1967], vol. 5, 542). "Ontology," however, is used by many writers to designate what "metaphysics" meant, namely "an analysis of the structures of being." "The preposition *meta*," says Tillich, "now has the irremediable connotation of pointing to a duplication of this world by a transcendent realm of beings. Therefore it is perhaps less misleading to speak of ontology instead of metaphysics" (*Systematic Theology*, I, 20). In this connection, see also John Macquarrie, *Principles of Christian Theology*, ch. 5, "Being and God," pp. 94ff.

17. *Systematic Theology*, II, 12. What it seems to me one must ask of Tillich's system is whether he took seriously enough the alternative ontology that is behind the symbols and theological concepts of the scriptures, especially the Hebraic scriptures. Was he too content, perhaps, to regard the biblical material as a more "primitive," dramatic, or historical representation of the same basic ontology that he found in the tradition of Athens? "Systematic theology," he writes, "cannot, and should not, enter into the ontological discussion as such . . . although the theologian must be familiar with it" (*S.T.*, I, 164). The assumption here seems to be that the ontological "categories" and content are determined within the framework of a thought world quite extraneous to that of the biblical tradition, and that the representatives of the latter ("theologians") ought not to import content regarding the nature of being from the side of their tradition. But what if their tradition, i.e., the tradition of Jerusalem, assumes certain things about the nature of being that are different from, and possibly in conflict with, the assumptions coming out of Athens and worked upon by the human mind "for thousands of years" (*ibid.*)?

Precisely this was at the bottom of Reinhold Niebuhr's quarrel with Tillich, though Niebuhr did not phrase it in these terms, because he too assumed that "ontology" bore the indelible mark of the tradition of Athens. My point in this study, however, is that if "ontology" refers to the *logos* of being (*ontos*), i.e., is the attempt of the human mind to grasp the fundamental meaning of being, the Hebraic tradition must certainly be said to have an (implicit if not explicit) ontology. But it is not, so far as its content is concerned, identical with the characteristic ontological thought of Greek civilization and philosophy, for instead of thinking in substantial or reified terms, it thinks relationally. If this is taken seriously, Hebraic and Christian theology cannot simply accept as final those theories of being that emanate from Greek or other philosophical-religious traditions, but must develop its theory and praxis on the basis of its own ontological pre-understanding.

18. Reinhold Niebuhr's *The Self and the Dramas of History* (New York: Charles Scribner's Sons, 1955), a work that is foundational for this present study and touches its concerns at many points, also designates three dimensions of human relatedness — or, to use Niebuhr's own language, "three dialogues" in which "the self" is engaged. "The implications of these three dialogues may give more accurate content," Dr. Niebuhr writes, "to the original metaphor 'image of God' than the Greek emphasis on reason" (p. 14). In naming these dialogues, Niebuhr does not include (what others like Martin Buber and Joseph Sittler, writing within the same historical context, did include) the dialogue with nature. He discusses rather the self's dialogue with itself, with its neighbors, and with God.

The self's dialogue "with itself" may be regarded as an omission in my own analysis here. In defense of my decision not to include it, I would only say that I regard the self's internal reflections as being of a different order than the dialogue with the three counterparts of our being I have designated. Each of these — God, the neighbor, and nature — is objectively "other," and confronts the self with its otherness, its refusal to be incorporated, to be coopted. I think that the term *dialogue* presupposes this kind of otherness. What the self has by way of conversation with itself should probably be called monologue — or better, soliloquy. I consider that the *dialogical* character of the self's conversation with itself is implicit in its dialogue with its counterparts.

The more important question, however, is why nature was not included in this profound work of Reinhold Niebuhr. The answer is probably more complex than could be suggested by the fact that at the time he wrote this work, it would not be expected to contain the same consciousness of nature, since the crisis of nature had not yet made itself conspicuous. Beyond this obvious explanation, however, one must certainly consider the long neglect of nature by theological traditions that were primarily interested in *history*. Professor Niebuhr was very much shaped by those traditions — as were we all!

19. Augustine finds traces of the trinitarian structuring of creation especially within human being as the integration of reason, memory, and will. This, of course, reflects Augustine's essentially substantialist frame of reference. In line with the relational conception of human being as *imago Dei*, I am suggesting here a triunity in the outward orientation of our being rather than its internal qualities or endowments.

20. Sittler registers the following complaint about that school of theology that replaced the "natural theology" of nineteenth-century liberalism with a theology of revelation in which nature had little part: "I have felt a

deepening uneasiness about the tendency in Biblical Theology, generally known as neo-orthodoxy, whereby the promises, imperatives, and dynamics of the Gospel are declared in sharp and calculated disengagement from the stuff of earthly life." Then, in an intuitive deduction which three decades after its composition has the ring of the prophetic, Sittler adds: "When theology does not acknowledge and soberly come to terms with the covert significance of the natural, the world of nature is not silenced. . . . When Christian orthodoxy refuses to articulate a theology for earth, the clamant hurt of God's ancient creation is not thereby silenced. Earth's voices, recollective of her lost grace and her destined redemption, will speak through one or another form of naturalism. If the Church will not have a theology *for* nature, then irresponsible but sensitive men will act as midwives for nature's unsilenceable meaningfulness, and enunciate a theology of nature. For earth, not man's mother—which is a pagan notion—but, as St. Francis profoundly surmised, man's sister, sharer of his sorrow and scene and partial substance of his joys, unquenchably sings out her violated wholeness, and in groaning and travailing awaits with man the restoration of all things" ("A Theology for Earth," pp. 369–370).

21. I include the human *species* here because, while religion in the post-Reformation period could still discuss the human individual and the state, the species as such—its fate as species—has hardly interested theology. If there has come to be in our time something calling itself a political theology, it is in part a reaction to this neglect. It has this in common with ecological theology.

22. "The world is not God, but it is God's. Or to put the same issue another way, nature and grace belong together" (Sittler, "Ecological Commitment as Theological Responsibility," p. 178).

23. See *Institutes*, bk. I, ch. 16, 217. Calvin begins his treatment of "God's Preservation and Support of the World by His Power and His Government of Every Part of It by His Providence" with this lively sentence: "To represent God as a Creator only for a moment, who entirely finished all his work at once, were frigid and jejune; and in this it behooves us especially to differ from the heathen, that the presence of the Divine power may appear to us no less in the perpetual state of the world than in its first origin."

24. The three dogmas that may be regarded as the primary doctrinal vehicles of the biblical theology of grace (*creatio ex nihilo*, justification of the sinner, and resurrection of the dead) all point to the faith-experience of finding, unexpectedly, the wherewithal to live ("go on") despite the consciousness of life's impossibility. There are, of course, parallel experiences in nature (spring follows winter, etc.), and it is neither accidental nor reprehensible, wholly, that Christianity chose these natural points of discontinuity and transformation, Easter being chief among them, on which to fasten its recall of the facts of "salvation history."

25. Joseph Sittler, *Essays on Nature and Grace* (Philadelphia: Fortress Press, 1972), p. 86.

26. *Ibid.*

27. So it is chastised, implicitly, in the postbiblical formulation of much doctrine. For example, testimonies to the life of the Christ that violate his genuine humanity (the apocryphal gospels) are rejected as canon: the obviously "miraculous" in the popular sense of the word, involving superhuman feats and capabilities, is not what the early church was after. Think what might have been made of the virgin birth and the resurrection if it had been left up to some of our contemporary literalists and workers of miracles, for whom wonder seems possible only where nature's laws are utterly and visibly set aside! Above all, the biblical modesty that looked for mystery in what was ordinary—for glory hidden beneath its opposite (Luther)—seems to have been persuasive enough to prevent classical Christianity, in its developing Christology, from espousing versions of the identity of Christ's person that clearly favored the jettisoning of the humanity principle in favor of a clear and undiluted statement of his divinity (e.g., the monophysite controversy). Given the enormous pressure under which faith in that age of the human race must certainly have found itself—namely, the pressure to come up with another god!—the Formula of Chalcedon is itself nothing short of a miracle.

28. *Essays on Nature and Grace*, pp. 87–88.

29. Cf. n. 15, this chapter.

30. The phrase occurs in Henryk Skolimowski's *Eco-Philosophy: Designing New Tactics for Living* (New York & London: Marion Boyars, 1981, p. 55), and the whole context is worthy of quotation here. Professor Skolimowski has developed a philosophy of "ecological humanism" as "an authentic alternative to industrial society." This philosophy, he writes, holds that: "1) The coming age is to be seen as the age of stewardship: we are here not to govern and exploit, but to maintain and creatively transform, and to carry on the torch of evolution. 2) The world is to be conceived of as a sanctuary: we belong to certain habitats, which are the source of our culture and our spiritual sustenance. These habitats are the places in which we, like birds, temporarily reside; they are sanctuaries in which people, like rare birds, need to be taken care of. They are sanctuaries also in the religious sense: places in which we are awed by the world; but we are the priests of the sanctuary; we must maintain its sanctity and increase its spirituality."

31. When the writer of Luke-Acts has Paul (Acts 20:35) "remembering the words of the Lord Jesus, how he said, 'It is more blessed to give than to receive,' " he is in a real sense providing a summary statement of the gospel. So copious are the references to receiving and giving in the Synoptic Gospels and John—and especially to giving—that they constitute what may be the primary metaphor of these writings, a hypothesis that ought not to surprise anyone reared on the Reformation teaching of the priority of grace, i.e., the gift quality of all life.

32. This well-known dictum of St. Thomas Aquinas was quoted "with great approval" by both Luther and Calvin (see Sittler, "Ecological Commitment as Theological Responsibility," p. 180).

33. Loren Eiseley, *The Immense Journey* (New York: Random House, 1946), pp. 173ff.

CHAPTER FIVE

1. In an interesting remark in *Being and Time*, Heidegger acknowledges this alternative tradition that passes through the Reformation: "*Theology*," he writes, "is seeking a more primordial interpretation of man's Being towards God, prescribed by the meaning of faith itself and remaining within it. It is slowly beginning to understand once more Luther's insight that the 'foundation' on which its system of dogma rests has not arisen from an inquiry in which faith is primary, and that conceptually this 'foundation' is not only inadequate for the problematic of theology, but conceals and distorts it" (p. 30) (cf. the discussion of Tillich's acceptance of non-Hebraic ontology in n. 17, ch. 4).

2. A splendid and well-known example of Luther's employment of this concept is his Christmas sermon: "There are many of you in this congregation who think to yourselves: 'If only I had been there! How quick I would have been to help the Baby! . . . Why don't you do it now? You have Christ in your neighbor. You ought to serve him, for what you do to your neighbor in need you do to the Lord Christ himself" (Roland Bainton, *The Martin Luther Christmas Book* [Philadelphia: Westminster Press, 1948], pp. 37f.).

3. However, it is false and dangerous when ecological and justice concerns are kept in separate compartments, with enthusiasts for each doing battle with the other camp. That is why, in this study, I have attempted to state an onto-theological foundation for contemporary social ethics that assumes the inseparability of human relationships to nature, humanity, and God ("The Triunity of our Being-With").

4. Unlike both of the older theories of atonement (the classical or "ransom" theory developed, e.g., by Irenaeus, and the sacrificial-satisfaction, or Latin, theory of Anselm), Abelard's conception of the meaning of the work of Christ assumes the human response as a necessary aspect of the work itself. This may be criticized (as it was by Bernard of Clairvaux and many since) for its "subjectivism," yet it belongs to the biblical understanding of the nature and providence of God that the human response (as in the whole of covenant theology) is central, and not merely a secondary or consequent consideration.

5. *Church Dogmatics*, III, 3 (Edinburgh: T. & T. Clark, 1961), pp. 240–243.

6. One of the most provocative and systematic statements of the nature of authority in Christian theology is Paul Tillich's sermon "By What

Authority?" (see *The New Being* [New York: Charles Scribner's Sons, 1955], pp. 79ff.).

7. *The Self and the Dramas of History*, p. 30.

8. *Ibid.*, p. 31.

9. John R. Williams, *Martin Heidegger's Philosophy of Religion* (Waterloo, Ont.: Canadian Corporation for Studies in Religion, Supplements, No. 2, 1977), p. 150.

10. Niebuhr, *The Self and the Dramas of History*, p. 31.

11. *Ibid.*, p. 32.

12. *God as the Mystery of the World*, p. 320.

13. For an extended illustration and documentation of this statement, I refer the reader to one of the great (and neglected) novels of our era, the first of the antiutopian genre, *We*, by the ex-Bolschevik Zamiatin. (trans. Gregory Zilboorg [Boston: Gregg Press, 1924]). With its sharp and stinging criticism of the kind of communality that sacrifices the personhood of persons to the group, this work is relevant reading not only for contemporary Marxists but for members of every "mass culture," and for all religious traditions that provide the cultic basis for this sacrifice of the individual person.

14. See above, pp. 120–121.

15. In addition to *We*, I am thinking of George Orwell's *1984* and *Animal Farm*, Huxley's *Brave New World*, Ray Bradbury's *Fahrenheit 451*, and Kurt Vonnegut's *Player Piano*, among others.

16. Of course the only reason why the bride-bridegroom metaphor can be made to apply to the relationship between Christ and the church is that it is assumed that this dialectic already applies in marriage.

17. But see Phyllis Trible, *God and the Rhetoric of Sexuality* (Philadelphia: Fortress Press, 1983), ch. 1.

18. As Jonathan Schell does in his *The Fate of the Earth* (New York: Avon Books, 1982), pp. 186ff.

19. Both of the present-day superpowers appear invincibly naive about this. They do not understand how their "redemptive" intervention in the affairs of lesser states could be perceived by peoples they aim to "protect" as threatening not only to their national sovereignty but destructive of their very culture. Living on the edge of empire, Canadians (when they are not wholly taken in by the "good life" à la the U.S.A.) are able to sympathize with Central and Latin American peoples, as well as victims of the "fraternal affection" of the U.S.S.R. who fear for the total eclipse of their cultural heritage and identity.

20. The Canadian experience is very valuable in this connection, since this country has been able thus far — with difficulty! — not only to contain within itself two quite different founding cultures, French and Anglo-Saxon, but to make it possible also for later immigrants from a great variety of nations and races to live under one jurisdiction while at the same time re-

taining much of their various cultural and linguistic heritages. It is precisely this "mosaic" (patchwork quilt) pattern of community, however, that is in danger of collapsing under the burden of a mass technological culture bringing ever greater uniformity (to be distinguished from unity). See my book *The Canada Crisis* (Toronto: Anglican Book Centre, 1983).

21. This is illustrated graphically today by the many ways in which the ecumenical church cuts across national and "world" boundaries, achieving a network of communication and cooperation that is rare if not unique. Where churches have sufficiently de–Constantinianized themselves to become distinguishable from the dominant classes of their host societies, they are able to overcome much of the harm that is done through the propaganda of *Feindbilder*-creation (creating images of the enemy); they can join in international quests for world peace without succumbing to the ideologies of politically motivated peace movements; together with other human agencies, they can achieve humane economic, ecological, human rights, and other goals, and help build trust between mutually suspicious and competitive governments and movements.

But the church has only begun to explore this potential for an enlightened global consciousness and care; and it is greatly impeded by dimensions of its own life that fear Christian catholicity and react against its practical application (e.g., by the World Council of Churches or the World Alliance of Reformed Churches) by retreating into even more chauvinistic and imperialistic forms of "Christendom."

The greatest challenge to the church of Jesus Christ today, consequently, is to extricate itself from the Constantinian quest for power through proximity to power, and to elaborate a gospel and ethic that is truly world-affirming, and therefore not affirmative merely of parts of the world. Only in this way is it possible for the church today to make good its ancient claim to "catholicity."

CHAPTER SIX

1. Charles Neider, ed. (New York: Bantam Books, 1954), "Introduction."

2. "A Theology for Earth," pp. 371–372.

3. The pamphlet is entitled "For Them, Life or Death is Up to You!" text by Bob Cummings. The publication date is not given, but the pamphlet was circulated in 1985.

4. New York: Scribner's, 1952.

5. As I write, news of a deadly chemical "blob" deep in the waters of Lake Saint Claire has startled all who depend on the Great Lakes, those rare repositories of fresh water, for their water supply, i.e., an estimated 35 million. Another report announces that by recent test these are the most polluted waters on the continent.

6. The idea of a lake being "dead" would have seemed senseless to our grandparents. Like so many other contemporary expressions, the "dead lake" reflects the negative dimension of the technological society we have become. Lakes are regarded as being "dead" when they will no longer support life, and the primary cause of this growing phenomenon is acid rain. "Acid rain eats into food crops, trees, materials, buildings and aquatic life. It is a negative factor in the environment of the United States, Canada, western Europe, Scandinavia, Japan, and other industrialized areas. The United States has planned to build 350 coal-burning power plants between 1979 and 1995. Under existing air pollution standards, this could add 10 to 15 percent more acid rain to the atmosphere. Already more than 300 lakes in the Adirondack Mountains are so acidified that they no longer contain fish, and Canadian scientists estimate that if their acid rain continues at present rates, 48,000 Ontario lakes will be devoid of life by the year 2000" (John Carmody, *Ecology and Religion: Towards a New Christian Theology of Nature*, p. 18).

7. Michael Ignatieff, *The Needs of Strangers* (New York: Viking, 1984), p. 40. In connection with the dark side of nature, see also George S. Hendry, *Theology of Nature* (Philadelphia: The Westminster Press, 1980), pp. 183f.).

8. William Golding's novel *The Inheritors*, depicting the transition from Neanderthal Man to anxious *Homo sapiens*, is perhaps one of the best commentaries on the mythic "history" conveyed by Genesis 3, and especially regarding the multiple character of the alienation suggested by the biblical saga (New York: Harcourt, Brace and World, 1955).

9. *The Technological Society* (New York: Alfred A. Knopf, 1964), p. 16.

10. Toronto: Bantam Books of Canada Ltd., 1957.

11. Clarence J. Glacken, "Man's Place in Nature in Recent Western Thought," in *This Little Planet*, ed. Michael Hamilton (New York: Charles Scribner's Sons, 1970), p. 199.

12. *Being and Time*, p. 30 (the full quotation is given in n. 1, ch. 5 above).

13. This is certainly related to the renewed interest in the theology of creation, which after a long period of redemption-centered theological reflection has been gradually introduced into the discourse of the Christian community (see the Introduction of Claus Westermann's *Creation* [Philadelphia: Fortress Press, 1974]).

14. Philadelphia: The Westminster Press, 1978.

15. *Ibid.*, p. 102.

16. *Ibid.*, p. 104.

17. *Ibid.*, p. 113.

18. *Ibid.*, p. 119.

19. *Ibid.*, p. 120. Joseph Sittler agrees: "When . . . one reads the

104th Psalm, one becomes conscious that this Psalm speaks of the relation-ship between man and nature in a quite new way. The poetical naiveté of the images must not blind us to the majestic assertions of the song. In this Psalm nothing in the world of man and nothing in the world of nature is either independent or capable of solitary significance. Every upward-arching phenomenon, every smallest thing, is derived from the fountain of life. . . . Natural and mortal life are incandescent with meaning because of their mutual dependence upon the will of the ultimate and Holy one. . . .

"Here is a holy naturalism, a matrix of grace in which all things derive significance from their origin, and all things find fulfilment in praise. Man and nature live out their distinct but related lives in a complex that recalls the divine intentions as that intention is symbolically related on the first page of the Bible. Man is placed . . . in the garden of earth. This garden he is to tend as God's other creation—not to use as a godless warehouse or to rape as a tyrant" ("A Theology for Earth," p. 372).

20. Birch and Rasmussen, p. 120.

21. *Ibid.*, p. 121.

22. *Ibid.*, p. 122.

23. Pp. 189ff.

24. *Ibid.*, p. 189.

25. *Ibid.*, pp. 189–190.

26. *The Land: Place as Gift, Promise, and Challenge in Biblical Faith: Over-tures to Biblical Theology* (Philadelphia: Fortress Press, 1977).

27. Santmire, *Travail of Nature*, p. 192.

28. *Ibid.*, p. 194.

29. *Ibid.*, p. 197.

30. *Ibid.*, p. 200.

31. *Ibid.*

32. *Ibid.*, pp. 208ff.

33. *Ibid.*, pp. 217–218.

34. Birch and Rasmussen, p. 118.

35. See, in particular, Paul Tillich, *Biblical Religion and the Search for Ultimate Reality* (Chicago: University of Chicago Press, 1955).

36. See Reinhold Niebuhr, *The Self and the Dramas of History*, p. 112.

37. Jürgen Moltmann writes: "Humanity is . . . not subject ruling over nature as object, but rather the product of nature. In theological terms we must not understand ourselves primarily as *imago Dei*, but rather as *imago mundi*" ("The Alienation and Liberation of Nature," in *On Nature*, ed. Leroy S. Rouner [Notre Dame, IN: University of Notre Dame Press, 1982], p. 142). While appreciating Moltmann's point as a corrective to the substan-tialist overstatement of *imago Dei*, I should be loath to see the two terms jux-taposed as alternatives. My attempt here has been to render the *imago Dei* symbol in a manner that incorporates our being of the earth earthy.

38. "Canticle of Brother Sun."

39. "Nature undergoes history, but she does not experience it. She is history but does not have history, because she does not know that she is history. And why does man alone have a conscious, experienced history? Because he alone has consciousness and experience. And so it does seem to me meaningful after all to see man's distinction not in his historic existence as such, but in his awareness of his historic existence" (C. F. von Weizsäcker, *The History of Nature*, trans. Fred. D. Wieck [Chicago: University of Chicago Press, 1949], p. 9).

40. Quoted by Richard E. Wentz, in "The American Spirituality of Loren Eiseley," *The Christian Century* (April 25, 1984):430.

41. See Desmond Morris, *The Naked Ape* (New York: McGraw Hill, 1967).

42. See Margaret Laurence's splendid novel *A Jest of God* (Toronto/Montreal: McLelland and Stewart, 1966).

43. See the final subsection of the book, "Homo loquens: Representative Creaturehood", pp. 203–204; and see Dorothee Sölle, *Christ the Representative* (London: S.C.M. Press, 1967).

44. Loren Wilkinson, ed., *Earth Keeping: Christian Stewardship of Natural Resources* (Grand Rapids: Eerdmans, 1980), p. 227.

45. Conrad Bonifazi, "Biblical Roots of an Ecologic Conscience," in *This Little Planet*, pp. 226–227.

46. See my essay, "Rethinking Christ," in *Anti-Semitism and the Foundations of Christianity*, ed. Alan T. Davies (New York: Paulist Press, 1979), pp. 188ff.

47. The contextual dimension in theology must be held in tension with a critical stance vis-à-vis the historical context. The purpose of theology is to engage the context, not simply to reflect it. Too often in the past (and still today) where this critical distance is missing, influences from the immediate situation determine the church's theological and ethical decisions. A theology that *knows* that it is in some real sense conditioned by its context is likely to be more conscious of the temptations implicit in this than is a theology that merely *is* contextually conditioned. See my essay "On Contextuality in Christian Theology," *Toronto Journal of Theology*, I, 1 (Spring 1985):3ff.

48. "For Paul, the Crucified One is weak, subject to death. But Paul does not celebrate this thought with melancholy; rather, he thinks of it as the gospel, as a source of joy. What is joyful about the weakness of the Crucified One? The weakness of the Crucified One is for Paul the way in which God's power of life is perfected (II Cor. 13:4). Weakness is then not understood as a contradiction of God's power. There is, however, only one phenomenon in which power and weakness do not contradict each other, in which, rather, power can perfect itself as weakness. This phenomenon is the event of love. Love does not see power and weakness as alternatives. It is the unity of power and weakness, and such is certainly the most radical

opposite of the will to power that cannot affirm weakness. Pauline "theology of the cross" (*theologia crucis*) is accordingly "the most stringent rejection of all deification of self-willing power" (Eberhard Jüngel, *God as the Mystery of the World: On the Foundation of the Theology of the Crucified One in the Dispute Between Theism and Atheism*, p. 206).

49. John Carmody, *Ecology and Religion*, pp. 6–7.

50. Senator M. Lamontagne, "A Science Policy for Canada" (reported in *Consumer Society Notes* 1, no. 2 [Dec. 1975]; published by the Science Council of Canada).

51. *The Ontario Public School History of Canada*, authorized by the Ministry of Education for Ontario (Toronto: The Macmillan Co. of Canada, 1913).

52. Christopher Derrick, *The Delicate Creation*, p. 95.

53. *The Brothers Karamazov*, trans. Constance Garnett (London: Wm. Heinemann Ltd., 1912), p. 332.

54. Conrad Bonifazi, "Biblical Roots of an Ecologic Conscience," p. 210.

55. *I and Thou*, p. 8.

56. "Because the Hebrews understood consciousness to be distributed throughout the body, it was possible to conceive of psychical qualities in the natural world. After all, our bodies are the one part of nature of which we have an inside view, and the body seemed to show how nature felt and acted when viewed from within. It seems natural to extend this awareness to the external world, to regard one's environment anthropomorphically, as though animated, capable both of fellow-feeling with human beings and of obedience to its own sustaining depth of force.

"Therefore, *nephesh* is not peculiarly human; there is no ultimate division between human and animal *nephesh*; indeed, life and sensibility extend throughout the animal kingdom into the world of objects. Perhaps because of their volatile contents, perfume bottles are 'houses of the soul,' and mountains shake or trees 'clap their hands.' These personal propensities of a glad earth are more than poetry; they betoken an intricate connection between man and the earth, understood by analogy. The relationship between them, however, may properly be described as *living* because men visualized their surroundings as sharing in their own psychic nature" (Conrad Bonifazi, "Biblical Roots," pp. 207–208).

57. In this connection, see Richard Selzer, *Mortal Lessons: Notes on the Art of Surgery* (New York: Simon and Schuster, 1974), especially the essay "The Exact Location of the Soul."

58. Loren Eiseley, quoted by Richard E. Wentz in "The American Spirituality of Loren Eiseley," p. 430.

59. *Ibid.*, p. 431.

60. It is not accidental that the author of this well-known concept, Albert Schweitzer, was reared on Lutheran piety.

61. Rosemary Radford Ruether, *Sexism and God-Talk: Toward a Feminist Theology* (Boston: Beacon Press, 1983), p. 85. The entire discussion of the chapter "Woman, Body, and Nature: Sexism and the Theology of Creation," should be studied in connection with the present topic.

62. Linus Pauling, "The Prevention of Nuclear War," from a speech delivered at the Hotel Vancouver in October 1982, edited by Thomas L. Perry, Jr., and published privately by the Physicians for Social Responsibility, British Columbia Chapter, in the "Proceedings of a Symposium Held at the University of British Columbia, March 5–6, 1983," page iv.

Index

SUBJECTS

AUTHORS

SCRIPTURE REFERENCES